EUROPEAN DEMOCRATIC CULTURE

Contributors

Alain-Marc Rieu • Jean Baudoin • Rodney Barker
Francesco D'Agostino • Hans-Joachim Schmidt
Gérard Duprat • Pierre Avril • Jean-Pierre Cot
Richard Corbett

Edited by Alain-Marc Rieu and Gérard Duprat
English edition prepared by Noël Parker

The Open
University

The Open University, Fédération Interuniversitaire de l'Enseignement à
Distance, European Association of Distance Teaching Universities

ROUTLEDGE

London and New York

A note for the general reader

European Democratic Culture forms part of a second level course in the humanities and social sciences. The English language version of the *What is Europe?* course is produced by the Open University in conjunction with the European Association of Distance Teaching Universities. Open University students are provided with supplementary teaching material, including a *Course Guide*, which gives a complete list of all printed and audio-visual components.

What is Europe?

Book 1   *The History of the Idea of Europe*

Book 2   *Aspects of European Cultural Diversity*

Book 3   *European Democratic Culture*

Book 4   *Europe and the Wider World*

First published in 1993 by
The Open University, Walton Hall, Milton Keynes, MK7 6AA
Revised edition first published in 1995 by
The Open University, Walton Hall, Milton Keynes MK7 6AA
                    and
Routledge
11 New Fetter Lane, London EC4P 4EE
Simultaneously published in the USA and Canada by
Routledge
29 West 35th Street, New York, NY 10001

Edited, designed and typeset by the Open University
Printed in the United Kingdom by Bell and Bain Ltd., Glasgow
British Library Cataloguing in Publication Data
A catalogue record for this book is available from the British Library
Library of Congress Cataloguing in Publication Data
A catalogue record for this book has been requested
ISBN 0-415-12418-2
ISBN 0-415-12419-0 (pbk)

The other institutions which participated in the creation of *What is Europe?* were:

Open universiteit,
Valkenburgerweg 167,
PO Box 2960,
6401 DL Heerlen,
The Netherlands

Deutsches Institut für Fernstudien an der Universität Tübingen,
Post Fach 1569,
7400 Tübingen 1,
Germany

Jysk Åbent Universitet,
Nordre Ringgade 1,
DK – 8000 Århus C,
Denmark

Fédération Interuniversitaire de l'Enseignement à Distance,
l'Université Paris X
200 Avenue de la République,
92001 Nanterre,
France

Contents

Part III   Public opinion and the role of criticism

Part IV   The institutions of democracy

NOTE: Where there is no English-language published version, the quotations from German authors that appear in these essays have been translated by Monica Shelley; quotations from other foreign authors have been translated by the author or editor.

General preface to 'What is Europe?'

Kevin Wilson, Chair of the European Association of Distance Teaching Universities (EADTU) Humanities Programme Committee

The four books in the *What is Europe?* series are the product of a collaborative enterprise under the direction of the Humanities Programme Committee of the European Association of Distance Teaching Universities (EADTU). The universities involved in the project are:

- The Open universiteit, The Netherlands

- Jysk Åbent Universitet (the Jutland Open University)

- The Deutsches Institut für Fernstudien an der Universität Tübingen

- The Centre d'Analyse des Savoirs Contemporains at the Université des Sciences Humaines de Strasbourg on behalf of the Fédération Interuniversitaire de l'Enseignement à Distance

- The UK Open University

The Humanities Programme Committee of the EADTU was established in late 1988 with a brief to promote joint course development. The four books in this series were designed as the academic core of its first course which was first presented by the Open University in 1993. For this new edition, the course team have revised and updated the original materials so that they can be made available to students of European Studies at universities and colleges not involved in the EADTU programme in Europe, the United States and beyond.

Starting to plan a course on Europe in the heady year of 1989 was both a challenge and an opportunity. With Europe in a state of flux, we quickly rejected as too narrow the idea of a course focused only on the European Community. We dismissed just as quickly the idea of a European history course, not on grounds of irrelevance, but because numerous such courses were already available. Instead we agreed to write a course on European identity in its various historical, cultural, social, political and economic aspects. This topic was is at the centre of the debate on Europe, called for a wide-ranging approach across academic boundaries and stood to benefit from the different national perspectives that could be harnessed to the project.

The course has four objectives:

1 To provide a context for the understanding of contemporary European developments through a consideration of the history of the idea of Europe.

2 To consider aspects of European cultural diversity through investigations into language, education, mass-media and everyday culture.

3   To examine the theory, function and practice of democracy as, arguably, fundamental components of European culture.

4   To locate Europe as a political and economic entity in a context of global change.

These objectives – and the European nature of the course – are reflected in the titles and provenance of the respective books:

1   *The History of the Idea of Europe* is a Dutch–Danish collaboration.

2   *Aspects of European Cultural Diversity* emanates from Germany, though one of the authors is British.

3   *European Democratic Culture* is a French product, though there are Italian, German and British, as well as French, contributors to the book.

4   *Europe and the Wider World* comes from the UK.

We have framed the title of the series as a question – *What is Europe?* – yet we are under no illusion that there is a simple, straightforward answer, or even a series of agreed definitions that satisfy. Nor are we making the assumption that Europe is stamped with a unique identity, or that it has a manifest destiny, or that a singular meaning is revealed in its history.

We follow in the footsteps of Hugh Seton-Watson, who tells us that 'the word "Europe" has been used and misused, interpreted and misinterpreted in as many different meanings as almost any word in any language. There have been and are many Europes...'[1] The question, then, is a provocative device to set you thinking, and to prompt further questions. Instead of rushing into definitions we have approached the topic from a number of points of view and from the standpoint of various methodologies, raising questions as we go about how 'Europe' has been conceptualized, organized, structured and utilized, both in the past and in the present. The contributors to this series do not have any particular axes to grind. The essays are not propaganda pieces for a 'European spirit', cultural unity, a single market, political union, or any other European project. On the contrary, they are scholarly explorations designed to enhance our understanding of the many facets of European identity.

So, the essays cover a wide canvas. They deal with various ideas of Europe in the past and present; with different aspects of everyday life and associated tensions making for cultural uniformity or accentuating cultural difference; with a political culture founded on public opinion, law and democracy; and with Europe's relationship with the United States, Russia and the developing countries and with its place in the world economy.

The series as a whole presents Europe as a work in progress rather than a finished product, a construction yard rather than a museum. As a project Europe can never be completed. It will always need to be re-made, emancipated from the past, re-invented.

---

[1] SETON-WATSON, H. (1985) 'What is Europe, where is Europe?: from mystique to politique', *Encounter*, July/August, vol. LX, No. 2, p. 9.

Introduction to Book 3

Prepared for the Course Team by Alain-Marc Rieu
Translated by Noël Parker

This book is at once modest and ambitious. Its ambitious purpose is to summarize European democratic thought, setting out the principal organizing themes and problems in our knowledge of politics. Our aim is not to compare the different democratic systems, because that would tend to narrow each one down to its own special character, origins and history. Rather we aim to interrogate political practices and institutions, to explore how political situations and problems are resolved. In this way, we identify how the political is thought about and how political activity is sustained.

Yet this book has the modesty befitting its ambition: it cannot claim to be exhaustive, clear or clear-sighted enough. It is intended to be a tool of development, of learning and of reflection, offered to readers who may deepen and fulfil its purpose by their critical responses. The hope behind it is that by presenting the political culture which flows from Europe's history and feeds into its present, we will play a part in the growth of a European public opinion.

Why study European democracy as a culture? Our first goal is to show that democracy cannot be understood if it is divorced from the conditions of its emergence and evolution, or from the institutions through which it articulates – and sometimes resolves – problems. This is not to say that European democracy does not have universal value: that it is entirely relative to the historical and social conditions of its formation. European democracy is not a model, but it is an instance of a type of politics which can exist in other forms. As a type, democracy displays a number of distinctive requirements and criteria which amount to a certain way of thinking about, understanding and dealing with political matters. It is in Europe that politics of this type has taken shape most fully and explicitly, and in the greatest diversity.

So it is the way this development came about – rather than the resulting model – which is exemplary. European democratic culture is distinguished less by its supposed level of achievement than by the endless efforts through which European societies have acquired the knowledge to criticize and reform themselves, so as to direct their own future. It is this shared endeavour, rather than its results, that characterizes democracy. One of the dominant ideas behind the work we have undertaken is that if Europe is ever to achieve a political existence and touch all of its citizens, then this critical endeavour has now to stimulate a European type of democracy.

By taking European democracy as a culture, we underline also that it cannot be reduced to a system, to a range of political techniques, or to institutions and their mode of operation. On the other hand, an understanding of democracy can no more be grounded in *a priori* conceptions of human nature, reason or society. For these things are themselves products of history, arising from the very thing we wish to explain by reference to them. By 'culture' we mean precisely an organized ensemble of attitudes, values, patterns of individual or group behaviour, forms of knowledge and discourse – all of which have a history. They arise from formal and informal education, are transmitted and evolve with the passage of time in different ways which depend on individuals, groups, regions and nations.

That means democracy is passed on by being thought about, practised, experienced and reflected upon. It is not a natural, spontaneous, inherent feature of humanity or society. It is a historical product sustained by effort and, in consequence, both sturdy and fragile: grounded in a long history, but dependent on its practitioners having a shared capacity to discover its benefits and its meaning again and again. Democracy is not reducible to a system of government, because it embraces the entire social and cultural environment presupposed by a particular type of state. Yet it could not exist without the institutions in which it finds expression, since it exists at the heart of a society by virtue of their operation.

Democracy establishes a relationship between political institutions and collective activity which makes institutions sensitive to the evolution of society. Institutions cannot function alone, like machines, to produce consensus independently of the collective activity they presuppose. If inherited attitudes and values fade because democratic culture is not passed on, understood and reinvented for changed circumstances, then the institutions are cut off from the social practices which give them meaning and enable them to be controlled.

New forms of tyranny then arise, though these do not necessarily follow the great models of the past. When democratic institutions lose that symbiosis with society which is the condition of their operation, they themselves become empty collective rituals to which the political class meticulously renders homage. The institutions then sustain political life by draining it of all meaning, and monopolize the administrative and financial means of control over people and territory. Consulting the electorate becomes nothing more than a technique of legitimation for policies decided on high, and political activity is reduced to passing power from one party, or one leader, to the next. The political class then treats the country as its property, imagining that its constant presence in the media guarantees its benefit to the people. Democracies themselves produce their own particular forms of authoritarianism.

Denunciations of the Eastern bloc countries have long served to mask the inadequacies of Western democracies. The collapse of communism and its 'people's democracies' does not entitle us to preach lessons in democracy, so much as to assess the political evolution of the capitalist countries of the present. It is our wish to contribute to this. Our only lesson is the diversity of perspectives.

All that accounts for our way of proceeding. The book begins with an anthropological approach analysing the conditions for the emergence of democratic thinking in ancient Greece, and ends with an account of the operation of contemporary European institutions. Between these two points, democracy's function and practices are considered, its two distinctive characteristics (the status of law and the place of public opinion) are examined, and the institutions on which it necessarily depends are described. The course of discussion presupposes a thesis: that the Europe which is coming into existence before our very eyes does not need some collective myth or political epic, but rather an acquaintance with its own history and reflection on the forms of knowledge which preserve the memory of that history. It is not a *belief* that Europeans need in order to exist together and build their future. The emergence of European political culture rests on *knowledge of its diverse lines of development* and hard-won construction. That is the deeper meaning of modernity, which is indeed the gradual, ongoing break with all founding myths.

It is the technicians, the experts and the under-labourers of European construction who wish Europe to have a 'soul', a spiritual side or a great project which can bind together this mosaic of peoples, histories and traditions. Many think that Europe needs collective myths and beliefs if it is to become a community rather than a mere market. Do the effects of the market need to be corrected by a 'soul'? What can this spiritual soul or this culture do that such hopes are vested in it? Where can it be found? Does Europe have to be a sacred thing in order to exist? The approach we pursue gives the answer No.

Europe simply needs to reflect on democracy, political institutions, law and the means by which public opinion will be formed and heard. Europe is the outcome of debate, thought and negotiation. It is enough that, rather than dreaming and building ourselves illusions about Europe, we watch carefully over its social, political and economic construction. In this, it is the university – rather than any universal claim for truth – that has most to offer. Collective inquiry and thought are needed which reach across national and discipline boundaries, straddling our separate histories. In this volume that we offer you to read and criticize, with its discordant concert of voices, note the true stamp of knowledge: the primacy of reason over myth. That is why this is a work by universities, embarking on a debate with its readership in Europe and elsewhere.

Part I
The growth of democracy

Essay 1
Scientific revolutions and ideas of democracy

Prepared for the Course Team by Alain-Marc Rieu
Professor of Philosophy, University of Strasbourg II
Translated by John Williams and Noël Parker

Introduction

The resonance between the words 'science' and 'democracy' reveals a connection which is both obscure and obvious. More than anything else, they symbolize European thought, its history, its present and its future. In order to give an account of European democratic culture and, at the same time, examine it critically, we need to have a long-term perspective and study the conditions which enabled political thought and democracy to emerge. It then appears that democracy arises in very specific historical conditions: not simply political or economic crises, but what can only be called revolutions. These are revolutions in the conceptions that individuals have of themselves and their relationship with the world, and also of their society and their relationship with it. These revolutionary periods occur very rarely in history. Fundamentally, they are characterized by crucial scientific changes which are both the product and the logical consequence of certain social and cultural changes. The object of this essay is to study these interrelationships – not to offer a history of political thought, but to set out the problems around which the evolution of political thought has been organized.

The word 'science' does not here refer to any particular science, but to what is generally known as 'the scientific spirit'. That term does not denote only certain methods, certain knowledge, certain theories and conceptions of matter, life and humanity. First and foremost, it signifies an intellectual discipline whose source lies in the European scientific tradition, and which sustains today a world-wide network for producing and communicating well-founded knowledge. Similarly, to define democracy we cannot be content with describing the various political systems recognized as being democratic, seeking what they have in common and what distinguishes them, and hoping thereby to grasp its essence. The resulting criteria would be so abstract and general that we would be hardly any the wiser. 'Democracy' refers to many things at the same time: a mode of organization and administration, a set of institutions, an intellectual discipline, a code of ethics, an ideal of individual and collective behaviour, a developing historical reality. Just as we used to speak of the 'scientific spirit', we must also speak of the 'democratic spirit'. The task before us, therefore, is to examine the relationship between the 'democratic spirit' and the 'scientific spirit'. One idea will become apparent as we proceed: there can be no science without democracy and no democracy without science.

The emergence of democracy

An anthropological approach to science and politics

We must first pursue the problem of the emergence of democracy on the basis of work by anthropologists specializing in ancient Greece. In fact, their approach, which is scientific in its own specific way, is the only one which sheds light on the problem. I shall take as my authority the works of Jean-Pierre Vernant. In a famous study, Vernant (1965; 1983 edn) records the emergence around the sixth century BC of a geometric conception of the cosmos which was not based on the gods of mythology. He points out that there was no established scientific tradition in Greece at this period, and that the astronomical data available at the time had been inherited from the Babylonians. However, in Babylon these astronomical data were interpreted within a frame of reference totally alien to that of the early Greek astronomers: in an astral religion which identified the stars with divine powers. Furthermore, the observation of the stars was the prerogative of a class of scribes working exclusively in the service of a king who mediated between earth and the heavens. Finally, the positions of the various stars were recorded without developing any spatial schema or any kind of geometry. One question therefore needs to be answered: if this knowledge of the positions of the stars was imported, how did the geometric conception come about?

Vernant wonders whether the source of this spatial representation of the heavens lies in Greek culture itself. Yet in Homer and Hesiod we find no trace of a cosmology, merely a theogony: any account of the origins of the heavens is inseparable from myths and religious beliefs. We can measure the extent of the shift towards science that was taking place by quoting Aristotle describing how his philosophical predecessor, Anaximander,[1] conceptualized the position of the earth:

> ...there are some, Anaximander, for instance, among the ancients who
> say that the earth keeps it place because of its indifference. Motion
> upwards and downwards and sideways were all, they thought, equally
> inappropriate and indifferently related to every extreme point; and to
> move in contrary directions at the same time was impossible: so it must
> needs remain still.
>
> *(Aristotle, 1930 edn, book II, ch. 13, 295b)*

The central position of the earth follows from a simple deduction based on the constant distance between the centre and the periphery of the cosmos, when the

---

[1]   Anaximander (c.611–c.546 BC) was one of the triumvirate of thinkers from Miletus in Ionia credited with starting the tradition of Greek philosophy, largely by asking questions about origins and the nature of matter which called for abstract explanatory principles (such as balance, development, condensation, etc.). (NP)

latter is posited as a sphere. The differentiation of space according to myth has been superseded by one founded on the geometric properties of the sphere. The emerging cosmology of these Ionian physicists showed a new requirement for explanation, for the construction of a *theoria* – that is, a vision or conception yielding insight into the world without reference to religion. These physicists were searching for new explanatory models. They drew on the activities and the forms of knowledge around them, which they refashioned to formulate a non-religious conception of the world.

Was it a radical innovation, then, this geometric conception of the world and the requirement for explanation which it implied? It arose at the same moment as other phenomena which were causing great upheavals in Greek society and culture. The key phenomenon was the advent of the city or *polis*. Vernant shows that the expansion of commerce and the development of a money-based economy precipitated the break-up of traditional Greek society. How did Greek society, in Athens or Miletus, react to this process? By posing the problem of institutions and inventing 'the political'. It was derived from a distinction between what belongs to the clan and its domestic economy (*oikonomia*), and what is common to all (*ta koina*), to every clan. The political was 'public affairs': that which concerned the unity of society and its capacity to respond to the processes which transform it.

Now, what is common to all cannot simply be proclaimed by a king, a unique individual or someone chosen by providence, since he will always have origins in a particular clan, and will seek to extend that clan's vision and particular interest to all members of society. What is shared in common is not obvious and observable; it is neither as tangible as a simple object nor as vague and distant as a divinity. It is intelligent, abstract, a formal property determining human actions – just as the properties of a circle determine the actions of carpenters or architects. But with one, decisive difference. What is 'common' is not so definable and demonstrable as to be logically necessary without further discussion: the political is not reducible to the certainties of a science. Yet it is not, for all that, irrational.[2] It has to be discovered, defined and established by all those who hold a position of responsibility or leadership in their clan. They must take shared responsibility for a process of change on which the very existence of their society hinges.

Politics emerges as an autonomous social activity whose object is the evolution of a people and its collective capacity to determine the direction it is taking. It implies the collapse of the existing authoritarian hierarchy and brings into being a new reality: the people (or *demos*). The question of *democracy* (the power of the people) therefore first arose at the very moment that the concept of the political was beginning to appear.[3] What is common became the object and the main issue

---

[2] That is why the invention of politics is a collective apprenticeship for an entire people. Today, as in the past, the process transforms society as a whole.

[3] In Greece this process was linked to a series of deep social cleavages: men gained access to the public sphere; women remained shut inside the home; slaves were still excluded from the household; strangers and misfits were merely tolerated within the city. [continued]

of a debate which, through negotiation between private interests, brought out the common good and the collective interest. This new discipline first became evident in the layout of the town itself: the disorganized pattern of houses belonging to different clans slowly gave way to one centred around the market place – a place of exchange which became the forum for the discussion of common affairs. The *agora* – that is, market place and place of assembly – was taking shape. It was a kind of city within a city, because it was there that the city reflected on itself, that a society became a city. The *agora* was not merely the mirror of the city; it brought the city into being.

The political sphere that was beginning to take shape was revealed, to be sure, in the layout of the town. But it corresponded primarily to an intellectual discipline and an activity of mind that had previously been unknown: namely, thinking about and formulating what is 'common'. The instrument for achieving this, the only one that people share for transcending their conflicting passions and interests, was to be speech. But new rules and principles arose out of the practices required by the situation of people discussing common affairs. Politics, understood as a collective approach to common affairs, was embodied in the *logos*, a term which signifies both 'the word, the speech pronounced by an orator at the assembly' and 'reason', the faculty of argumentation which defines a human being as being not just an animal, but a 'political animal', a 'reasonable being' (Vernant, 1965; 1983 edn, p. 182). Speech and politics are inseparable from each other: each contains the possibility of the other.

The birth of political thought

Politics was born at the same time as cosmology. The same intellectual posture, the same methodological rigour can be found in the work of the Ionian physicists and in the shared reflection of those who, awakening from the world of myth, learned from within their households to apply their minds to matters which affected their common future. But we cannot say either that the rules of the political game were projected into a cosmology, or that the new vision of the heavens was mapped onto social life. All we can do is observe that the two arose simultaneously. The most important point is that philosophy appeared at the same time as science and politics. From the very beginning, it was pursued in relation to the other two. It was to be linked to the development of the sciences, and had its finger on the pulse of the political evolution of societies.

Though they embrace individuals and groups, these cleavages are not simply 'inequalities'. In fact, they are ways of differentiating (women), segregating (foreigners) and excluding (slaves), which constitute the social system and define a society's very way of life. That is why they seem obvious to the members of that society. These cleavages take up simple or immediately recognizable indicators: sexual difference, coming from abroad, not coming of one's own free will, doing work that no one wishes to do, not having the same skin colour, not speaking the same language, etc. The list of differentiations is infinite and, in the end, matters little in itself. For it is the social system as a whole that is at issue. The idea of inequalities should be reserved solely for differences where a social group pretends to be homogeneous. There is little point in struggling to suppress any particular inequality which is inherent in the social system itself and the status it assigns to individuals. To denounce such inequalities, rather than the system that generates them, can amount to a whitewash.

For the pre-Socratic thinkers,[4] the primary task of philosophy was to ask questions about nature, about the order and balance (or justice) which govern the cosmos. It was already attempting to include human destiny within this, to discover the connection uniting the cosmic order with the social order, and find the law (in the sense both of model and norm) which might serve as the organizing principle of the life of the community. That is why philosophy was a form of wisdom.

However, the philosophers gradually realized that the *logos* is not only the instrument of politics: it contains the very possibility of sustaining political life. It contains the potential to discover what is general to all human beings at all times – beyond their private interests and individual opinions. The general is revealed not in figures of rhetoric, but in unfolding the structure of reasoned argument. When it is structured by argument, discourse is reason itself – reason can be discovered only through such argument. And reasoned argument is not simply a means to an end. It is prior to, rather than dependent on, actual discussion – as those who practise it gradually come to realize. A valid form of argument is one which can be reproduced by anybody. What is merely personal opinion will exhibit internal contradictions as it is exposed to the deductive power of the *logos*. The *logos* therefore contains the criterion to judge truth and falsehood.

Socrates is the historical figure who embodies this new awareness; in his dialogues he does not place himself opposite his protagonist, as if he was putting forward an opposing set of ideas in the hope of winning him over. The *logos* is always a third party in the argument: both moderator and judge. And Socrates places himself on the side of the *logos*, embodying and unfolding the logic hidden within it. He is not expressing his personal views or those of public opinion, but the internal necessities of discourse itself. In seeking what is general or universal (the essential), philosophy sets out to formulate, one after another, the very rules of thought and discourse. The *logos* has not only the power to reveal contradictions within opinions. The most profound discovery to be made about it was that it produces knowledge which cannot be extrapolated from the community's own experience.

Through logical demonstration, the *logos* gives access to the 'True' and the 'Good', realities transcending the human sphere. In Greek civilization it was to remain attached to the cosmos; it was the link between the science of the heavens and human lives. Plato epitomized this new stage: he wanted to construct a science of politics by discovering the place of the city in the cosmic order. This was the meaning of the first great work of political thought, *The Republic* – whose title means the 'common thing' or 'commonwealth'. Plato pursues these questions: how can a city be founded on the true and the good? How can we evaluate the capacity of different political systems to express the 'True' in politics? It emerges

---

[4]   That is, those active before Socrates (469–399 BC). Anaximander and the other Ionian physicists, as referred to above, are therefore pre-Socratic. Socrates transformed philosophical thinking by focusing on evaluating and reformulating key ideas – including socially significant ones, such as justice – through rational interrogation and intuition about them. He pursued this process in dialogue where various contentions were counterpoised and their implications and internal weaknesses exposed. Plato (c.428–c.348 BC) – who advanced his own ideas as Socrates' – and, to some degree, Aristotle (384–322 BC) are the principal philosophers to follow Socrates. (NP)

that cities are born of human beings' need to come together in order to ensure their survival; the principle behind the city lies in human nature itself. Human beings and cities are thus subject to the order of 'nature': they cannot escape its law. Science therefore plays an essential role. By discovering the order of the cosmos, science formulates the norm to be applied to society, the order which it is the function of politics to establish and preserve. For Plato, politics must be subordinate to science, which is in turn bound by a conception of nature.

This conception of nature, for its part, has no scientific foundation. But Plato's conception of science, society and politics has the following consequences. Human beings differ from each other according to their capacity to reason, their courage, and the importance they attach merely to their individual well-being (*Republic*, book IV). Each man's nature bestows on him a destiny and a role in the city, which he cannot depart from without endangering the city as a whole.[5] If rationality is the prevailing quality in a particular person, he belongs to the class of leaders; if it is courage, his nature is to be a soldier or 'guardian'; if his immediate well-being is the decisive factor, he belongs to the class of craftsmen and merchants. Only those who have sufficient rationality to attain wisdom, which is the science of the good and the true, are capable of governing the city justly. These governors may be only a minority, but the wisdom of the 'philosopher-king' teaches him what is good for everybody.

This is the principle of Plato's utopia. Utopia consists in starting from a conception of science and deducing from it a conception of the social order or the perfect society. Plato's utopia arises from devising a society on the basis of a principle which transcends it and assigns to it an ideal order. Society must then seek, in the ordinary time-bound world, to live up to that ideal order; everything must be subject to its underlying principle.

Taking all this as his foundation, Plato develops the famous theory of the degeneration of forms of government (book VIII). When the governors cease to govern in accordance with justice, the warriors take power but can rule only through coercion. The wealth they need to raise armies and fight makes them dependent on the oligarchy which, when the interests of the rich are threatened, takes power too. However, the rich know only how to make themselves richer. The people become poorer and, wishing to get rich in their turn, they revolt. Hence democracy is born: government of the people by the people. The unity and order of the city are then shattered by the ceaseless conflict of private interests; disorder sets in, to the point of threatening the security of each individual. To restore order, tyranny is imposed. But it is devoid of justice and can only rule by terror.

Thus Plato condemns democracy in the name of science. It is an historical fact that the Greek cities could not establish a stable political system that ensured

---

[5] For Plato, revolt is either an error or an act of madness. An error because nobody can escape their own nature; revolt is then simply a momentary lack of awareness. An act of madness where an individual's revolt is a genuine expression of his nature. That makes him different from others, and thus threatens the order which ensures the survival of all. Infinitely varied and continually reinvented throughout history, Plato's argument against revolt has invariably been the basis for repressing opposition.

peace between them, nor a lasting autonomy in the face of external dangers. It is also a fact that Plato condemns 'the power of the people' because he sees in it nothing but the clash of individual opinions and private interests. He condemns 'public opinion', that ever-changing, many-sided babble of voices created by sharing social life.

In the end, the error of Plato the philosopher was to believe that philosophy can govern. It was born, it is true, at the same time as science and political thought. But that does not mean philosophy only amounts to formulating scientific knowledge and applying it to the human sphere – as if the method by which knowledge is established ensures it would be valid in all aspects of individual and collective existence. Philosophy cannot legislate for science or society. The only thing worth preserving which Plato represents in Greek thought is the historical stage when a rational approach to the world and to society were linked (while the two were distinguished one from the other), and which made philosophy possible. That does not mean that philosophy is either useless or dangerous. Quite the contrary: it is still today the discourse in which we reflect upon the processes transforming society.

One, more complex point remains to be elucidated. We have said that there was no relationship of cause and effect between democracy and science. How then are we to account for the fact that they came into existence simultaneously? Between the political and the study of the heavens, there developed an attitude of mind and a requirement for rigorous method which were reflected in that application of the *logos* known as philosophy. Situated between the heavens and the city, philosophy was to seek out the strands running through science which make it possible to conceive, explain and communicate. Philosophy was to construct forms of argument which philosophers would introduce into debate and hence spread throughout society. Philosophy creates concepts and uncovers forms of valid argument which gradually modify the way human beings engage in debate, their view of themselves, and their connection with each other and their environment.[6]

That is philosophy's historical function: to construct models of representation, explanation and organization, and to introduce them into discourse. It follows that there cannot be a rigid science, scientific method or ideal applied to politics. Nor is there any political ideal which can be superimposed on nature or life. There is only this work of the mind finding its bearings, at the heart of society, in contact with the sciences, learning at every moment new ways of thinking about the problems which confront human beings and their societies. This quiet, silent work of the mind – which we know as philosophy – goes hand in hand with science and democracy; it uncovers and expresses in discourse the link which, at each stage of history, unites them.

The democratic ideal and the conditions of its emergence

If we wish to refute Plato's view of democracy as a philosophical error, we have to go back to Vernant and imagine the city at the moment of its formation. How

---

[6]   This is what is meant by the motto attributed to Plato's academy: 'Let no one who is not geometer enter here.' (See Boyer, 1968, p. 93.)

did it think of itself? Just as the earth was thought of by Anaximander as the centre of the cosmos, the *agora* was the centre of the city: that which ensured its autonomy and guaranteed its stability. It was the centre from which the city was governed, in which it took the true measure of itself. That is to say, in the *agora* the city discussed matters relating to its own nature: its population, geographical situation, history, neighbours, etc. The *agora* was the symbolic space in which the city was revealed to itself and its citizens (and only to them) in the ideal form from which it was constituted. The *agora* was a sort of stage. When people entered the stage to act out their role, 'citizens' were made; individuals transformed themselves into 'political actors'.

Now the Greek language employs two synonyms to express this function of the *agora*: *en meso* (in the middle) and *en koino* (in common). What is common to all is that which is in the middle, at a constant distance from the outer edge of the city. The same geometric model is in play in both the heavens and the city. Thus the city's place in the cosmos is marked out, and it is that which justifies Plato's utopia. But what matters to us in this Greek vision of the city is the conception of the citizen it engenders: the image each citizen forms of himself and his relationship with others. Alongside private houses, there exists a public sphere, a centre where what is common to all is discussed, negotiated and exchanged. In this centre, everyone is equal to everybody else, and no one is subordinate to anyone else. From the moment they enter the *agora* – this place which belongs to nobody and everybody – citizens define themselves as 'equals' and 'peers'. Relationships between individuals are then thought of and lived as relationships of identity, symmetry and reciprocity. At the very moment of its origin, democracy was the ideal which provided the norm for the city. The political arose at the same time and out of the same principle as democracy. Democracy is contained in the very principle underlying politics.

Vernant goes further. On the strength of his anthropological approach, he rejects the idea that science and the city were conjured up from nothing by an act of genius, or that the transition towards science can be detected in the way mythology itself was evolving. He attempts to locate a source for the *agora* in Greek culture: to identify a practice which, transformed and reinterpreted as society itself was transformed, might have become the model on which politics was founded, transforming in its turn the organization of the town by providing people with a space to think through their development together. In Book II of Homer's *Odyssey*, Vernant finds an account of the military practice of 'convening the *agora*': of assembling the army in a circle. The circle thus formed opens up a space for discussion and free speech:

> Once the circle is formed, Telemachus enters it and stands *en meso*, at the centre. He takes the sceptre in his hand and speaks freely. When he has finished he steps out of the circle and another takes his place and replies to his speech. This assembly of 'equals' constituted by the meeting of the warriors creates a circular space with a centre in which each man can freely say whatever suits him. Following a series of economic and social transformations, this military assembly became the *agora* of the city where all the citizens (first a minority of aristocrats

and later the whole of the *demos*) were able to argue out and decide in common upon the affairs that concerned them collectively.

(Vernant, 1965; 1983 edn, p. 194)

Vernant's account provides us with an important lesson: everybody must make an effort to find in their own history a means of breathing life into the democratic ideal, of assimilating and reinterpreting it in order to give it meaning. Democracy is not simply a technique of government, a way of managing societies so as to increase their total efficiency by obtaining the participation of the largest possible proportion of the population. The invention of democracy was a slow and bumpy process internal to Greek civilization. To be sure democracy is a model for politics.[7] But it can only be successfully implanted elsewhere if the model is reinterpreted within each society, and if the agents of democratization have the will to seek out the democratic potential in their societies, developing through education the understanding already shared among the people. All that democratic systems have in common is their 'family resemblance'; the differences are more important than this basic ideal which the Greeks were the first to nurture out of their own past.

Democracy makes no sense unless it is the collective construction of a people as a whole, responding to internal and external changes which threaten to fragment it. Similarly, the sciences are not simply a set of mechanisms to produce and communicate knowledge that is well founded and hence capable of being applied. Science is born at the same time as democracy, and among people who, to ensure their survival and autonomy, are learning how to sustain a democracy.[8] At a time when Europe (by virtue of its own efforts at construction) is faced with a new democratic challenge, and when there are countries emancipating themselves from the totalitarianism which has crushed their people's spirit, the example of the Greeks still offers lessons. But only as revealed by modern anthropologists rather than by the Greek philosophers.

A few points need to be emphasized by way of a conclusion. The city was a response to the transformations undergone by archaic Greek society, in particular to the increasing level of commerce. The fragmentation of the kingdoms led to the fragmentation of the cities. From then on, commercial success was the deciding factor in rivalries and conflicts of interest, so that certain towns (particularly Athens) had the wealth to become military powers that could measure up to the new situation. Again democracy is shaped by the historical conditions of its emergence: in Greece its principal function was to enable the cities which in-

---

[7]   Democracy is not a procedural panacea which one merely needs to put cheerily in place for tyranny to cease, the economy to develop and the population to grow wealthy and peaceful. To reduce democracy to a set of political mechanisms is a form of manipulation, and a snare which will lead in due course to its devaluation. The failures which follow may then be used to justify a return to authoritarianism.

[8]   Democracy is the means to obtain access to the sciences and to technical skills since, through it, people create the conditions to develop, disseminate and make use of knowledge. That brings them into the fold of those peoples enjoying the benefits of science and liberty.

vented it to retain their autonomy and internal cohesion. Its undoing was to be the conflicts between the cities which required that it be suspended in pursuit of military expeditions, which slowly impoverished the whole of Greece. Such commerce and rivalries required a change in the scale of political organization, but war remained the principal mode of exercising power and resolving conflicts. Ancient Greek civilization did not know how to create the 'city of cities', the common *agora* where they might have forged a collective autonomy. Unification was to come about only through tyranny and conquest, under the power of one king or people over all the others. That is what made possible the emergence and triumph of Macedonian domination.[9] Greek democracy was, in the end, a failure, but the democratic ideal was to have a permanent place in the European political memory.

The age of empires was beginning. The collapse of the Macedonian empire paved the way for Roman domination. Military dominion became the only available solution. Yet it too was undermined from within; the conditions which made it possible precluded it from finding an adequate response to its long-term needs as a form of organization. Outside of the wish for security and the hope of gain, authoritarian domination was incapable of providing a common legal framework, a 'common good' or a 'general interest' which might have legitimized it in the eyes of its subject populations.[10] Empire, too, has its place in the European political memory.

The Copernican Revolution: the conditions for the emergence of modern democratic thought

The medieval world

The political culture and scientific development of modern Europe were not born in ancient Greece. To understand the origins of modern science and political thought, we must develop a fresh anthropological approach, which will reveal the nature of their relationship. Our route to understanding modern history must pass, albeit briefly, through that long epoch known as the 'medieval world'.

One cannot dissociate the feudal system and its political order[11] from a conception of the world which intertwined science and theology. Medieval Christian religion succeeded in integrating those three poles. The world was grounded in religious

[9]   From 357 BC armies from the country of Macedonia, north of Greece, under the leadership of their king, Philip II, gradually intervened (partly by invitation) in the Peloponnesian Wars between the Greek states. By 338 BC Philip had control of the whole of Greece via the 'League of Corinth' which he set up and led. The Macedonians continued to rule Greece until both countries were absorbed into the Roman Empire in 168 BC. (NP)

[10]   No empire has any other destiny than its own downfall. But the most serious danger it faces is that, while draining its energies, its own accumulated power may enable it to postpone its final end.

The Christian medieval world from a thirteenth-century psalter (credit: British Library).

[11] Feudalism was the hierarchical social order dominant in western Europe from the ninth to the fourteenth century. Within this hierarchy, land and authority within the territory of that land (or 'fief') were granted by the higher power holder to the one below (his 'vassal'). In return, the vassal swore an oath of personal loyalty, tribute and/or military service to the 'lord' above him. Notionally, across a large area of central northern Europe all owed ultimate allegiance to the Catholic Church and the 'Holy Roman Emperor', crowned by the Pope. This is discussed in Book 1, *The History of the Idea of Europe*. (NP)

and theological modes of thought. The complex evolutionary process which, in ancient times, had made society and the cosmos objects of secular forms of inquiry disappeared. So the very conditions of science and political thought had ceased to exist. Not that the sciences had disappeared, but they were wholly subordinate to a theological conception of the world which gave them a framework and orientated their investigations. To observe this enormous backward step confirms the fragility of the scientific and the democratic spirit.

The main characteristic of the medieval world was that it derived its organizing principle from an all-powerful God. He ruled over heaven; he ruled over nature by organizing the world which he had created; he ruled over the earth by the law he revealed in the sacred texts of the Gospels. Natural science and the organization of society were inseparable from theology. Divine law was the organizing principle of both the natural and the social order; the latter had to try to bring itself into line with the former by overcoming the obstacles in the path of social existence. Both were subject to an authority which claimed to transcend them and constitute their foundation. This is what is meant by 'theocentrism', which also has a place in our political memory.

In this vision of the world, society exists only because there is an authority which founds it and forces individuals to live together. The underlying principle of authority is outlined by St Paul:

> Every person must submit to the supreme authorities. There is no authority but by act of God, and the existing authorities are instituted by Him: consequently anyone who rebels against authority is resisting a divine institution ...[12]

Individuals may come together to elect one of their number as leader, but from the moment he is appointed, the authority he assumes over his peers, and the difference in status which his power confers on him, derive from God alone. Earthly authority takes its origin and principle from divine power, which sustains its legitimacy as long as those who exercise it are capable of enforcing and commanding respect for it. They can achieve this only by using the means available in the material world – tainted as it is by sin and subject to violence and conflict. Certainly, authority must respect the commandments and the message of the Gospel. But the kingdom of God, if it is to come to pass,[13] is forced to start from the reality of the human world: evil is a means of combatting evil. In this nether world, the exercise of authority entails the use of violence. The principle of feudalism, based on theocentrism, is that the social order exists only by coercion.

This conception of the world was the model for a social order which was meant to mirror the hierarchy of creation. It called for and legitimized a hierarchical order which assigned people a function in society according to their status. Power was

---

[12]   Romans 13: 1–2, *New English Bible*, 2nd edn, OUP/CUP, 1970, p. 270.

[13]   This expectation was founded on the orthodoxy of Christian history established by St Augustine's *City of God* (412–27). In it, he contrasted the 'heavenly city' of God and the imperfect 'earthly city' which is the stuff of human history, pending the second coming of Christ. (NP)

exercised over both people and the land, from which they were inseparable. Those who 'earned their bread by the sweat of their brow' were at the bottom, condemned to obey those who, by virtue of birth or rank, were in charge. Society was thus a pyramid of interlocking status groups; at the top was the sovereign, who embodied and enforced divine law, while leaving his lords the power to impose order in exchange for their allegiance. The arbitrary will of the lord was the mark of his power; he managed his fief in the interests of his 'house' – as a domain which belonged to him and where he was master.

This conception of authority based on possession was a form of domination which precluded any truly mutual bonds between people (i.e. bonds between equals, by agreement). For there were some who were responsible for establishing order in their territories. They embodied the social order in their persons, their behaviour, their castles, their soldiers, their taxes, the law itself. In the feudal world, one was always subordinate to a higher power: the only autonomy was in the exercise of the authority which that power left one over those below.

Political authority was inextricably bound up with religious authority. The Church took up where the political system left off. It kept a watchful eye on individuals and their behaviour, whatever their place in the hierarchy, and at the same time guaranteed the legitimacy of the political system. Nevertheless, there was a constant, latent conflict between the spiritual and temporal powers.[14] For the theological-feudal conception of the world differed from the Christian message founded on the Bible and the Gospels, which embraced the brotherhood of humankind, irrespective of social divisions, and charity to guarantee a right of subsistence to those who owned nothing. This conflict was visible within the Church itself. Some of its members lived in religious communities which had set themselves apart from the temporal law and renounced an impure world in order to submit themselves directly to divine law. Thus, there existed at the very heart of the feudal hierarchy a religious community expressed in the faith of its members and in its own rites and dogmas. This community appears in its purest form in the great monastic movements which developed throughout the Middle Ages.

Feudal society was shot through with great tensions: between the lords and their sovereign, between the temporal power and the Church, between the Church and the religious orders who wished to live in accordance with divine law. The common ties of humanity only existed within religion, faith and the ideal of life hereafter. They were continually repressed and violated by the feudal order's obsession with the ownership of land and the domination of men. The monstrosity of feudalism embraced everything – except the towns. They gradually escaped because they were places of exchange and commerce, and because peasants who managed to get away from the land took refuge there and acquired new customs, knowledge and patterns of behaviour which slowly integrated them into a different world. They became enclaves in which a new world began to take shape.

What became of science in the Middle Ages? Paradoxically, its subordinate position left it with a degree of freedom which eventually opened up the opportunity

---

[14] It would therefore be wrong to speak of full-blown 'theocracy' – rule by the priesthood.

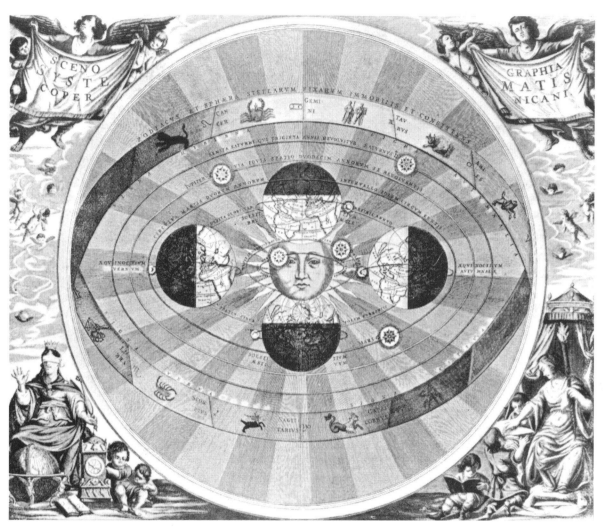

Representation of the system of Copernicus from 'Harmonia Macracosmica' by Andreae Cellarii, 1660 (credit: Mansell Collection).

for the construction of a new conception of the world. In fact, the subordinate role of science was what made it possible to transform the way the world was conceived. In the early sixteenth century, without the benefit of new observations, Copernicus constructed a new, simpler and more economical 'hypothesis' by which to 'save the appearances' – that is, to account for the available observations.[15] But his model was heliocentric: he assumed that the sun, not the earth, was at the centre of the universe. Before the revolution could be complete, it remained for it to be proved that the world did indeed conform to the Copernican

[15]   The expression, used by Copernicus and his contemporaries to mean that observations would fit established doctrine, gives priority to the latter over the former. The doctrine was taken not to be at issue; rather, observed 'appearances' and theories embracing them could be accepted or rejected according to whether they could square with doctrine. (NP)

model and, above all, for European civilization to take in the broader consequences of the adjustment it had registered. These developments would not occur until the time of Galileo (1564–1642). Copernicus's *De revolutionibus orbium caelestium* was published in 1543. The hypothesis was seen as scandalous and strenuously resisted, but its consequences could not yet be fully appreciated. The book was not put on the Index[16] until 1616, which was too late.

Why do we speak of a 'Copernican Revolution'?[17] Because the medieval world was entirely undermined as the full repercussions of a heliocentric hypothesis were revealed. This subsequent process of evolution, which gave birth to the modern world and brought it to the threshold of the twentieth century, was organized along three major axes: a new methodology, a new attitude of mind, and a new politics.

A new methodological discipline

The first axis was purely scientific: the new scientific spirit revealed in a methodological discipline which came to be known as the experimental method. On its own, it enables us to understand the fundamental role played by the sciences in the development and organization of the emerging Europe.

The all-encompassing conception of the universe inherited from Aristotle was being dismantled. It had supposed that the world was an enclosed space, circumscribed by a sphere of fixed stars, and by the principles of movement and life which Christianity had later identified with God. Physics had thus been rooted in astronomy. But Copernicus's astronomy brought about a break with that past. Once its astronomical foundations were lost, physics – the science of nature – had as its source only the world as observed by perception. Throughout the sixteenth and seventeenth centuries, physics sought to reconstruct itself. This gave rise to the 'New Science' of Galileo and Newton, in which astronomy no longer underpinned physics; rather, physics explained the movements of the planets in terms of the principles of falling bodies.

A new relationship appears between thought and reality. Knowledge can no more be based merely on observation than on the astronomy sanctioned by the Church. It may come from the senses, but since the earth is not, as the senses suggest, at the centre of the universe, knowledge cannot be equated with the senses.[18] It re-

[16]   The Catholic Church's list of proscribed books. (NP)

[17]   The idea originates from Emmanuel Kant (1724–1804) in his preface to the second edition of the *Critique of Pure Reason* (Kant, 1787; 1933 edn, pp. 18–25). Kant pointed out the revolution brought about by Copernicus's rethinking from scratch the interpretation of the established data on planetary movement. The 'Copernican Revolution' has since become a cornerstone of the history and philosophy of science. (NP)

[18]   In addition, at the end of the Middle Ages the available observations, derived from perception and instruments to extend its reach, did not allow a choice to be made between the Copernican hypothesis and the previous, geocentric description of the universe as developed by Ptolemy (c.90–168 AD).

quires that sense data be rectified by a type of mental activity. And that cannot be reduced merely to the practices of discourse: talk, debate and ever more subtle arguments cannot hope to uncover the order of the universe. Knowledge calls for hypotheses to be forged and verified by experiments. There was a gradual move away from observation with instruments and towards rationally organized experimentation, carried out on the basis of theories, hypotheses, measuring instruments and 'experimental machines'. Reality is not as given in sense data; it is no more nor less than the hidden order of the universe, as revealed by natural science through the efforts of scientific thinking. This is the underlying principle of the modern world.[19]

The experimental method also tallies with another tendency of modern thought. Considerations of method became intrinsic to physics, and necessary to guarantee its results. But modern science also generated another set of problems concerning the idea of human beings, the relationship between human beings and science, the human capacity for knowledge, and the ability of science to know reality as it truly is. Thus, from the beginning of the sixteenth century, science responded to its own need for first principles with a new conception of human beings, defined as possessors or 'subjects' of knowledge. These problems gave rise to modern philosophy. To deal with them, philosophy had to break with its traditional models.

The ultimate foundation of science being in humans, it was in them that philosophy was to seek the origins of knowledge. The modern conception of human beings is anchored to their function in the acquisition of knowledge. Various versions have been put forward, a number of which are worth recalling. Descartes (1596–1650) located humanity's being in the act of thinking, which derives a criterion of truth from its own character. Hume (1711–76) reduced scientific laws – that is, the principle linking causes to effects – to a habit born of human nature and the repeated experience of similar sense impressions.[20] Kant (1724–1804)

---

[19]   The complete situation is still more complicated. The reconstruction of physics took place in the context of the technological transformation during the Renaissance. In fact, the technical problems posed by ballistics, hydraulics and mechanics supplied physics with the questions it was to consider and the means for formulating them – especially as they had already been arithmetically quantified and set out in geometrical terms. Physics became truly experimental when its link with technical problems came into play, when the activities of engineers met up with the researches of physicists. Galileo's essay, *Le mecchaniche* (On mechanics – c.1600), was a typical example. The most famous of the 'experimental machines' was Galileo's inclined plan [which demonstrated the uniform acceleration of falling objects regardless of differences in weight – NP]. This association of science with technology, which gathered momentum towards the end of the sixteenth century, was decisive for the modern world. The interaction between scientific progress and the development of machines created the conditions for the Industrial Revolution, which, from the eighteenth century, was to overturn the old monarchical societies. The origin of classical science can be traced back to the Copernican Revolution, but it was fed by sixteenth-century technology. Henceforth, technology was to develop in symbiosis with the sciences, with industrialization as the major outcome.

[20]   *Treatise on Human Nature* (1739–40), book 1, part 3, especially section 14.

sought to define the structure of understanding from the human faculty of knowledge.[21]

Philosophers extended the issues regarding human beings and science. Are the laws of physics the laws of nature itself? Can science claim to grasp the essence of reality?[22] Since the laws of natural science establish causal connections between phenomena, are human beings simply natural creatures subject to an all-encompassing determinism? If so, what becomes of the freedom they have discovered and begun to explore in this new world? These questions bear witness to a new attitude of mind.

A new attitude of mind

This is the heart of European thought. Why was scientific change gradually able to engender a new civilization? Because it developed within the framework of a new relationship of human beings to themselves, to nature and to the deity. Scientific change provided new ways of thinking, organizing, communicating and representing reality. In short, a new conception of reason. This attitude of mind had developed during the Middle Ages but emerged fully during the transitional period known as the Renaissance.

The Renaissance found deity in everything and, being 'pantheistic', it came to deify nature. The world was no longer under the shadow of original sin. It was the world where humans had sinned, but also where they would obtain redemption. Pantheism marked an essential step in the 'desacralization' which set aside the direct links between nature and the God who had created it. It led to thinking of nature in terms of the being who has knowledge of it: man. This new conception of humanity was, first and foremost, a new experience of themselves and their abilities. It was founded on liberty. Sin itself was proof that God had created people free in nature, and it fell to them to understand the meaning of this freedom. Furthermore, as natural beings, humankind held a prime place in nature; they were its most perfect creation, an expression of its final purpose. For they had the ability to know it and the duty to use it to aid their development, and realize the potential with which God had endowed them. Thus, Renaissance pantheism transformed human beings' image of themselves and their role.

---

[21] In 'Transcendental analytic' (Kant, 1787; 1933 edn, pp. 102–275). One of the aims of this essential work of European philosophy was to refute the scepticism about the validity of knowledge which Hume's position implied.

[22] For scientists, the universe is just as science knows it, no more and no less. This implicit assertion in science is not simply a form of atheism. The order which they gradually discovered took on, to the scientists' eyes, an immensity and perfection which could not have been the work of chance, and so must reveal a 'design'. This was, after a fashion, a proof of the existence of God, which allowed some of them to formulate a new conception of deity and religion – for example, the general *Scholium* (or commentary) with which Newton concluded his *Philosophiae Naturalis Principia Mathematica* (Mathematical Principles of Natural Philosophy) of 1687. It was no longer God that made it possible to understand nature; it was physics that made it possible to conceive of God.

Pico della Mirandola (1436–94) set out this foundation of Renaissance humanism in an exemplary fashion in his *De Hominis Dignitate Oratio* (Discourse on Human Dignity) of 1486. He had God address Adam thus:

> Neither a fixed abode nor a form that is thine alone nor any function peculiar to thyself have we given thee, Adam, to the end that according to thy longing and according to thy judgement thou mayest have and possess what abode, what form, and what functions thou thyself shalt desire. The nature of all other beings is limited and constrained within the bounds of the laws prescribed by Us. Thou, constrained by no limits, in accordance with thine own free will, in whose hand We have placed thee, shalt ordain for thyself the limits of thy nature. We have set thee at the world's centre that thou mayest from thence more easily observe whatever is in the world.
>
> *(Quoted in Cassirer et al., 1948, pp. 224–5)*

The modern notion of freedom makes its first appearance in European thought: human beings are defined by their freedom, their autonomy within nature and their ability to know, create and build.

This new attitude sprang up in a world that was still geocentric, and so would be profoundly modified by the methodological discipline of the 'New Science' and its conception of the universe. It found means of expression and articulation in science. Pantheism set up a kind of private dialogue between humanity and nature, which physics would make so much its own as to appear the ultimate expression of reason, the model for all knowledge. The idea of an all-encompassing nature was to continue to inspire a whole range of philosophies right up to the beginning of the nineteenth century. The basic problem they pursued was this: just as Newton had discovered the fundamental law of nature in universal attraction, was it not possible to do for human nature, and even for society, what Newton had done for the physical universe?

How can we sum up the attitude towards human beings in nature? The world is no longer an enclosed space, but has become infinite. A rift has gradually opened up: human beings perceive nature at a distance from them, a vista which is set out before them yet contains them. They must get to know it objectively by learning how to rectify the data of perception. Hence the science they develop and their experimental method, which bring home to them the power of the human mind.

This power is expressed in the progress of the sciences, particularly physics, and also in the development of technology. Science formulates technologies' principles of operation and progressively adapts them to different types of production. This is summed up in Descartes' famous formulation:

> ... it is possible to attain knowledge which is very useful in life, and ... we may find a practical philosophy by means of which, knowing the force and the action of fire, water, air, the stars, heavens and all other bodies that environ us, as distinctly as we know the different crafts of our artisans, we can in the same way employ them in all those uses to

which they are adapted, and thus render ourselves the masters and possessors of nature.[23]

Through science, humans take possession of nature. They acquire control over it because they learn to acquire knowledge of it. At the same time, through technology they know how to make nature satisfy their needs.

This rift with nature also extends to humans themselves, by dividing them into a body and a soul. Through their bodies, human beings are natural beings. They therefore become objects of science and can be studied by the experimental method. However, through their souls – which, from now on, would be defined as consciousness, thought or reason – people escape from the laws of nature and perceive themselves as free agents in nature. Humanity has a destiny that is not governed by determinism. Can they then establish a human world governed by laws which their freedom and capacity for thought allow them to formulate? In order for the natural and the human worlds to exist each within the other, the former must be controllable by the latter. This is the attitude of mind which runs through modern civilization. But this control tends to be rather precarious: in the gap between body and soul, a certain emptiness appears in human beings, a fractured unity threatening their coherence.[24] This rift, which reproduces that between humans and nature, is fundamental to modern subjectivity, and to individuals' relationship with themselves and with other people.

In this gap, new relationships between God and humanity are conceived and lived out. From now on, the relationship with God is built within subjectivity – in the conflict between body and soul, the feelings of guilt which that gives rise to, and the solitude of the individual consciousness. Faith and belief became more intense, more rigorous, and took as their foundation an activity of the spirit divorced from both the collective rituals of popular religion and the ceremony of established religion. As it came to be more internalized, religion became distinct from the Church, which appeared more obviously a temporal institution with its pomp and ceremony, its hierarchy and dogmas. Religion became an individual and collective morality, capable even of opposing the Church and reproaching it for its compromises with political power. The historical sign of this evolution was the Protestant

[23] *Discourse on Method*, part 6 (Descartes, 1637; 1911 edn, p. 119). In view of the historical context, it would be wrong to see this formula as an early advocacy of the violation of nature which is the root of contemporary ecological problems: nature is at the service of human beings, but they cannot exempt themselves from it.

[24] Renaissance men and women were fully physical beings who were thereby able to live as part of nature. Since then, however, for modern men and women the body has been at the disposal of mind and consciousness, seeking to control it through the exercise of will. Though the body may be an object of science, to be known about and cared for, it is also the source of disturbance to the soul and danger to knowledge. It is the locus of passion and desire, as manifested in sensuality and sexuality. Modern human beings are obliged to define their consciousness in relation to their sexuality, and reduce all their sensual, affective nature to that.

Reformation,[25] the Catholic Counter-Reformation and religious movements such as Jansenism,[26] which were to play a crucial role in undermining the old, pre-Revolutionary regime in France.[27] Henceforward, theology yielded supremacy to philosophy. The Church was no longer grounded on cosmology, but purely on the faith of its members, its own dogmas, and the hold it had (principally through confession and education) over people's consciences. The relationship between God and nature would be confined to the province of religion, and religious discourse and dogma would have to stay within the bounds marked out by physics. The historians have described this slow but inexorable secularization of society, arising from a religion which no longer ruled over nature but over human beings, their consciences and their moral conduct.

Under the combined influence of this methodological discipline and attitude of mind, human beings could not live, understand or organize their collective life in the same way as before. The result was a new relationship with society, and thus a new kind of political thought.

New thinking in law and politics

With the Renaissance new opportunities were opened up, both for individuals and for entire peoples, not only in philosophy, art and science but also in politics. The social and political concepts born then still constitute a major reference point of European thought – indeed the only one dating back as far as that period. This is the third axis along which the modern world has evolved.

The human community and natural right

In the pantheistic Renaissance view of the world, nature is harmony and its order is the 'natural law' which, inscribed in each living being, rules over all of them. Natural law is reflected in human beings and, through them, reaches the level of conscious-

---

[25]   The Reformation marks a rift between the temporal Church and its religious message; there was a desire to rediscover the original message, and to establish a religion based on an interior dialogue between the individual and God.

[26]   A rigorous conservative tendency within Catholicism established by the writings of Cornelius Jansen (1585–1638), who opposed the Jesuits' teaching (developed as part of the Counter-Reformation) and advocated a return to the thinking of Saint Augustine regarding the sinfulness of the world and the need for God-given grace in order to achieve salvation. In France in particular, the other-worldly gravity of this way of thought appealed to many, both among the poor and the untitled bourgeoisie, who saw in it a condemnation of the alliance between wealth, monarchical pomp, the Jesuit Order and the upper echelons of the Catholic Church in general. (NP)

[27]   For a synthesis of current research, see Roger Chartier (1991, ch. 5).

ness: each individual discovers that he or she is capable of action grounded in natural law, which contributes to its realization – that is, to a situation of 'natural right'. Human beings are the repository of natural law. Their destiny is to follow natural law, and so extend its rule over this world. Most importantly, this implies a 'state of nature':[28] that is, a natural community preceding each 'body politic' and transcending them, in which all living beings are under nature and its law. It posited harmony and established a principle of equality between human beings.

The idea of a human community originates in Greek thought. But Christianity had claimed it as its own by affirming a brotherhood embracing all peoples, nations and conditions of humanity. The Renaissance formulated a new conception of society by reinterpreting the political thought of antiquity, especially Stoic philosophy. Thus Cicero (106–43 BC) had written in his *De Legibus*:

> Law is the highest reason, implanted in nature, which commands what
> ought to be done and forbids the opposite .... Law is a natural force; it
> is the mind and the reason of the intelligent man, the standard by which
> Justice and Injustice are measured .... [I]n determining what Justice is,
> let us begin with that supreme Law which had its origin ages before any
> written law existed or any state had been established .... Therefore, since
> there is nothing better than reason, and since it exists both in man and
> in God, the first common possession of man and God is reason ....
> Further, those who share Law must also share Justice; and those who
> share these are to be regarded as members of the same commonwealth.
> If indeed they obey the same authorities and powers, this is true in a far
> greater degree ...
> *(Cicero, 1928 edn, book 1, ch. 6 & 7, pp. 317–23)*

Within the framework of Augustine's dichotomy between a 'heavenly city' and an 'earthly city',[29] an old, Greek idea of cosmopolitanism was revived and a new cosmopolitan idea was born: that of citizenship transcending all social divisions. The state of nature, postulated on the spontaneous community of human beings, was a pantheistic substitute for universal brotherhood in the Christian community. Just as nature, once divine, had become profane, so in the state of nature the human community was sanctified and the Christian community desanctified. Not that natural law, the state of nature and natural right were merely new dogmas, modern beliefs arising from a non-religious sentiment of belonging to a community. This new conception of politics was primarily an effect of various threads of the Copernican Revolution. The attitude of mind described above generated a radically new collective experience of society, individuals and their relationships. The methodological discipline showed itself in the way problems were posed and dealt with, and in the way the results were communicated and criticized. The concept of the state of nature was the point of convergence which brought together this attitude, this experience and this discipline.

---

[28]   The phrase seems to make its first appearance in 1625, in Grotius's *De Jura Belli ac Pacis* (The laws of war and also of peace). This work is discussed further in the section below on the authority of Law (pp. 44–5).

[29]   See note 13 above. (NP)

The meanings and implications of the idea were set out by Puffendorf in *De Officio Hominis et Civis juxta Legem Naturalem* (The duty of man and the citizen derived from natural law) of 1682:[30]

> Insofar as it can be known by the light of reason alone, the state of
> nature can be looked at from three points of view: in relation to God the
> Creator; or by imaging individuals as they would be on their own,
> without the support of their fellows; or, lastly, in terms of the social ties
> that exist naturally between human beings.
>
> *(Puffendorf, 1682; 1747 edn, p. 2)*

These points of view illustrate how the notion has evolved. The first two have disappeared from view. The reference to a God who made human beings 'the most excellent of the animals'[31] still bears the trace of the Renaissance period. Likewise, by the end of the eighteenth century, people no longer thought of society in terms of a state of affairs that had preceded it. The contrast between natural life and civilized life 'made comfortable by industry and commerce with other men' – which Marx denounced as 'Robinsonades'[32] – had lost its force. The third point of view is still relevant today because it is fundamental to European democratic ideas of human rights and the various declarations of them. 'The state of nature in the last sense', wrote Puffendorf:

> is that where one conceives of men with nothing in common
> except the similarity between their natures, which exists inde-
> pendently of all conventions and any human act to subjugate
> some to others.[33]

[30] Translated into French by Jean Barbeyrac as *Les Devoirs de l'homme et du citoyen tels qu'ils sont prescrits par la Loi Naturelle*. Quotations are taken from the 4th Trévoux edition (1747) of this translation (which includes Leibniz's 'judgment of this work' and Barbeyrac's replies), mainly from volume 2, book II, chapter 1. I have chosen this particular Puffendorf work because his 'digest of natural law' was probably the most popular text on this theme in eighteenth-century Europe. Puffendorf's principal work is *De Jure Naturae et Gentium Libri* of 1672 (trans. *The Law of Nature and Nations*, Oxford, 1710).

[31] From which, as Puffendorf put it, 'it follows that man must acknowledge the author of his existence, admire His works, render Him worship worthy of Him, and behave in a quite different way from animals devoid of reason' (1682; 1747 edn, p. 3).

[32] The term refers to Defoe's Robinson Crusoe. In using it, Marx is drawing attention to the self-congratulatory anachronism of models of 'natural' human life devoid of social relations: 'The individual and isolated hunter and fisherman ... belongs amongst the unimaginative conceits of the eighteenth-century Robinsonades ... [The economists] Smith and Ricardo ... stand with both feet on the shoulders of the eighteenth-century prophets, in whose imagination this eighteenth-century individual ... appears as an ideal, whose existence they project into the past' (Marx, 1857; 1973 edn, p. 84). See also Marx (1867; 1970 edn, ch. 1, pp. 76–7). (NP)

[33] Puffendorf (1682; 1747 edn, p. 4). This passage may be contrasted with the definition given by John Locke: 'To understand political power aright, and derive it from its original, we must consider what state all men are naturally in, and that is a state of

This was the moment when the modern form of citizenship was defined. Puffendorf abandoned fiction in favour of a universal morality which established a secular community of all humanity running across formally constituted societies. Rather than a fictional state that dissolved at the advent of society, the state of nature had become a universal morality, constituting the pivotal reference point of society and the norm by which each body politic can be assessed. As members of the human community, human beings demand equality before the law and individual liberty, and they are entitled to judge their societies and the governments exercising authority over them according to universal morality.

This universal moral community transcended the distinction between the 'heavenly city' and the 'earthly city'. It replaced opposition between the two with a connection between what we might term real-world societies and a transcendental, or even an 'ideal', society (provided we note that, though the 'ideal' acts upon the present, its focus is on the long-term future). Second, it established not only a right and duty to criticize despotism but, above all, a right of resistance for oppressed populations. In effect, it furnished the principles to justify opposition to any government which conflates the interests of a single individual or group with the interests of society as a whole.[34] Finally, it introduced the possibility of the progressive transformation of societies in the real world.[35]

This condemnation of despotism was not a rejection of monarchy as such, which was considered as legitimate a type of government as any other provided it remained subservient to natural right. Nevertheless, the definition of natural law imposed severe constraints on those who exercised authority. The introduction of a moral dimension made it possible to define principles of liberty and equality, leaving the legitimacy of absolutist[36] regimes perpetually in question. From now on, natural rights were to be precisely the attributes that all individuals had in common. They were to constitute the common good which underpins the republic,[37] because they were present in each individual, irrespective of the use he or she might make of them. Modern democracy was initially a

---

perfect freedom to order their actions and dispose of their possessions and persons as they think fit, within the bounds of the law of nature without asking leave, or depending upon the will of any other man.
'A state also of equality, wherein all the power and jurisdiction is reciprocal, no one having more than another ...' (Locke, 1689, 1956 edn, ch. 2, paragraph 4, p. 4).

[34]   The right to intervene in the affairs of a sovereign state on humanitarian grounds is in fact an extension of resistance justified by the universality of human rights.

[35]   Though our view of history no longer corresponds with this conception, the everyday life and the administration of modern societies are conducted in terms of a future which transcends the contradictions of the present.

[36]   The dominant form of state in seventeenth- and eighteenth-century Europe, in which the monarch claimed unrestricted authority. (NP)

[37]   That is, the idea of '*res publica*' or 'commonwealth' [see the section above on the birth of political philosophy – NP].

notion of lawfulness.[38] In considering individuals apart from the society where they lived, and offering them the opportunity to use their reason to think for themselves, the theory of natural right affirmed their liberty. They no longer owed obedience to anyone but their own selves, via a law of their own nature, guided by the proven capacity of reason. At the same time, by availing themselves of developing scientific knowledge, they were able to question the ways of their society. The experience of liberty is inseparable from human beings' experience of their own capacities. It provides them with an ideal and a project: to free themselves of oppression, habit and subjection.

The critique of authority

In effect, the state of nature and a morality based on human rights struck at the very foundation of authority by proposing a new concept of society: as a free association of individuals entered into by mutual consent – that is, a covenant, contract or compact. There are numerous, quite distinct notions of the contract. But Rousseau's in *The Social Contract* (1762) is exemplary because it is one of the later ones, and reveals the function of this kind of argument. Rousseau's starting point is the prevailing situation of subjection and despotism. He explains that it was underpinned by a conception likening society to a family, with the king as the father.[39] But in modern times the king is no father of a family, and the submission underpinning the social order is founded solely on the habit of obedience and the fear of punishment. To conceive of society according to the model of the family is to treat human beings as children dependent on a father, and think of oneself as a subservient being incapable of exercising the faculty of reason – in other words, as a sort of slave. The objective of that kind of reasoning is clear: 'Slaves, in their bondage, lose everything, even the desire to be free' (Rousseau, 1762; 1968 edn, p. 52).

For Rousseau, existing societies can no longer conceal the fact that they are founded on absolutist despotism and the implicit enslavement of their subjects – that is, on the more or less overt use of force, fear and intimidation. But as Rousseau says, 'might does not make right' (p. 53). He proposes to abandon this conception of society and replace it with a different one founded on 'the act by which people become *a* people' (p. 59). He develops a new way of experiencing

---

[38]   Francesco D'Agostino's essay in this volume on the state under the rule of Law develops the claim that law is an essential medium to identify and enforce the common good inherent to democracy. (NP)

[39]   Thus, in the beginning, the children freely consented to remain with their father, whom they felt naturally inclined to obey as he was their progenitor and protector: 'The family may therefore perhaps be seen as the first model of political societies: the head of the state bears the image of the father, the people the image of his children, and all, being born free and equal, surrender their freedom only when they see advantage in doing so. The only difference is that in the family, a father's love for his children repays him for the care he bestows on them, while in the state, where the ruler can have no such feeling for his people, the pleasure of commanding must take place of love' (Rousseau, 1762; 1968 edn, pp. 50–1).

society and a different discourse, offering a new relationship to other people and to authority.

> 'How to find a form of association which will defend the persons and goods of each member with the collective force of all, and under which each individual, while uniting himself with the others, obeys no one but himself, and remains as free as before.' This is the fundamental problem to which the social contract holds the solution …
>
> If, then, we eliminate from the social pact everything that is not essential to it, we find it comes down to this: 'Each one of us puts into the community his person and all his powers under the supreme direction of the general will; and as a body, we incorporate every member as an indivisible part of the whole.'[40]
>
> *(Rousseau, ch. 6, pp. 60–1)*

The theory of the social compact was, then, a hypothesis to replace the analogy with a family, just as Copernicus's hypothesis replaced Ptolemy's. Its value (though not its validity) can be measured by its effect on the thinking of the period.

The social contract argument was inextricably bound up with the 'New Science', though it is not possible to establish a relationship of cause and effect between the two. Just as physics was attempting to discover the fundamental laws of the universe, the aim of the new legal and political thinking was to discover the fundamental law which governed human societies, so that human beings might act on the basis of it. Modern people were seeking to become 'owner and master' of their society as well as of nature and themselves. Thanks to their faculty of reason, whose power had been proven by science, they had the capacity to create a properly human world – one which had both a moral and a political dimension. Experiencing their reason and the freedom it offers in nature and society brings humanity to adulthood. This rebirth was the political equivalent of the Copernican Revolution.

Some questionable presuppositions of the new thinking

This line of argument contains certain presuppositions which need to be made explicit. The body politic was being rethought from the point of view of its origin. The object was not to show this or that origin as historical fact or fiction. It was to show that society has its formation in its own hands – as if it were possible to go

---

[40] That does not mean the will of the majority necessarily reflects the will of each individual. Rousseau's hypothesis may be compared to Locke's: 'For when any number of men have, by contract of every individual, made a community, they have thereby made that community one body, with a power to act as one body, which is only by the will and determination of the majority. For that which acts any community being only the consent of the individuals of it,… every one is bound by the consent to be concluded by the majority' (Locke, 1689; 1956 edn, ch. 8, para. 96, p. 49). [The relationship between government by the people and majority rule is explored in Rodney Barker's essay in this volume – NP.]

back to a moment at the beginning of society, where the legitimacy of its established order (that is to say, an oppressive one) is suspended and thrown into doubt. At the moment of origin the eternal motives that bring human beings together can be rehearsed.[41] Ideally, by pursuing the question of the origin, individuals obtained the means to reinvent society, as if unmaking and remaking it. In this way, the idea of revolution – of abolishing history and starting anew – made its first appearance in political thought.

In the final analysis, the explanation in terms of a state of nature comes down to a discourse or collective fiction recounting the origin and development of societies. It presupposes that the account it gives has the power to take us who read it back to the moment of origin, to be present at that fictitious time when human beings, with no intermediaries, formed themselves into a society. With this discourse, it was imagined, the people of the seventeenth and eighteenth centuries would be able to free themselves from their historic enslavement and reinvent the body politic. These texts about origins were all variations on the same theme. They functioned as a kind of collective myth woven by philosophers. The myth had a power which was both real and illusory for the people at that time: it could lead them out of humanity's childhood, free them from slavery and, by appealing to reason, open up the possibility of a new society. This political discourse functioned as a kind of collective psychoanalysis for Europeans. It allowed them to relive the establishment of society and the conditions of their acquiescence in their own oppression.[42] It left them in a position to submit to oppression or to dare to follow their reason and their urge for liberty – fortified by the idea that one is alone in fear and submission, but never in criticism and the pursuit of liberty.

Since the discourse in which reason is to transform society is a kind of collective myth, this political philosophy cannot be considered a form of knowledge, much less a science. But that does not mean it is devoid of interest: it reflects the new state of mind which inspired it, and which changed the course of western European societies. However, this discourse becomes dangerous when translated into a programme which a political group seeks to impose on society, sometimes by resorting to violence. It becomes criminal when this programme draws on particular sciences and theories in order to develop an ideology justifying its objectives, or, even worse, when it co-opts them to obtain the technological means to

---

[41]   Humanity is a natural community in which *civitates* have developed – that is, individual societies built around a specific compact or consensus. As S. Goyard-Fabre puts it in his introduction to Locke's *Second Treatise of Government*: 'Although the great human community in which life is lived according to reason is a natural society, it falls to human beings to actualize it in particular societies *(civitates)* which, insofar as they are based on a contract expressing consensus, supplement their natural roots with an artificial aspect' (Goyard-Fabre, 1984, p. 97).

[42]   The therapeutic strategy of psychoanalysis is for the patient to recover what appear to be suppressed memories of traumatic past experiences, especially from childhood. This empowers the patient to make a free, conscious choice of his or her own future behaviour, untrammelled by psychological burdens from the past. The 'myth' of a social contract might function in that way, regardless of its claim to historical accuracy. (NP)

realize these objectives. That is why it is necessary to stress the methodological discipline described above which underpins the sciences, and show that they amount to something over and above the actual content of the knowledge they engender.

The problem of sovereignty

This methodological discipline was gradually to transform modern European political thought, supplying its definitive shape as well as the problems and concepts which constitute its historical reference points. The problem of politics has two sides to it: first, to formulate a notion of the human community by defining natural right (that is, the imprescriptible and inalienable rights of individuals[43]); second, to establish how individuals could choose, or freely consent to, a form of rational government capable of putting the authority of natural right into effect.

What could it mean to be the 'sovereign power' in the state?[44] It could no longer be identified as the basis on which society was established or as the agent of authority originating in God.[45] The problem for the modern age is no longer, 'Who should govern?' It has split into two questions: 'How should one govern?' and 'How can the government be controlled?' In these reflections on sovereignty, the future of the old, monarchical regimes was at stake, as was the idea of a new political system whose sole legitimacy lay in the debate over its principles, institutions and purposes. The sovereign could no longer be anything other than the natural human community – 'brothers, free and equal' – which gradually came to be known as 'the people'. That was the Copernican Revolution in politics: authority could no longer set itself up as the sovereign power; rather, reflection on the principle of sovereignty formed the basis of government.

The solution to the problem of sovereignty gave birth to the modern idea of the state under the rule of Law, which is fully expounded by Francesco D'Agostino in this volume. Puffendorf leads the way to it: 'Where the state is properly formed, there must be two covenants and a set of constitutional instruments' (Puffendorf, 1682; 1747 edn, vol. 2, pp. 64–6). The fundamental covenant is as follows:

> Everyone first commits himself, with all the rest, to join together for all time in a single body, and to administer by common assent whatever affects their conservation and security.

This assent embraces natural right. From that there follows:

> a set of constitutional instruments which establish the form of the government, without which there would be no means, effectively and by

---

[43] Rights which can be neither taken away nor surrendered by those endowed with them. (NP)

[44] This debate on sovereignty gave rise to the distinction between the executive and legislative powers, which is fundamental to modern democracy.

[45] The theory of natural law excludes both these options: society is now founded on the common rights of humanity, which replace God-given authority. (NP)

common accord, to take clear measures for the public good. Finally, there has to be yet another covenant, by which, once one or more persons have been chosen on whom to confer the power of governing society, those endowed with this supreme authority commit themselves carefully to protect the common security and interest; at the same time, the rest promise faithful obedience to them.

These are the modern principles of a constitution. Three distinct levels are identified and distinguished: the principles of Law; the type of government they entail; and the relationship whereby the government commits itself to the people, and the people can control the government in the name of those original principles.

In effect, as Rousseau puts it, the sovereign now corresponds to the body politic itself:

> ... each person, in making a contract, as it were, with himself, finds himself doubly committed, first, as a member of the sovereign body, in relation to individuals, and secondly as a member of the state in relation to the sovereign ...

> However, since the body politic, or sovereign, owes its being to the sanctity of the contract alone, it cannot commit itself, even in treaties with foreign powers, to anything that would derogate from the original act of association; it could not, for example, alienate a part of itself or submit to another sovereign. To violate the act which has given it existence would be to annihilate itself; and what is nothing can produce nothing.

> *(Rousseau, 1762; 1968 edn, pp. 62–3)*

The problem is very complex. Law brings the people together and constitutes them as a state. Hence, the state under the rule of Law is the necessary condition of modern democracy: it defines the political sphere, where problems susceptible to collective formulation and treatment belong. Ideally, government then mediates between Law and the people.[46] The people can make Law and the constitution their own in order to influence the government. But to make use of Law, they must behave like a people rather than a mere assemblage of individuals. They must demonstrate sovereignty in their unity and cohesion by expressing themselves unanimously, or at least in a solid majority.[47] The core of the problem is to establish what is Law and what is a people. Modern democracy plays out that tension.

To assert that 'the people' is sovereign requires us, then, to clarify what 'the people' is. Three radically divergent conceptions appeared, forming the lines of

---

[46] Though there are enormous problems about this. Can we assume unmediated communication between government and people? Is 'the people' not an abstraction? Does the bureaucracy express the true function of the modern state? What are the relationships between government, the people, individuals and so on?

[47] That is where the function of elections lies: participating in them makes individuals into members of a people. That counts at least as much as who is in power as a result of the election.

tension drawn within European democracy. For some, what constitutes 'the people' is shared traditions and customs because these are the distillations of the group's history, activities and knowledge. This is the British conception, which sees the essential principle inspiring resistance to authority in collective practices and customs. Democracy is accordingly believed to lie in the control of the government's prerogative and the limitation of its field of action. Ultimately, it matters little who governs, so long as the government intervenes as little as possible in the life of the community, or does so only in accordance with the law.

This first conception, spreading right across Europe, was to be reinterpreted in Germany during the eighteenth century,[48] with results, at the beginning of the nineteenth century, that contradicted the British version. The state was defined as itself a product of the collective history: its function was therefore to reflect that history and preserve those traditions. Hence, the problem was no longer how civil society could control the state, since the latter was in fact the expression of the former, above the conflict of individual interests and opinions. On the contrary, the role of the state was to acquire sufficient authority to protect the people against anything which might threaten their unity, identity or territory. The people were considered not as a society of individuals and groups, but as a living historical community, an organic totality.[49] Whereas the British version limited the role of the state, the German version tended to expand it.

In eighteenth-century France, within the current of political thinking which led to the revolution of 1789, shared traditions and customs were no longer thought to be what individuals have in common. The existence of the people (or society) is accounted for by individuals' exercise of universal reason. That enabled each individual to partake of natural right, claim his or her liberty, and seek to put both into practice within the body politic. Customs and traditions were no longer the means of protecting the people against the government; on the contrary, they came to be considered as the means by which the people were enslaved, and from which they needed to be liberated by changing the government and modernizing the state. Sovereignty thus came to be conceived of in terms of the 'general will' of the sovereign people: a unanimous opinion expressing universal reason, which the

---

[48]   For example, by the philosopher and poet Herder in his *Ideen zur Geschichte der Menschheit* (Thoughts on the history of humankind) of 1784–91, which was refuted by Kant.

[49]   See, for example, Hegel, in *Grundlinien der Philosophie des Rechts* (1821), paragraph 258: 'If the state is confused with civil society, and if its specific end is laid down as the security and protection of property and personal freedom, then the interest of the individuals as such becomes the ultimate end of their associations, and it follows that membership of the state is something optional....' He goes on to contrast what I call the German view: 'Unification pure and simple is the true content and aim of the individual, and the individual's destiny is the living of a universal life' (Hegel, 1821; 1952 edn, p. 156). See also paragraphs 273 and 274. Monarchy was the form of government which expressed this political philosophy: 'Taken without its monarch and the articulation of the whole which is the indispensable and direct concomitant of monarchy, the people is a formless mass and no longer a state' (p. 183).

government must proclaim in order to carry out the transformations supposedly necessary to the country. This French conception ascribes a dominant role to the state, which brings it into simultaneous opposition with the British conception of civil society and the German conception of the role of the state.

These divergent views on sovereignty contain the essence and the meaning of democracy. They generated different types of political culture which have come into violent conflict in the past. The political construction of Europe cannot expect to rise above these conflicting views until it has studied and confronted them.

The authority of Law and natural right

The fiction of a state of nature was absorbed into the theory of natural right, which is the basis of the modern conception of sovereignty. From the beginning of the seventeenth century, this theory, by virtue of the role it fulfilled in the debate, displayed the modern methodological discipline. For it articulated its principles in such a way that their universal validity was guaranteed by reason alone. The recognition of Law as the only route to democracy is an essential feature of modern thought. To govern all societies and be valid for all times and places, Law cannot be derived empirically from elements drawn from existing legal regimes. The idea of natural right has to provide a standard to judge which regimes conform to Law. What is required is to delineate an idea of what might be called a transcendental democracy.

This is the task undertaken by the great theorist of natural right, Hugo Grotius – politician, humanist and jurist. His work was dominated by the desire to ground natural right in a manner consistent with the modern methodological discipline. He shows that Law, if it is to guarantee its validity, must develop within a framework modelled on mathematical proofs. Right and justice must be abstracted from all contingent, historical realities. Just as a geometrical proof does not depend on the precise shape of the diagrams constructed by geometricians, even if there is no society where natural right is applied, that does not mean it has no value. It is possible to deduce just laws from self-evident axioms. Right is thus a matter of eternal truths. These are the ideas Grotius developed in his principal work, *De Jura Belli ac Pacis* (The laws of war and also of peace) of 1625.[50]

One essential point had been grasped: Law can be detached from the social, political and cultural conditions of its emergence, transcend what is merely relative to those conditions and, on the strength of its universality, demonstrate its validity. If natural right is not constructed merely on the strength of the conditions in which it is formulated, then it is not tied to any individual state, civilization or period of history. On the contrary, it is the product of a special type of endeavour whose aim

---

[50] Grotius was writing during the Thirty Years War, 1618–48. [This was a religious war fought largely in Germany, but with the participation of most other European powers, partly to sustain the power of the Holy Roman Empire. – NP] With its shifting alliances and, even then, the massacres of large numbers of innocent civilians, the war played a major role in the development of the modern notion of natural right.

is to transcend relativism.[51] On several occasions, Grotius shows his admiration for Galileo. Natural right partakes fully of the modern methodological discipline which seeks knowledge that is independent of those who obtain it because it is generated by reproducible and communicable procedures guaranteeing its validity. Without (of course) actually becoming a science, right thus acquires certain characteristic features of all scientific activity: its construction and formulation can never be completed once and for all, and it involves a series of progressive steps which develop out of criticisms and subsequent corrections. Just like science, then, right has a history. But its history has not been merely a development confined to the historical conditions where it developed. It has been a process of construction to free itself from those conditions, with a view to securing its autonomy and universality. That does not mean natural right is subordinate to science; on the contrary, it shows its autonomy and its common ground with science. In very different guises, the same methodological discipline can be found in various separate branches of knowledge or social life.

Within this framework of rational law, the content of the human community was taking shape. The theory of natural right engendered the theory of the state under the rule of Law. From now on, right was to be grounded solely in the rational activity of formulating it – through, that is, the activity of jurists. Thus the meaning of law was modified. It was no longer the decrees of any *de facto* power; it was the application of the right which underpinned it. The legislative power within the state was based on rules which were not limited by the conditions in which it was exercised. Right is independent of government: it is the central principle of the political system, to which citizens suffering injustice have recourse. What we might call its transcendental republic, quite separable from the contingent realities, is the principle of modern politics.

Politics is never conducted in accordance with right: it is always subject to more or less explicit forms of domination and oppression, to the violence of conflicting interests and inequalities, and to resistance from the subject. As Gérard Duprat argues in this volume, this twofold nature of politics has a major consequence: modern individuals can never fully subscribe to the political set-up in which they live. They belong both inside and outside: immersing themselves in it only to resist it, participating only to criticize. This tension at the heart of society drives its evolution and shapes political life.

[51]   One cannot therefore speak of 'European' or 'western' human rights on the pretext that they originated in Europe, or refuse to apply them on the pretext of not being European or western. Human rights are not European in the sense that a law may be Dutch or American. At the same time, however, this imposes a certain obligation to be continually removing from the concept of natural right whatever may make it merely relative.

A new social and political philosophy

A different conception of society

The metaphysical notion of a community of human beings founded on natural law is the first axis within the development of modern democratic thought. Even to-day, it still remains a major point of reference and a criterion of judgement. However, this current of thought came in for a great deal of criticism on the grounds that its moral principles were too abstract and thus ill-equipped to explain societies, much less reform them. A second, more radical axis for debate was therefore opened up, adding a dimension of change to the first. It rejected the equation between natural law, the foundation of society and the order of nature. Rather, it pursued questions about the nature of abstract entities such as the state, the people and so on. Originally English and Scottish, this current of thought focused not on the 'natural law' which supposedly gave rise to the natural community of human beings, but on the relationships between the members of this actual community. It rejected the transcendent model, whether natural or divine, as a premise from which to deduce the political order. The problem it pursued was twofold: (a) to account for a social order which nobody had intended, but which would not have come into being if nobody had wanted it; and (b) to explain how human beings were able to create a political order which oppressed them.

John Locke was the philosopher in whose works this discourse took shape. His argument is often blurred at the edges, as if his own doctrine is in the process of generating another. For Locke, society is natural; it cannot therefore be the out-come of an explicit, conscious act of association by which individuals quit the state of nature in order to create a 'state of society'. Likewise, he is dismissive of the idea that society is brought into being by an act of submission to a ruler on the part of the subjects. The truth of the matter is that there is no departure from the state of nature; society is simply one of its manifestations:

> The only way whereby anyone divests himself of natural liberty and
> puts on the bonds of civil society is by agreeing with other men to join
> and *unite into a community* for their comfortable, safe, and peaceable
> living one amongst another, in secure enjoyment of their properties, and
> a greater security ....
> *(Locke, 1689; 1956 edn, para. 95, p. 49; emphasis added)*

Society is in fact a spontaneous order arising out of existing relationships between individuals. It is not fixed by the members acting together, nor by any one of them: it emerges as the chance result of a certain kind of interaction between an unknown number of people. Not having been decided upon or chosen, neither can it be re-decided or established anew. But all this should not be viewed as a critique of the state under the rule of Law so much as scepticism towards its underlying metaphysics. The fact that nobody willed society into being, that nobody had in mind a plan of what it should be or become, does not mean existing societies are the best possible. Quite the contrary: it means that society is not grounded in any transcendent principle, model or norm, be it God, natural right or an act of will

John Locke, 1632–1704 (credit: Hulton Deutsch).

(ideal or imaginary) made by individuals to establish a 'body politic'.[52] Society is formed between individuals as the outcome of interactions they develop in the natural course of events, and of their gradual efforts to devise a legal framework for their relationships.

A psychology of social ties

Locke attempts to clarify the relationship between individuals and the social order they find themselves in without asking for it. He describes the origins of politics at the level of an individual experience which he takes for granted because, for individuals, that is where the political set-up finds its justification. It might seem unsatisfactory to conceive of politics simply in terms of a psychology of social ties, or the feeling of being a member of a society. But the problem needs to be

---

[52]   There is a fundamental paradox in the attempts to establish the grounds of the state. The previous metaphysics of natural law made them a matter of contingency. For one can ground natural right on either a self-evident proof or a deduction from universally accepted principles. Either way, the case is blocked: it ends merely by making the state contingent on something other than itself, leaving its foundations relative rather than universal, as was intended.

looked at from a different angle. For Locke, without the metaphysics of natural right, this psychology is all that remains of the social bond, of the renunciation of freedom on which it is founded, and of the consent which ensures its continuance. The emergence of civil society represents, first and foremost, a renunciation of personal 'executive power', in other words, of the use of force to settle disputes.[53] That is the initial condition of all social existence, insofar as it opens up the possibility of any order within social reality. It is a version of the state of nature for people who understand that renunciation is not a sign of weakness but, on the contrary, a way of redirecting one's powers.[54] Renunciation is the essential mark of entering civilization[55] and citizenship.

This emergent[56] order, which individuals find themselves putting into effect, cannot be said to be universal in the sense of valid for all people, at all times and places. It is 'impersonal' in the ordinary sense of common to all, and as a kind of impartial arbiter expressing the origin of social existence. It is both part of, and separate from, interactions between individuals, appearing to each one as a judge. A human judge is an individual who tries to embody this arbitrating function by reflection which, in the thick of the rivalry between different interests, enables him or her to identify what is implicitly required for the political existence of society. This is a vital point: the judge is just as important as right itself.[57] The law is no longer transcendent; it is human. But it has not, for all that, been made relative. It is invented by human beings not merely in response to circumstances, but in a continual endeavour to give fresh expression to the requirements of society's political existence.

[53]   The use of force would result in generalized warfare between individuals, the negation of any kind of society or 'living together'. The central idea is that war is the negation of the social bond or, more precisely, a type of social bond that negates all social bonds. This is a critique of Hobbes, for whom fear and violence drive human beings to submit voluntarily to one of their number, who then guarantees peace by exercising a monopoly of violence, which thus becomes lawful. For Locke, this kind of peace is no peace at all. [Hobbes's idea of the so-called state of war is discussed further in Jean Baudoin's essay in this volume. – NP]

[54]   One obvious objection needs to be met – namely, that this renunciation can only be a token of weakness because it amounts to a submission to 'voluntary servitude', to use Hobbes's expression. In fact, it can only demonstrate power: only those with choice, and the courage to put it into practice, can renounce something.

[55]   This is Locke's meaning in his paragraph 89: 'Wherever, therefore, any number of people are so united into one society, as to quit every one his executive power of the law of nature, and to resign it to the public, there, and there only, is a *political, or civil society*' (p. 45; emphasis added).

[56]   An *emergent* feature of a system is one which is more than can be expected merely from the sum of its component parts. (NP)

[57]   This approach implies a distinction between justice and what is good in itself: the former assumes nothing more than the efforts of the judge as he or she reflects on the meaning of right and the principles underlying civil society, whereas the latter calls for an

The loss involved in renunciation is immediately compensated for by the gain in consent, which is the other side of the coin. Consent is the very foundation of the body politic. It is the acknowledgment of its existence and legitimacy – not once and for all, as in Rousseau, but at every moment, on every occasion that a relationship to other people or to society is engaged in. The performance of consent is trust, by which one belongs to something that does not exist until consent creates it. Locke's civil society is therefore by no means an ideal or transcendental society. But neither is it equivalent to 'real', historically existing societies. It shows up the despotism of those societies as something which cannot be trusted or consented to. The act of renunciation and consent takes place between individuals. Each one grasps his or her identity as a citizen,[58] as a member of a society which exists only in the terms which individuals consent to, even though, at the same time, it exists through forms of domination and subjection. The spontaneous order of society is not all-embracing. On the contrary, it removes the need to treat society as a totality. It leads us instead to conceive society as an aggregate not of individuals but of micro-societies, chance associations between individuals based on reciprocal acts of consent which form and dissolve. Society, therefore, does not possess a unity which transcends individuals; they are not members of a community or parts of a larger whole.

Natural law's idea of the human community has been challenged, questioned and superseded in two different ways. First, it has broken up into the diversity of individuals defined by their interests and inclinations, or by the unstable micro-societies which they shape and reshape as their relationships change. Sometimes they obey and sometimes they disobey the laws, the customs and the institutions it codifies. They wrestle with the economic structures which ensure their survival. Second, the focus has now shifted from natural law and its basis in religion or cosmology to custom, the administration of justice, and the liberties which individuals seek to acquire in order to affirm their autonomy – and governments seek to reduce. In bringing right and law down to the profane level of customs, practices and individual inclinations, this political philosophy does not merely make them relative. On the contrary, its greatest virtue is its conception of the individual, which does not reduce him or her to the distinction between body and soul. It tries to observe how individuals really are: following their interests and their inclinations, their egoism and their altruism. It thus becomes pointless to ascribe to

---

effort to specify its content. The problem of good, considered as an 'idea of reason' in the Kantian sense, is that historically it has tended to confuse the common good with the general interest. The weakness of the first is to remain merely formal and abstract; the weakness of the second is to confuse the interest of the greatest number with that of particular individuals or minorities. The definition of justice becomes confused with the method whereby justice is arrived at and implemented.

[58]   Individuals do not continuously live out consent as a process of becoming a part of a larger whole or members of a community; they simply become citizens – that is to say, participants in politics and members of a 'collective' entity. As Schmidt's essay in this volume makes clear, this is what is experienced in the 'public sphere'. It is therefore necessary to distinguish the Greek notion of 'community' from the modern notion of the 'public'.

them a moral essence, 'divine instinct', or other elements of that metaphysical superstructure. Though it lacks the old appeal to reason and geometric methods, this new conception has a higher degree of rationality because it is more economical.[59] Reason need not be a property of individual human beings, residing in the soul or the conscience. Indeed, it is an emergent effect of interactions between individuals striving for their own survival and their personal interests or those of their micro-society. They gradually discover the best means of achieving their aims: that is, the means with the least risk of provoking conflict. Reason is gradually born to human beings in society to the degree that they secure their autonomy and exercise their freedom, eventually realizing that the best guarantee they can have of their own freedom is that which they accord to others.

Modern political rationality

The rationality of politics thus underwent a profound change of direction towards the end of the seventeenth century. It was no longer simply the pursuit of the *res publica*, the common good, natural right or human rights. Not that it excluded these; rather, it provided a deeper analysis of the problem which these notions had sought to resolve. It led to a distinction between *civil society* (individuals, their interests, inclinations and interrelationships) and the *state* (political institutions, their history, mode of operation and activities). Political rationality henceforth addressed two levels. It required consideration of the interconnections between the two: of the capacity of the political system to reflect ongoing changes in civil society, and of civil society to exercise control over the government and state institutions. Political rationality from the eighteenth century to the present was bound to be dominated by this division. Certain thinkers, such as Hegel (1770–1831), would identify reason with the modern state, the organs society creates for its own administration; others would locate reason in individuals and their calculations of self-interest,[60] or in the evolutionary processes of society. The whole of our political history has been played out in this gap between society and the state, in the conflict between them, in the means of managing it, and in the recognition of the logic specific to each level. One thing is now certain: the state cannot claim to be identical with society, whose autonomy is thereby secured.

This cleavage displays the methodological discipline common to political thought and scientific development. By dividing state from society, political rationality created the theoretical preconditions for two separate groups of disciplines. First, a space was opened up for sciences of society, 'human' sciences that would study the relationships between individuals and societies. As an autonomous entity subject to analysis in terms of various concepts and problems, society became the potential object of new sciences to describe and explain it. These new sciences (economics, sociology, psychology, demography, etc.) embrace the territory of

---

[59]   That is, uses fewer superfluous and hypothetical structures to sustain its explanation. (NP)

[60]   The most important movement initiated by this tendency was Utilitarianism [also discussed in Rodney Barker's essay – NP].

modern politics. But as they developed and became more specialized, they gradually lost touch with the political questions which underlay them. The challenge before philosophy today is to reopen these questions. For politics is always *the* critical issue. It is also a specifically philosophical problem that cannot be equated with those of the human and social sciences, though it is inseparable from them.

At the same time, a second space gradually opened up for a *political* science. The object of the science of politics or government would be the state, its institutions and political systems in general. These two great discipline groups (the social and the political sciences) are characteristic of modernity. Their methods and objectives are distinct, and will remain so. They will always clash around the insoluble conflict that is the key issue within modern political rationality: the difference between political principles and practical politics. This means that, though they can achieve nothing without the human sciences, the political sciences cannot be reduced merely to sciences of 'administration' or government. And neither political nor social sciences can dispense with the questions which, thanks to the conflicts over the ground they share in common, political philosophy poses them.

Modern political rationality is thus fundamentally fragmented. The task of philosophy lies in the spaces between the fragments. Political thought is continually reinvented outside the practice of politics. Its key question is the interconnections between the different levels and disciplines where the life of society is lived, made, thought about, and where politics breaks down and questions of its legitimacy are raised. Thus modern democratic culture slowly took shape in the meeting of the political sciences, the human sciences and philosophy. Now that, at the end of the twentieth century, we can look back over this political thought and its consequences, it offers neither the unity for putting forward a European model of democracy nor the certainty to serve as the basis of a plan, a programme or a long-term ideal. As Duprat shows in this volume, it is a *type* of political activity rather than a model. The utopianism of the seventeenth, eighteenth and nineteenth centuries has evaporated. Reflections on European political culture today do not concern the failure of ideologies and utopias; they teach us to look at political practice afresh and reinvent democracy. To achieve that, it is necessary, again and again, to refine and re-examine modern political thought with a view to identifying what needs to be reformulated or left behind.

The concept of public opinion

The history of modern political thought is the history of the evolution towards democracy and the resistance to it. Thus modern political thought as a whole leads to democracy. It is no longer simply one of three possible forms of government[61]

---

[61]   The distinction between 'forms of government' – any of which could in principle be put into operation in the one, given state – was implicit in Plato's account of the degeneration of forms of government (see the section on the birth of political philosophy). Systematized by Aristotle into monarchy, aristocracy/oligarchy, and democracy, it was considered basic to political theory until the late eighteenth century. Since democracy was merely one possible form among others, it had no status (as is being claimed for it here) as the essence of the just state. (NP)

to bring natural law into the real world; it is the essential mode of operation of the state as natural law envisaged it. Democracy has become the only political system that adequately reflects modern political rationality, or the state of collective thinking in which human beings consider together the societies that they create, and how to conceptualize them and transform them in accordance with carefully thought-out goals. The ideas of Locke express this attitude at the very moment of its emergence:

> ... when any number of men have, by the consent of every individual, made a *community*, they have thereby made that *community* one body, with a power to act as one body, which is only by the will and determination of the majority. For that which acts any community being only the consent of the individuals of it, and it being necessary to that which is one body to move one way, it is necessary that body should move that way whither the greater force carries it, which is the *consent of the majority*... And thus every man... puts himself under an obligation to every one of that *society*, to submit to the determination of *the majority*, and to be concluded by it...
> *(Locke, 1689; 1956 edn, ch. 8, paras 96 and 97, pp. 49–50)*

Whereas Rousseau conceived democracy as only a limiting case of government (since it would ideally have to be founded on unanimity), Locke formulated the majority principle, which has become the basis of modern democracies rooted in an electoral system and legislative control over the executive. Within the conceptual framework of the democratic state, the common good – impossible to define, justify or ground in itself – comes to be seen in terms of the principle of the majority.[62]

The notion of the political community has also been dissolved into that of 'public opinion', which Hans-Joachim Schmidt will discuss in this volume. The chaotic mass of individuals (each different from the others, ruled by inclinations and interests setting them against each other) generates a spontaneous order which no one wanted or willed into being. This spontaneous order is not a norm or a definition of the good. Public opinion is paradoxical: at one and the same time, the opinion of nobody and everybody. It is a collective opinion, possibly that of the 'greatest number'. It is a statistical notion recording a collective state of mind, and thus cannot constitute a norm. Using the right polling methods, one may establish what it is at a given point in time, but publishing the results transforms the reality they are supposed to have grasped. In the eighteenth century, the idea of public opinion showed individual attitudes and collective demands: it was the expression of those members of society who exercised their reason in public, who demonstrated their liberty and took advantage of their individual rights to explain, communicate, discuss and modify their ideas. Public opinion is an emergent characteristic of modern politics and constitutive of democracy. It is democracy's most sensitive point, where order seems to teeter on the edge of the disorder that is the diversity of opinion in a democracy. Public opinion is the people's truth: not

---

[62] The relationship between government by the people and majority rule is explored in Rodney Barker's essay in this volume. (NP)

a precisely determined collective opinion identifiable with that of the greatest number, but something residing in the diversity of individual opinions, in their conflicts and rivalries.[63]

We must distinguish between the two levels of modern political rationality: the state and society. The majority is an essential institutional norm for the political system, implicit in the practice of elections.[64] But to reduce public opinion to the views of the greatest number is to misunderstand the way it develops and evolves. It also runs the risk of changing public opinion into a strategy to reduce diversity by silencing minorities or invalidating what they have to say. In the eighteenth century, challenging majority opinion meant entering into debate with it, publishing one's ideas, supported by argument, in a process of discussion which formed and developed public opinion. Public opinion is most alive not in the majority but in marginal, dissident opinions. The whole value of minority opinion lies in its starting a debate which then becomes part of majority opinion and transforms it. The contrast between majority and minority should therefore not be seen as a choice between alternatives or a principle of exclusion. It is the essential circumstance of democratic debate, where the aspiration to become the majority view is the principal justification.[65]

Today the 'message' of the greatest number is inaudible. There is an urgent need to rethink public opinion and free it from the powerful forces that have grafted themselves on to it, claiming to speak for it. In the past, the press formulated and communicated public opinion, but today the mass media try to monopolize it or even substitute themselves for it, anaesthetizing and sterilizing it in the process. This is the main focus of Schmidt's essay.

It is vitally important that we rediscover the meaning of public opinion and do not let it drown in the illusion of mass communication, or reduce it to a seamless consensus which distorts the conditions of its formation and development. Over and above the opinion of the majority, we must understand the collective intelligence of an entire people. Public opinion presupposes individual and collective ethical principles for thinking and debate: those of acquiring, developing and communicating ideas, and knowing how to argue them through and compare them so that they may be criticized and modified. In a nutshell, these principles require

[63]   It corresponds to what Marx was to term an 'ideology' when he studied the mechanisms of its formation in a given society, namely the capitalist societies of the early nineteenth century. To secure the conditions for the free development of public opinion is the first duty of a democratic government. This is a matter, first and foremost, of education and culture.

[64]   Regardless of whether the aim of elections is to form a solid parliamentary majority or to express the diversity of opinion, the electoral system evokes the relationship between the government, the people and public opinion.

[65]   The idea that the majority is an exclusive body that represses the rest of society is a recently formed notion based on a particular interpretation of history. It does not contradict the argument being put forward here.

that knowledge be given priority over spontaneous opinion and prejudice.[66] It is the very same discipline that we find operating in the sciences.

Afterword: Crisis and the conditions for democracy

The key problems that will be explored in this volume have now been set out. There are others which go beyond our remit, two of which must be mentioned. First, the present essay does not explain how the Copernican Revolution gave birth to the Industrial Revolution, and with it the deep social problems that were the source of European democracy's two great reverses: Nazism and Stalinism, the living negation of the very idea of a human community. The trace of horror and shame they evoke in all Europeans reminds us of the fragility of human rights, public opinion and the state under the rule of Law. But that trace does not show that such reverses are inevitable. Rather, this century's tragedies demonstrate that democracy's underlying objective has to be to maintain the liberty which under-pins it – that is, to give individuals the means (not only constitutional but also so-cial and economic) allowing them to enjoy their rights. There lies the way to resist regressive tendencies eroding the principles of democracy.

The second, broader problem brings this essay's long-term perspective further for-ward. Since the beginning of the twentieth century, the conditions in which science and modern democracy first appeared have fallen away. Alongside enormous politi-cal crises, new transformations have broken up the Copernican universe – first in science, then in technology and production. European societies are therefore being sucked into a new revolution. Once again, democracy will have to be reinvented; its one essential task will be to find means of controlling technological development. But one thing is certain: only democracy can furnish the means to develop society's collective understanding so as to answer to these enormous problems.

The starting point is the division in modern political rationality between the sci-ences of society and the sciences of politics. Philosophy straddles this fissure: it links and distinguishes these two opposed, yet mutually dependent fields of in-quiry. Future analysis of these fields will address their relationship and the ques-tions they raise.

I have shown the relationship between scientific transformations and the formation of the two great conceptions of democracy, the classical and the modern. In the process, we have identified what one could call 'revolutionary situations', in which the social system gradually comes apart and another is formed. The thesis I

---

[66]   Democracy and religion are incompatible as regards their attitude to the world and the type of thinking they require. But this does not mean that democracy is entitled to prohibit the practice of religion. For religious liberty is a fundamental democratic right. What it does mean is that religion can only exist as something affecting individuals and contributing to the necessary diversity of public opinion. In this respect it enjoys the same status as sex, ethnicity or national origin.

"BABY PLAY WITH NICE BALL?"

The cartoonist Low comments on one of the technological outcomes of the scientific revolution of the twentieth century (credit: Solo Syndication).

advance is twofold: such situations are extremely rare in history and quite peculiar; and, in them, the idea of democracy is invented or reinvented.

We must contrast revolutionary situations, which confront or even cast doubt on the political system and its institutions, with mere 'political crises' (see also Dobry, 1986). Notwithstanding contemporary usage, such crises cannot be called 'revolutionary'. They are simply 'extraordinary' in the sense that they depart from the 'ordinary' run of political life. In normal political life, which covers what we can call 'political problems', individuals display no great political passion. They vote at regular intervals, but outside of (or even during) election time, they seem to take no interest in public affairs, preferring to devote themselves to their private concerns. Political apathy is often more apparent than real: individuals tacitly trust

55

in the mechanisms of control they can exercise, within the constitution, over the government and their own representatives. Generally, ordinary political life comes down to electing the government and representatives of the people, and to arranging for arbitration between opposed values, between the demands of particular groups and the needs of the community, and between partial interests and our shared obligations.

Mere 'political' problems do not call for the mobilization of the people. But an absence of satisfactory solutions to problems met by the social system can bring about (sometimes rapidly) the mobilization of various groups, which leads in extreme cases to a crisis in the political system. Two types of political crisis must then be distinguished. On the one hand, a crisis may be resolved within the established framework of the constitutional state under the rule of Law. Such crises lead to reforms in the system of government and reinterpretations (in keeping with changes in public opinion) of the basic ideas of law and justice. Constitutional amendments or even a change of constitution are their outward signs. On the other hand, a crisis may call into question the role of Law itself, the idea of the people and the capacity of the state to govern. The crisis then falls outside the constitutional state's political resources for dealing with conflict.

There is one particular historical case we must touch on, because it obsesses European culture. The German crisis of the 1920s engulfed the economic, social and political systems all at once. In due course, the constitutional state was swept aside, the democratic idea of the people rejected, and the normal function of government suspended. That is not to say that the state under the rule of Law is fundamentally weak and illusory, unable to deal with exceptional situations where the very existence of the people is at risk. Tragically, the Weimar republic,[67] incapable either of mastering the country's problems or of putting into effect the solutions it could envisage, was bereft of means to reassert its legitimacy in the eyes of various groups suffering from the situation. The bankruptcy of the state under the rule of Law created an exceptional situation. Sovereignty was stripped down to the mere practice of authority and power; the government was fused with the state; civil society was made to identify itself with the state or be declared its enemy. On the other hand, the social, economic and political crisis prompted by the fall of the Nazi dictatorship could, in its turn, be resolved only by the establishment of a state under the rule of Law.

Because they cast doubt on the existing political system, we must now go on to examine these extraordinary crises. In the past they have sometimes led to the formation of a democratic regime and sometimes to its rejection. What are the essential conditions of this? In the next essay, Jean Baudoin shows that democratic political regimes form under varied and yet quite specific conditions. He examines some paths and settings for the process of democratization. There is a strong underlying claim: all democracies carry with them the traces of the conditions in which they were established.

---

[67]   Constitutional republic of Germany established in the town of Weimar in 1919 following Germany's World War I defeat under the monarchy, and replaced in 1933 at the Nazis' accession to power. (NP)

References

ARISTOTLE (1930 edn) *De Caelo* (On the heavens), trans. J. L. Stocks, in *The Works of Aristotle*, vol. II, ed. W. D. Ross, Oxford, Clarendon.

BOYER, C. B. (1968) *A History of Mathematics*, New York, Wiley.

CASSIRER, E., KRISTELLER, P. O. AND RANDALL JR, J. H. (eds) (1948) *The Renaissance Philosophy of Man*, Chicago, University of Chicago Press.

CHARTIER, R. (1991) *The Cultural Origins of the French Revolution*, trans. Lydia G. Cochrane, Durham, North Carolina and London, Duke University Press; first published (1990) *Les Origines intellectuelles de la Révolution Française*, Paris, Editions du Seuil.

CICERO, M. T. (1928 edn) *De Legibus* (The laws), trans. C. L. Keyes, London, Heinemann, and Cambridge, Mass., Harvard University Press.

DESCARTES, R. (1637; 1911 edn) *The Philosophical Works of Descartes*, vol. 1, trans. E. S. Haldane and G. R. T. Ross, Cambridge, Cambridge University Press.

DOBRY, M. (1986) *Sociologie des crises politiques* (The sociology of political crises), Paris, Presses FMSP.

GOYARD-FABRE, S. (1984) 'Introduction' to John Locke, *Second Traité de gouvernement civile*, Paris, Garnier-Flammarion.

HEGEL, G. W. F. (1821; 1952 edn) *Hegel's Philosophy of Right*, ed. T. M. Knox, Oxford, Oxford University Press.

KANT, I. (1787; 1933 edn) *Critique of Pure Reason*, ed. N. Kemp Smith, London, Macmillan.

LOCKE, J. (1689; 1956 edn) *The Second Treatise on Civil Government*, ed. J. W. Gough, Oxford, Blackwell.

MARX, K. (1857; 1973 edn) 'Introduction' to the *Grundrisse: Foundations of the Critique of Political Economy*, trans. Martin Nicolaus, Harmondsworth, Penguin.

MARX, K. (1867; 1970 edn) *Capital*, vol. 1, London, Lawrence and Wishart.

PUFFENDORF, S. (1682; 1747 edn) *Les Devoirs de l'homme et du citoyen tels qu'ils sont prescrits par la Loi Naturelle* (The duty of man and the citizen derived from natural law), Trévoux.

ROUSSEAU, J.-J. (1762; 1968 edn) *The Social Contract*, book I, trans. M. Cranston, Harmondsworth, Penguin.

VERNANT, J.-P. (1965; 1983 edn) 'Geometry and spherical astronomy in the First Greek Cosmology', in *Myth and Thought among the Greeks*, London, RKP; trans. of *Mythe et pensée chez les Grecs*, Paris, Maspero.

Essay 2
The conditions for the development of democracy

Prepared for the Course Team by Jean Baudoin
Professor of Political Science, University of Rennes
Translated by John Williams and Noël Parker

Introduction

The face which western Europe presents today was quite simply unthinkable a mere half-century ago. It has become both a peaceful continent, no longer under the shadow of centuries-old national rivalries or territorial disputes, and a community of liberal values and rules whose democratic resolve has been further strengthened by the disappearance of the last surviving dictatorships along the Mediterranean rim (Greece, Spain and Portugal).

The sudden disintegration of the communist system in eastern Europe constitutes the most striking outward sign of democratic revival. In these societies, which had all, to a greater or lesser degree, experienced pure forms of 'totalitarianism', political democracy and the market economy have appeared spontaneously as the only plausible alternatives – although simply establishing them is not sufficient to make them function correctly or to produce immediate and beneficial effects.

The aim of this essay is to help clarify certain fundamental questions which are central to a proper investigation of democracy's slow progress on the European continent since the end of the eighteenth century. There is little hope of being able to weave together and make sense of the various, often chaotic paths that have led to this modern-day flowering of democracy unless, in the first instance, we keep strictly to an approach based on *historical sociology*. Historical sociology elucidates the diverse routes which have led to the democratization of society, the factors which have encouraged or retarded it, the actors on the social and political scene who have embodied it, and the institutions which have contributed to its consolidation.

This approach, based on an initial prejudgement about the issue, allows us to avoid a number of theoretical dead-ends. It avoids institutionalism because it invites us to look beyond the formal procedures for appointing leaders, and consider the whole range of problems posed by co-existence in society. It avoids developmentalism because it saves us from having to consider the earliest democratic systems (those of the Anglo-Saxon[1] nations, in particular) as yardsticks against which later systems of government can properly be measured. It avoids relativism as it obliges us to pick out elements of universality from what appear to be entirely unique experiences. From this point of view, the gradual and uneven progress of the democratic model in western Europe can be assessed in relation to two variables: on the one hand, the strong tendency towards the *rationalization of social conflicts*, and on the other, *the internal logic of republican institutions*.

That said, it is also necessary to have a definition of democracy. This is not the preserve of sociology but primarily a matter of political philosophy. Let us reject the aphorism of the political scientist Giovanni Sartori that 'democracy is a pompous name for something that does not exist'. Democracy has been said to commend itself as 'the least bad system of government'. That is at least partly because it is based on certain values – those of *liberalism* – and on certain procedures – those of *democracy*. The value of those procedures emerges if we take into account the view of the seventeenth-century philosopher Thomas Hobbes, who supposed that any human community is necessarily undermined by quarrels and thereby exposed to an extreme risk of 'war of every one against every one'. Liberal values and democratic procedures together allow human societies to accommodate their contradictions, and go forward without tying themselves to some theological purpose or ultimate goal such as 'the withering away of the state'.

The rationalization of social conflicts

Democracy is a social condition before it is a political system. It emerges when the groups and individuals that make up a society are in agreement, or come to an agreement, over the need for conciliation in place of conflict and its destabilizing effects. Thus, rather than expecting a society to comply straightaway with the requirements of democratic constitutionalism, we should look carefully at those procedures and experiences which indicate a propensity towards the rationalization of disputes and prepare people for a culture of debate and compromise. Looked at this way, it appears that from the nineteenth century onwards, several historical factors have proved to be favourable, either simultaneously or in succession, to the implantation of an authentic democratic tradition.

- The *contingent* factor – in several countries there was the slow emergence among those competing for political supremacy of a preference for conciliation which, though not necessarily intended or thought out, eventually became an ingrained habit and encouraged the development of stable procedures for regulating disputes.

- The *intellectual* factor – the seed of democracy has more chance of germinating when it is planted in fertile intellectual soil which welcomes discussion

[1]   That is, British, North American and Australasian. The term 'Anglo-Saxon' has been commonly used in Europe since the nineteenth century to identify those nations and their history as a group. (NP)

and mutual criticism, and which encourages tolerance and the exchange of views. It will, necessarily, be more fragile in places where this liberal topsoil meets a bedrock of historic intolerance. Since no society can be more democratic than the individuals who compose it, the spread of a genuine spirit of liberalism throughout society is a crucial condition for the establishment of a lasting democracy.

- The *social* factor – the rationalization of conflict becomes more of a practical possibility if it is inscribed within a social structure characterized by the relative diffusion of sources of conflict. In dealing with this question, Anglo-Saxon political science associates the likelihood that disputes will be settled reasonably with a situation of 'cross-cutting cleavages', whereas situations of 'overlapping cleavages'[2] tend to exacerbate such disputes and prevent democracy from becoming institutionalized.

By combining these three factors that contribute to the gradual rationalization of disputes, and by observing how European societies and their politics have evolved in the modern era, we can identify two standard patterns under the following headings: *formative experiences* and *legacies of intolerance*. These are explored below.

Formative experiences

The British parliamentary system, on the one hand, and 'consociational democracy', on the other, represent crucial historical experiences which have left their mark on the revival of the democratic imagination across the European continent, and have had a powerful knock-on effect on other societies. We should also mention the development of 'republican compromises' in the second half of the nineteenth century.

The British parliamentary system

The emergence of the British parliamentary model and its subsequent stabilization seem to bear out the hypothesis that democracy is much more the product of chance events or the force of necessity than it is the result of deliberate construction or popular demand.[3] Great Britain presents a pattern that has long been considered exemplary because, at a given moment in history, the groups that 'mattered' in society reached certain decisive agreements, thereby banishing the spectres of absolutism and anarchy. A number of features deserve attention.

As the difference in social status between the old, titled élite and the bourgeois élite was narrowing, both groups came to an understanding in order to limit the power of the central government. They removed the vestiges of feudalism and

---

[2]   That is, where grounds for divisions between segments of the population cut across each other rather than reinforce each other. Thus, for example, manual workers might be predominantly Catholic and speak their own dialect (overlapping cleavages) or they might be divided into different religions and linguistic groups which also embrace other classes (cross-cutting cleavages). The implications of these two situations are explained in the section below on consociational democracy. (NP)

[3]   See the work of Guy Hermet (1983, 1986).

Parliamentary debate in the House of Commons, 1893 (credit: Hulton Deutsch).

kept the 'dangerous classes' lower down the social scale marginalized. This historic settlement was underpinned by institutions (Parliament) and procedures (rights granted earlier in the Magna Carta, the Bill of Rights, common law[4]) which had played their part in containing the dominant power of the monarchy, in defining the 'subjects' of the Crown as 'citizens' who possessed certain rights, and in the development of a system of justice that was independent of government. In short, until the great electoral reforms of the nineteenth century, British society was to be the scene of a continuous process of self-development by parliamentary government. Oriented more towards the limitation of central authority and the protection of individual rights than towards the search for a perfect reflection of the 'general will', this slow evolution eliminated, in a most effective way, all the ambiguities and dangers linked to the myth of 'popular sovereignty'.

However, we must not idealize the British experience. For a long period it remained confined to a social élite who strove to keep the mass of the people on the fringes of politics. Only gradually, and after many bitter struggles, did universal suffrage gain acceptance. However, if we focus only on the oligarchical excesses of the British system, we overlook the aspect of it that was radically new: the invention of a 'public sphere' (to borrow the expression popularized by Jurgen

---

[4]   These are further explained and discussed in Francesco D'Agostino's essay in this volume. (NP)

Habermas)[5] within which a disposition towards compromise prevails over the imposition of arbitrary power and over the appeal of populism.[6]

Consociational democracy[7]

As a general rule, situations of 'overlapping cleavages' within a society are particularly unfavourable to the emergence and growth of a democratic tradition. Instead of being dissipated across the body of society, overlapping cleavages – of social class, ethnic group, religious faith or political persuasion – harden and are echoed in the public arena by starkly opposed parties and groups. The search for compromise then becomes difficult. The Northern Irish and Lebanese examples offer particularly tragic illustrations of this. Only the intervention of forces from outside (the British army in the first case, the Syrian army and, at regular intervals, the blue berets of the UN in the second) allow these societies to escape from ever more bloody and devastating quarrels. These do not, however, have to be the inevitable consequence. Several western societies provide proof that extremely destructive overlapping cleavages can be overcome. The Dutch political scientist Arend Lijphardt has given the name *consociational democracy* to this form of social organization, which has allowed several deeply divided European societies (for example, Switzerland, the Netherlands, Austria, Belgium) to be ruled on the basis of values and procedures that ensure political stability. According to him, three circumstances arising one after the other permit the consociational gamble to come off:

1   Rival social élites are able to appreciate the hazards that overlapping, mutually exacerbating cleavages represent for society.

2   These same élites have the will to safeguard the unity of the social order and see the common interest take precedence over the mass of particular interests.

3   They manifest the will to transcend conflicts by setting up adequate procedures to overcome the lure of hegemony and address the needs of subcultures. These include the adoption of federalism, the introduction of proportional representation for the election of representatives, protection for minority languages, the proliferation of social benefits, and other strategies to stabilize these deeply conflict-ridden societies.

The republican compromise

In the second half of the nineteenth century, two other sorts of historical experience contributed to the stabilization of republican institutions. One was the his-

[5]   See Hans-Joachim Schmidt's essay in this volume for extensive discussion of this concept. (NP)

[6]   That is, the attraction of mobilizing mass support, often by demagoguery, to impose a single outcome upon dissenting minorities. (NP)

[7]   See also Pierre Avril's essay in this volume for further discussion of consociational democracy. (NP)

toric compromise that was established in most Scandinavian countries under the aegis of the social-democratic and trade-union movements. The other was the republican synthesis that was achieved in France under the Third Republic.[8] Let us concentrate on the second of these.

It may appear strange, indeed controversial, to credit the much maligned Third Republic as one of the progenitors of democracy. This role is more often attributed to the French Revolution of 1789. However, while there can be no question of detracting from the Revolution's greatness, not least its so-called immortal principles, the shortcomings of the Revolution need to be clearly and frankly acknowledged. On the one hand, it was hampered from the beginning by the fundamental dichotomy identified by the historian François Furet (1978). It experienced difficulty in regulating the tension between the liberal principle of the limitation of state power and the democratic principle of popular sovereignty. Most importantly, the preoccupation with what was regarded as the crucial problem – 'the expression of the general will' – pushed the search for mechanisms able to promote conciliation and compromise into the background. Generally speaking, the French Revolution was dogged by a fundamental reluctance to accept the reality and productiveness of differences of opinion.[9] It was not until the Third Republic (see the chart on forms of government in France) that the regulation of such differences became compatible with the idea of moderate government.

Forms of government in late eighteenth/nineteenth-century France

1789–1799	Original French Revolution, giving rise to constitutional monarchy, the execution of the king, and various republican regimes, including the extreme Jacobin period of the Terror (1792–4)
1799/1802–1815	Republic superseded by Napoleon Bonaparte's regime (latterly 'empire')
1815–1830	Return of old royal family to power
1830–1848	Revolution produces a more limited, constitutional monarchy (the 'July monarchy') under liberal wing of royal family
1848/52–1870	Further revolution leads to establishment of 'Second' Empire under Bonaparte's nephew
1870–1945	Defeat in Franco-Prussian War leads to new 'Third' Republic

[8]   That is, the French Republic created by the constitution of 1871, which remained in force until 1945. (NP)

[9]   In a similar manner to the 'philosophical' societies studied by Augustin Cochin (1925; 1979 edn), where the overriding wish to speak with a unanimous voice was plainly thought preferable to the peaceful regulation of differences.

There were a number of key points in this process:

- Although the Bordeaux Assembly (elected in the aftermath of defeat in the Franco-Prussian war of 1870) was dominated by monarchists, Adolphe Thiers[10] managed to reconcile the republican idea with the notion of liberalism not only by rebuilding the nation and respecting its institutions, but also by crushing the revolutionary Paris Commune. For traditionalist and Bonapartist elements, the traumatic episode of the Terror had been a point of reference *par excellence*, providing them with a convenient stick with which to beat the republican idea.[11] Thiers robbed them of this argument and demonstrated that the Republic was not necessarily synonymous with Jacobin Terror.

- The enactment of the constitutional laws of 1875 marked the invention of a political category previously unknown in France – the centrist compromise. It was on the initiative of the more liberal elements of the monarchist coalition[12] and the more moderate elements of the republican coalition that the Third Republic received its official consecration.

- This new political configuration started to show positive results as it gradually took root among new social forces, and enrolled them under the republican banner. It was instrumental in convincing the rural population that it was in their interest to rally to the Republic. By its very existence, it ensured the rise of a new ruling élite, the majority of whom were drawn from the 'new strata of society' Gambetta[13] was so fond of. It implied the need for a system of state schools and teacher training colleges which would carry out the daily task of republican education and persuasion. Later, it even went so far as to develop the social dimension of the state,[14] introducing 'welfare credits' for

---

[10]   Statesman and historian (1797–1877), who served as interior minister and prime minister under the bourgeois constitutional democracy of the 1830s and 1840s. He was elected head of the provisional executive and then president of the newly founded republic in 1870, though he lost power in 1873. (NP)

[11]   'Bonapartists' advocated a return to military-imperial dictatorship in the name of the Republic – as originally created by Napoleon Bonaparte from 1802 to 1815 and revived (from 1852 to 1870) under his nephew, Napoleon III. Traditionalists favoured a straightforward, monarchical autocracy. Both sustained their case against republicanism on the brutal demands of the urban poor and other radicals, which had underpinned the institutionalization of mass arrests and executions in the early 1790s known as 'the Terror'. (NP)

[12]   Notably the Orleanists, i.e. supporters of the liberal wing of the old royal family, to which the constitutional monarch of 1830–48, the so-called 'July Monarchy', had belonged. (NP)

[13]   Republican lawyer and politician (1838–82), elected to the legislature in 1869, who was minister of the interior responsible for the (ultimately fruitless) effort to reorganize French defences in the Franco-Prussian war on a broad popular base. He resigned from office in 1870 and remained in opposition, apart from one brief spell as prime minister in 1881–2. (NP)

[14]   'Inventing the social', to use Jacques Donzelot's well-chosen expression (Donzelot, 1984). [Donzelot and others examine the growth of the 'social sector' of government, which becomes the territory of new breeds of public servants such as social workers, judges in family courts, welfare administrators, doctors, teachers. – NP]

Rebels being executed after the suppression of the Paris Commune, 1871 (credit: Hulton Deutsch).

the benefit of underprivileged groups and thus heralding the arrival of the welfare state.

Certainly, this republican educational mission came up against its limitations. The Republic quickly degenerated into a system of government by assembly whose scandals and excesses revived the anti-parliamentary impulse as a permanent feature of politics, notably on the extreme right. Unlike later social-democratic parties, it did not succeed in introducing social compromise into the realm of civil society and into the practices of its supporters. It remained the responsibility of the legislators to create compromise. Nevertheless by the 1930s, when it came to the trial of strength with fascism, a republican spirit had percolated into society and, linked to the unity of the democratic forces, constituted an effective barrier to the appeal of totalitarianism.

Legacies of intolerance

Although the great majority of western European countries experimented, even as early as the latter half of the nineteenth century, with democratic institutions and procedures, these fulfilled their pacifying function only where there already existed a cultural climate which favoured discussion and compromise. The development of political democracy was all the more speedy in Great Britain and the Netherlands because it took place against the background of a tradition of conciliation and experiment going back many centuries. Similarly, in France the Third Republic played a particularly vital role in implanting the republican idea. The mechanisms it put in place gradually came to be associated with a feeling of confidence in the republican system among the majority of people. However, even the apparently most virtuous institutions are powerless when faced with a majority opinion which is consistently hostile or indifferent towards the democratic principle. Two forces inimical to that principle deserve to be mentioned: German authoritarianism and southern European clientelism.

German authoritarianism

The example of modern Germany shows the dangers of pursuing modernization through an unreformed authoritarian political system. In this respect, Germany under Bismarck in the 1870s and 1880s is a classic example. On the one hand, it is possible to credit Bismarck with the invention of the modern social-welfare state and with the establishment of a system of social security which was without parallel at the time. On the other hand, the social-welfare state was no guarantee that the German people would be socialized into democratic practice. On the contrary, democracy continued to be held in check by Bismarck's authoritarianism. This was directed towards consolidating the imperial structure and gagging the incipient parliamentary movement. The tragic impotence of Germany's Weimar Republic in the early 1930s was the natural consequence of this apprenticeship in the ways of modern politics. The humiliation caused by military defeat and the Versailles *diktat*,[15] the devastating scale of the ensuing economic and social crisis, and the overwhelming disunity which existed in the German workers' movement from the 1930s onwards succeeded only in opening up even more fissures in the republican fabric. The process of disintegration was implicit above all in the weakness and amateurism of the political forces committed to the democratic ideal, in the endemic hostility it incurred from the social and economic élites, and in the almost total absence (since the spread of the Hegelian doctrine[16]) of an intellectual tradition favouring debate and compromise. The powerlessness of republican institutions to stem the rising tide of National Socialism illustrates the time lag that can sometimes exist between the establishment of a democratic system and its consolidation: it is easier to set up a state under the rule of Law than to make it function properly.

Southern European clientelism

The example of regimes which flourished along the Mediterranean rim of Europe reveals the same kind of inadequacy, albeit in a different way. Let us look at Spain as an example. As early as the twelfth century, the rudiments of a 'moderate' organization

[15]   That is, the crushing terms (such as loss of territory, demilitarization and extensive war reparations) imposed on Germany at the post-World War I Versailles peace conference. (NP)

[16]   See Francesco D'Agostino's essay in this volume for a brief statement and defence of this. (NP)

of society had begun to emerge.[17] But two sorts of phenomena combined over a long period to act as parasites on these first seeds of liberalism. First, there was religion. Spain became the rallying point of the Catholic Counter-Reformation of the sixteenth century, with the state rapidly taking on the role of the Catholic Church's military arm. Second, there was the predominance of an agrarian economy characterized by extremely large estates (*latifundia*). This delayed the industrialization of the country and generated a lasting relationship of patronage between the great landowners and an illiterate and strictly controlled peasantry.

When the first moves were made towards an elementary form of parliamentary government during the nineteenth century, they were immediately driven off course. The parliamentary regime was merely a tactical settlement which allowed the landowning and city-dwelling élites to preserve the structure of domination. Above all, this venal and oligarchical regime, anxious to marginalize the 'dangerous classes', quickly aroused hostile reactions. This explains both the chronic temptation to solve political problems by military calls to resist legitimate authority (*pronunciamentos*) and, at a later date, the attachment of the majority of the workers' movements in Spain and Portugal to anarcho-syndicalist ideology.[18] The accommodation between clientelism and parliamentary government, plus the fierce conservatism of the Catholic Church, all helped to prevent democracy from taking root. The Francoist reaction[19] found fertile soil in which to grow. Even if, from time to time, the social élites conceived of the state as an arena where differences could be resolved, there was never any question of a 'republican settlement' which might have inspired stable loyalty among the people.

The virtuous logic of republican institutions

Although democracy is a condition of society rather than simply a political system, it would be wrong to deny all that political systems can do to consolidate society's condition. It is, moreover, remarkable to see how a whole set of procedures

---

[17] During the twelfth and thirteenth centuries, many semi-autonomous agrarian trading towns (*concejos*) were granted charters by the various kings in northern Spain which, for example, exempted them from paying tribute. In 1188 representatives of incorporated towns were for the first time admitted to the *Cortes*, the king's consultative assembly, in the city of Leòn. Other kingdoms followed suit: Catalonia (1218), Castile (1250) and Portugal (1254). Thus by the mid-thirteenth century, many representatives of *concejos* sat in consultative assemblies when the king chose to call them to obtain financial support. (NP)

[18] Which in 1934 came out in opposition to the infant Spanish Republic.

[19] In 1936 General Franco issued the most famous *pronunciamento*, against the republican government established four years earlier. This marked the start of civil war, which lasted until 1939 and ushered in 36 years of conservative dictatorship under Franco himself. Franco was replaced, on his death in 1975, by the present constitutional monarchy. (NP)

Republican forces during the Spanish Civil War (credit: Hulton Deutsch).

which were originally specific to Great Britain and the United States are, slowly but surely, being extended to the entire European continent. These procedures have contributed to the entrenchment of the democratic phenomenon – namely, the recognition of universal suffrage as the central regulatory mechanism of political activity, the development of political parties as privileged intermediaries between the state and the citizen, and the formation of a public sphere where deliberation takes precedence over force.

At this juncture, it may be valuable to shift the focus of our analysis. The overwhelming tendency of modern political science – and this applies to almost every part of the world – has been much more to describe and stigmatize the corruptions of representative democracy than to celebrate its virtues and practical benefits. Robert Michels and Moisei Ostrogorski were the first to mine this rich intellectual seam and throw light on the weaknesses and dangers of democracy. However, equal attention needs to be devoted to other, more virtuous kinds of logic, for which the contemporary development of mass democracy has provided both the original and the continuing impetus.

The gradual trend towards universal suffrage proved to be particularly decisive. In Great Britain and subsequently in France, Germany, Belgium, the Netherlands and Scandinavia, the franchise was widened during the nineteenth century. This was accompanied by an increasingly strict definition of the conditions and manner in which the franchise was to be exercised (relating to such matters as the type of ballot, boundaries between electoral districts, rules of eligibility, and the suppression of fraud and manipulation). The gradual transition from a suffrage based on property qualifications to a wider suffrage brought about profound transformations in the organization of political and social life.

69

Changes in political behaviour

Even in those societies which can be seen retrospectively as the most democratic, the introduction and subsequent refinement of universal suffrage was the focus of serious struggles, with much at stake. This eventually led to a general redefinition of the rules of the political game.

The apprenticeship of citizens

Probably the most important consequence was apprenticeship in the ways of citizenship. Although the French Revolution and its 'immortal principles' had done a great deal to promote the idea of the citizen on an intellectual level and to bring about the disintegration of social hierarchies, this was not translated into practical action until progress towards universal suffrage was well under way. In this respect, the example of France is quite instructive. It shows how a supposedly 'traditionalist' or 'authoritarian' regime can contribute to the extension of citizenship. Thus, the laws on municipal elections enacted under the constitutional 'July Monarchy' of 1830–48,[20] as well as the legislative elections and plebiscites that characterized the Second Empire, allowed the rural vote to be heard and enabled the vast numbers of peasant smallholders to become aware of their collective strength. Basically, all the Third Republic did was to extend and improve this early mechanism of political socialization, by accelerating what the historian Maurice Agulhon (1979) calls 'the social transmission of politics down to the masses', and by spreading republican imagery throughout those areas of the countryside that had remained indifferent, if not totally resistant, to it.

On a more general level, the invention of the voter-citizen created conditions which were, from the intellectual and the legal point of view, favourable to the political emancipation of the individual from all the networks of personal or traditional allegiance which had previously bound him (for example, to the landed aristocracy, to the power of the Church or to a private employer). Certainly, severing these allegiances was neither automatic nor absolute. In more than one region, landowners and peasants colluded in adapting republican rhetoric for their own purposes and in reintroducing, under this new guise, old forms of rural clientelism. Nevertheless, thanks to universal suffrage, social classes which had long been ignored or rendered powerless were given both an awareness of their sheer numbers (and therefore of their strength) and the chance to make it serve their particular interests. From this point of view, the republicans' greatest success in France must certainly have been the return of the Senate, nicknamed the 'Farmers' Chamber', from Versailles to Paris in 1879. This was followed in 1882 by what history has come to know as the 'revolution of the town halls'.[21] Henceforward, the republican mayor in his town hall was able to claim superiority over the lord in his *chateau*, while everywhere the 'Peasants' Republic' began to take a firm hold.

[20] The laws of 21 May 1831 and 3 July 1842.

[21] That is, the gradual rise, from 1877 on, of republican domination in local authorities. In due course, this produced a similar shift in the make-up of the upper house, the Senate, which presaged considerable extension of the autonomy of town halls by 1884. (NP)

The extension of political activity

The second consequence of the spread of universal suffrage was the extension of political activity throughout the nation. Such activity had, until then, been the preserve of the educated élite. The creation of a new public sphere where the free expression of individual opinions took precedence over old personal or corporatist allegiances led in most western democratic societies to the emergence of factions and later parties, whose energies were directed towards 'bidding for votes', as Moisei Ostrogorski (1902) demonstrated. This competition had two kinds of effect that were inseparable from each other. On the one hand, it led to genuine political parties being established, which worked to extend their influence. They transformed themselves, for this purpose, into more or less efficient machines designed to enrol citizens speedily on electoral registers and then capture their votes. On the other hand, political activity was gradually liberated from those shady intrigues and discreet deals which, under the cover of the property suffrage, had bound the various social élites together and made a travesty of elective office. In particular, the parties found themselves obliged to look beyond their own backyards and take an interest in much broader segments of the population.

The modern tendency of all major political parties to develop an appeal across classes (or to become 'catch-all' parties) puts the seal on this slow transformation set in motion by universal suffrage. Extending the suffrage obliges the players in the political game to make a bid for the votes of sections of the electorate other than those which are already socially and ideologically committed to them. The evolution of the British Conservative party during the nineteenth century is a useful example. In many respects, it had been the political manifestation of the landed aristocracy and the commercial upper middle class. The string of reforms extending the franchise which marked British history during that period (1832, 1867, 1884) forced the party, on each occasion, to modify its strategy and behaviour. Faced with the need to attract a wider spectrum of votes in order to compete with the Liberals and later with the Labour party, it was left with no choice but to adapt to this new environment and to overcome the handicap from which it suffered – namely, an excessively close identification with the well-to-do classes of society. Thus, under the influence of Disraeli in particular, the 1870s saw the rise of 'popular Toryism', which attempted to imitate its Liberal rivals and greatly increased the number of popular affiliated societies (such as the Primrose League[22]). Almost unnoticed, it also divested the Conservative party of its aristocratic heritage. Once again, widening the franchise had created a strong incentive for parties, if they wished to avoid being politically marginalized, to capture new audiences and, consequently, to modify their intellectual and organizational habits.

---

[22]   A network of associations begun in the early 1880s to spread support for established religion and conservative nationalism. While not formally allied to the Tory party, it was none the less a vehicle for popular Toryism because it gathered men and women from different classes around the ideas of traditional Tory figures such as Lord Beaconsfield. (NP)

The circulation of élites

The third and final consequence of universal suffrage was to ensure a degree of *circulation* among the political and social élites. Previously marginalized levels of society now contributed members to the élite groups. This struck at the concentration of government in the hands of a small, exclusive class which had characterized pre-democratic societies.

It was primarily a matter of *political mobility*, including the recognition of an opposition (or a number of oppositions) and the acceptance that power could change hands between political parties. In all democratic societies, this principle brings a healthy dose of suspicion to bear on the ruling élite, making it periodically vulnerable to what might be called 'the citizens' revenge'. Given this, the main purpose of elections (apart from periods when constitutions are being drawn up) is perhaps less to give governments a legitimate origin than to arrange for the removal of rulers from office in a calm, organized way. An election thus becomes, in any democracy, a 'judgement day' on which the party in power is obliged to present its record before it can renew its title to govern. It is a day on which the citizens have the power to dismiss them. It thus reintroduces a certain amount of uncertainty into political life.

But it was also a matter of *social mobility*. Although in practice no democratic society is governed by the 'sovereign people', the introduction of universal suffrage brought about a certain rotation of the ruling élites and, at the very least, weakened the 'natural' domination of monied classes. In his famous study of the city of New Haven, Robert Dahl (1961) masterfully demonstrated how universal suffrage, by encouraging a markedly wider distribution of 'political resources', enabled first 'entrepreneurs' and then 'ex-plebeians' to realize their assets: respectively, money from business activities and popularity with ethnic minorities. They were able to use these resources to challenge the local political establishment for the political and moral supremacy which it had exercised over the city, thus speeding up the replacement of a 'traditional oligarchy' by a 'functional polyarchy'.[23]

As far as Europe is concerned, several examples bear witness to the extent of the social transformation brought about by widening the franchise. In France from 1870 onwards, as the republican system became firmly established, political forces committed to republican ideals moved into positions of power within the state and, at the same time, managed to convince the 'new strata' of society that it was in their interest to rally to the new regime. A new generation of politicians, the majority of whom were drawn from the ranks of the middle classes and educated in state schools, successfully challenged the old legitimist and Orleanist[24] élites for

---

[23]   That is, a set-up where holding power depends on satisfying the interests and preferences of a range of minorities which, taken together, may even add up to a numerical majority of the electorate. (NP)

[24]   See note 12 above. (NP)

the political leadership of French society. Similarly, in Great Britain, Germany, Austria and Scandinavia, the growth of parties of a social-democratic persuasion allowed a new political élite, drawn for the most part from the trade union movement, to assume power and thus to contest the traditional dominance of the landlord, the squire or the *Junker*.[25]

The regulation of social conflicts

Although the overt function of universal suffrage is to contribute to forming an electorate, thus promoting the apprenticeship of citizens and legitimizing the selection of ruling élites, it also fulfils other functions which, though latent, are no less vital.

Ensuring peaceful outcome to social conflicts

First and foremost, democracy in its electoral and parliamentary form fulfils the beneficial function of ensuring peaceful outcomes to social conflicts. It offers a practical way out of endemically conflict-ridden situations which, if they are allowed to go unchannelled, could tear apart the social fabric and recreate a climate of civil war. 'In all modern democracies', wrote the American political scientist Seymour Martin Lipset, 'political parties have a responsibility to reflect the states of conflict which exist between various groups, thereby giving a democratic form to the class struggle' (Lipset, 1983). Even if this remark has lost some of its relevance in the light of the contemporary trend towards the corporatist fragmentation of societies,[26] it still underlines much of democracy's validity when applied to the past. Party rivalry has functioned as a sanitized form of social violence. It has offered opportunities for political forces and social groups to be integrated. If confined on the margins, these would have bridled at their isolation and helped to destabilize the system.

It may be useful to compare the evolution of political life in France and Great Britain in the second half of the nineteenth century. In Britain the enlargement of the franchise led the parties to internalize the rules of the political game. The Conservative party, concerned to attract the maximum number of votes, took a new interest in appealing to a wider public, while at a later period the Labour party, in order to fulfil the wishes of the working classes, accepted the constitutional conventions and loyally took its place within the machinery of democracy. In France, by contrast, the stubborn refusal of the July Monarchy[27] (particularly

[25]   The military-landowning nobility of Prussia. (NP)

[26]   That is, the organization of large, hostile classes into a variety of interest groups, each separately involved in peaceable campaigning and consulting with government. (NP)

[27]   See note 12 above. (NP)

under Guizot,[28] its principal driving force) to extend the benefits of the franchise and of genuine citizenship to a larger proportion of the people produced a number of disruptive effects. It opened the way to a mentality of civil disorder which, deprived of tangible outlets, turned to rioting in the street. It also encouraged a climate of suspicion to develop about republican political practices, thus preparing the ground for Marxist and libertarian invective against 'bourgeois democracy'. It was to require all the ingenuity of the founders of the Third Republic to convince the majority of the people that there was room for a middle way between Bonapartist authoritarianism[29] and revolutionary adventurism.

The success of social-democratic parties, mainly in the countries of northern Europe, provides further illustration of the learning processes of republicanism. It must not be forgotten that the choice of political democracy was not an automatic one in the early days of the social-democratic movement. First, the movement's most important objective was to change the means of production rather than political institutions. Second, it had inherited Marx's indictment of 'bourgeois democracy'[30] – that clever deception designed to perpetuate the dictatorship of the 'ruling classes'! Be that as it may, the broadly parallel paths followed by all the social-democratic parties are a perfect illustration of the *virtuous logic of democratization*.

- In the first phase, the struggle to widen the franchise, by involving the social-democratic movement in the workings of democracy, eroded its initial radicalism and integrated it in the machinery of the representative system.

- In the second phase, the parliamentary chamber came to be seen as the focus of a crucial balance of forces benefiting the social-democratic movement, which was already organized as a counter-culture within society at large, and which now set itself up as the vehicle of working-class aspirations in opposition to the ruling conservatism.

- The momentum of the third and final phase can only have been increased by the movement's later participation in the responsibilities of government. Social democracy extended its influence beyond the 'working class', which was itself undergoing major changes, and adopted a culture of compromise which most notably led it to endorse political democracy and the market economy.

The 1961 Bad-Godesberg Congress, where the German Social Democratic party publicly renounced all references to Marxism, appears in retrospect as the logical and symbolic culmination of a process of integration, common to all such parties,

[28] F. P. G. Guizot (1787–1874), historian, literary critic and statesman. He occupied various offices under the July Monarchy: minister of the interior, minister of education, ambassador to Britain, special adviser to the King, and finally (in 1847) prime minister. In the 1840s he was associated with repressive measures and withdrew from politics after the revolution that brought down the monarchy in 1848, which his measures were thought to have provoked. (NP)

[29] See note 11 above. (NP)

[30] Which goes back to his essay, 'On the Jewish question' (Marx, 1843; 1972 edn).

whose end result was to make the social-democratic movement not so much the vanguard of an alternative 'social democracy' as the specific modern-day version of liberalism.

The neutralization of political extremism

Modern democracy has perhaps performed another, even more beneficial, regulatory function: the eradication or, at the very least, the neutralization of political extremism. We might even go so far as to say that the manner in which extremist passions are dealt with (or, to put it more precisely, managed) shows most clearly how the lessons of democracy have been learned. If an extremist grouping can be defined as one which, in the name of certain radical ideals, aspires to transform society and subordinate it to an ultimate goal, and if we observe how such groupings have fared in contemporary democratic societies, our attention is drawn to a number of connected facts.

First, nowhere in western Europe since 1945 has an extremist grouping acquired sufficient purchase on the system to assume power or participate in government, much less to destroy the democratic order and install a 'fascist' or 'communist' society. In places where they represent a significant proportion of the electorate, 'extremist' parties have become in some cases parties of protest, in other cases the mouthpiece for a minority point of view. Second, the inevitable involvement of extremist groupings in the workings of representative democracy has gradually rubbed off on the extremists' rhetoric and strategy. For instance, in France and Italy the rather belated realization that republican values had become deeply ingrained in society encouraged the communist parties of those countries to rid themselves of more and more of their Stalinist legacy, and to recognize democratic institutions. The case of the Italian Communist party is all the more remarkable in that at the end of a long period of militancy, in the course of which it explored every avenue of 'transformist' strategy, it publicly admitted the failure of this ambition, renounced its outdated identity and retreated to a kind of social-democratic position. By contrast, the disgrace into which the French Communist party has fallen bears witness to the fact that it is impossible nowadays to reconcile revolutionary rhetoric with a practical policy of democratic participation.

It is perhaps, however, the fortunes of the extreme right that have the greatest exemplary value. Although the extreme right was dealt a serious blow by the defeat of Nazism and the devastation wrought by the end of the Second World War in 1945, the appeal of extremism has been revived by factors such as decolonization, immigration, unemployment and insecurity in general. This has led to the reappearance in certain countries of active extreme-right groupings capable of assuming a certain representative function. These include the *Movimento Sociale Italiano* in Italy, the *Nationaldemokratische Partei Deutschlands* in Germany and the *Front National* in France. Two points need to be mentioned. First, it is noticeable that these organizations are never mere replicas of the fascist movements of the inter-war years. Although they make copious use of nationalistic and xenophobic impulses, they do not draw from these an argument for rejecting democracy and calling for a 'new order'. Second, above all, the growing electoral success of these groups, far from spurring them on to greater levels of extremism,

Jorg Haider of the far-right Austrian Freedom party celebrating his election victory, 1991 (credit: Kurt Keinrath, Austria Presse Agentur).

has made them more inclined to seek out new areas of support, tone down their programmes and move towards a kind of robust neo-conservatism: 'far right' rather than 'extreme right'.[31]

Conclusion

It would be out of place to idealize democratic regimes. The collapse of communism in eastern Europe is no doubt a symptom that the revolutionary utopian ambition of those regimes has met with irreversible failure. Yet it does not seem to have brought to democratic thought the massive surge of legitimacy that the western countries had a right to expect. On the contrary, those countries are still beset by substantial problems which they struggle to contain with more or less success, provoking endemic discontents. Just about everywhere in Europe, it has become fashionable to evoke a crisis of 'democracy', daily evidenced by heightened disaf-

[31] *Droite extrême* as against *extrême-droite*.

fection *vis-à-vis* the democratic process, denunciations of 'politicians' or 'bureaucrats', and the accelerating power of organized interests by comparison with the impotence of the state. It now appears that, for the vast majority of former communist states, the route to democracy and the market economy is a fearsome trail. To be sure, most of them have managed, in a remarkably short time without major upsets, to break free of the habits of totalitarianism, reconstitute themselves as states under the rule of Law, and recreate a legal framework that encourages the market economy. But that does not alter the fact that they suffer from substantial handicaps in the economic, industrial and financial spheres thanks to the acknowledged inefficiency of the old system. This forces them into austerity measures which can only fuel resentment. The heavy rate of abstentions during the latest parliamentary elections in Poland indicates that the escape from communism – once seen as a fairy-tale road to material prosperity – does not automatically generate enthusiasm and commitment for a democratic regime.

This paradoxical mixture of satisfaction and disappointment illustrates the problematic character of creating a democratic government. Once complete, the democratic system generates few passions, and it calls for individuals with virtues that may be quite rare: lucidity, restraint, an impulse toward compromise and a concern for reasonable behaviour. The democratic regime does not have the seductive character of those 'total ideologies' which promised the people a rosy utopian future. On the other hand, we must not forget that democracy is a latecomer on the stage of human history – just a century old in the case of a country such as France with 'longstanding' democratic traditions. Moreover, it is still a marginal phenomenon on the global scale, where authoritarian regimes are legion. Above all, we must bear in mind that democracies are by nature fragile and unstable. They derive their 'superiority' less from some inherent central principle than from the evils they allow us to avoid: primarily their tendency to substitute compromise and dialogue in the management of society's affairs for violence and arbitrary power. The 'democratic melancholy' that Pascal Bruckner (1990) has recently evoked is sweet indeed compared to the war of attrition undertaken by Serbs and Croats. Today we can appreciate better than ever that Winston Churchill's famous remark,[32] 'Democracy is the worst form of government, except all those other forms that have been tried from time to time', was no mere pleasantry.

[32] Made in the House of Commons, 11 November 1949. (NP)

References

AGULHON, M. (1979) *La République au village: les populations du Var de la Revolution à la IIe République*, 2nd edn, Paris, Editions du Seuil; trans. (1982) *The Republic in the Village*, Cambridge, Cambridge University Press.

BRUCKNER, P. (1990) *La Mélancolie Démocratique*, Paris, Editions du Seuil.

COCHIN, A. (1925; 1979 edn) *Les Sociétés de pensée et la Révolution en Bretagne*, 2 vols, Paris, Presses Universitaires de France (Collection 'Sociologies').

DAHL, R. (1961) *Who Governs? Democracy and Power in an American City*, New Haven, Yale University Press.

DONZELOT, J. (1984) *L'Invention du social*, Paris, Fayard.

FURET, F. (1978) *Penser la Révolution Française*, Paris, Gallimard; trans. (1981) *Interpreting the French Revolution*, Cambridge, Cambridge University Press.

HERMET, G. (1983) *Aux Frontières de la démocratie*, Paris, Presses Universitaires de France.

HERMET, G. (1986) *Sociologie de la construction démocratique*, Paris, Economica.

LIPSET, S. M. (1983) *Political Man: The Social Bases of Politics*, 2nd edn, London, Heinemann Educational.

MARX, K. (1843; 1972 edn) 'On the Jewish question' in *Early Texts*, ed. D. McLellan, Oxford, Blackwell.

OSTROGORSKI, M. (1902) *Democracy and the Organization of Political Parties*, 2 vols, London, Macmillan.

Part II
Individual freedom and the rule of Law

Introduction to Part II

Prepared for the Course Team by Alain-Marc Rieu
Translated by Noël Parker

Having examined the various conditions for the emergence of democracy, we must now emphasize the parallel lines of evolution in democratic thinking, which produce two poles of attraction shaping European democratic culture.

The first line of evolution – discussed in Part II – stipulates that the political community exists between free and equal individuals. It culminates in the theory of human rights and of 'the state under the rule of Law'. Over the course of history, Law has become the very core of the community, the content of the common good: it establishes the meaning of *res publica* or 'public thing'. But to do this, Law cannot remain an abstraction: the state under the rule of Law must give the common good a real existence for individuals as political actors or citizens. The politics it generates entails an underlying constitutional principle that there is such a thing as a 'public service', which maintains the conditions for the exercise of personal liberty: education, national defence, law and order, public health, opportunities for employment. Political debate bears on the nature, extent and financing of public services. The state under the rule of Law does not stop, therefore, where the private economy begins. It is legitimized not only by the personal liberties it establishes, but also by the way that governments are able to develop public services which enable individuals to exercise those liberties, and thus become citizens in the full sense. This is ever an unfinished task.

The second line of evolution – covered in Part III – leads us to the status granted to public opinion. It affirms the autonomy of society *vis-à-vis* the state: the primacy of individual liberty and diversity over the internal logic driving political institutions. In democratic societies, public opinion is regularly denounced as the negation of the social order, encouraging indecisive government and anarchy. It is said to be the proof that democracy is a fragile system and has to be kept within bounds.

This is a double error. First, within this apparent disorder, there lies what is most essential to society: public opinion does not mean a cacophony of opinions, but the shared wisdom of a people, grounded in their education, their culture, their diverse capacities and experiences. In fact, the state's ability to adapt to its changing internal and external environment relies not upon the brilliance of its leaders but on the liberty of its people.

Above all, however, to condemn public opinion is to misunderstand how democratic politics evolves between two poles of attraction which balance each other – Law and public opinion. The tension between these two is at the heart of democracy. On the one hand, the state under the rule of Law fixes the rules of the game for politics, for social life, for economic activity and for public opinion itself. When public opinion loses its way in conflict and debate, it prevents society from taking the decisions that historical circumstances call for. Society then returns to the principles of Law and justice for guidance, re-examining and re-interpreting them. When the insights of the law have become too brittle to keep up with social and economic evolution, society makes its voice heard by opposing authority and demanding autonomy for the diversity of public opinion.

We have to admit that democracy is indeed a weak political set-up, always short on agreement, order and coherence. Indeed, the government in a democracy does not have a monopoly on sovereignty. When it exercises authority that is illegitimate or unchecked, society challenges it. It then denounces the weaknesses of democracy as justification for reinforcing its authority. The resistance it meets provokes disorders, which do not cease until society regains its autonomy. Should government succeed in inhibiting or destroying the forces opposed to it, it reigns over a dead society, peopled by shadows rather than citizens, which leads in the end to its own destruction. *Sovereignty, then, is rooted in society as organized politically by the state under the rule of Law.* As Gérard Duprat argues in Part III, the strength of the democratic set-up lies precisely in its weakness, for that is the guarantee of individual liberty and the autonomy of the citizens as a whole. Hence we must analyse these two poles.

Part II fulfils the vital function of elucidating two fundamental concepts of European political culture: democracy itself and Law. Up to now, they have been considered in terms of their history and their functions. Now we must consider what they are in themselves. In fact, there are different conceptions of democracy because there are different conceptions of the individual, of liberty, and of government, just as there are different critiques of democracy past and present. One idea runs through Rodney Barker's exposition: that democracy is not just one view among others but the experience of liberty itself. Thus it always entails a certain form of activity, certain demands, a certain kind of legitimacy. The criticism of weakness levelled against it points out problems society has yet to resolve.

The second concept is that of the state under the rule of Law or, loosely speaking, the constitutional state. Francesco D'Agostino defines it with all the rigour demanded by jurisprudence, in an argument that demonstrates its autonomy and its standing in theory and in the practice of politics. The jurist's work and ways of thinking – on which democracy depends – are thus illustrated too.

Part III starts from the other pole of European political thought: public opinion. Hans-Joachim Schmidt reveals its many ambiguities from the uses that have been made of the idea and the analyses undertaken by the human sciences. The idea of public opinion emerges radicalized: referring to a basic problem of democracy – the gap between society and the state. For his part, Gérard Duprat shows how this gap arises from, and is reinforced by, the practice of criticism. His thesis is that a political system can have criticism of itself as its underlying principle. Democracy is the practice of a paradox: politics as the perpetual crisis of politics. Once the reader has grasped this paradox by traversing the many historical experiences and forms of knowledge it embraces, the different democratic institutions of Europe can be considered in Part IV.

Essay 3
Democracy and individual freedom

Prepared for the Course Team by Rodney Barker
Senior Lecturer in Government, London School of
Economics

Introduction

We are all democrats now. So much so that though democracy is frequently advocated, it is far less frequently either defined or justified. We all know it is a good thing, and no one bothers to ask what kind of good thing it is. But it was not always so. The first use of the term 'democracy' by Aristotle was dismissive, an indication of a 'corrupt' form of politics, of misrule by the unfit masses who governed in their own interests rather than in those of the whole community. When the idea began to take shape in something like its present form as government by the people in late eighteenth-century Europe, 'democracy' was still for many a term descriptive of disorder and subversion. Throughout the nineteenth century democracy meant, for conservatives and for many liberals, the self-interested and ignorant domination of the state by the poor, the end of responsible government, and the inception of disorder. Good government, they argued, consisted of applying the correct principles in the correct manner, and only people of skill, wisdom and experience could do this. To place government in the hands of the people was to place it in the hands of those who knew neither what best to do, nor how best to do it.

Only in the present century has democracy been transformed into a term of the utmost respectability, and conservatives in the 1970s and 1980s could be found recommending to eastern European despotisms a form of government which their own intellectual and political ancestors had regarded with the deepest aversion. We can all recommend our proposals as democratic because it is generally accepted nowadays that democracy is a fundamentally desirable way of conducting political life.

But if democracy has become universally accepted, it is still frequently advocated in ways that leave it unclear what is being proposed. Calls for 'the restoration of democracy' or for 'more democracy' can often be more rousing than enlightening. When the Chinese popular movement of 1989 called for democracy, or when the Kuwait Democratic Forum in 1991 called for more democracy, the only thing that was immediately clear was that they were both confident of the approval of most of their audiences. It was not at all clear precisely what they were recommending or why.

We may reply that democracy simply means government by the people. But that is not, of course, the only definition that will be widely familiar. Democracy may be described as majority government, and that is perhaps an even more frequent use of the term. I have used 'government by the people' rather than 'majority government' because the first seems to me more fundamental, while the second is a means, if not to achieve it, then at least to approximate to it. But being a little dogmatic in this way at an early stage of the argument does not remove all the difficulties. It is not mere pedantry to point out that both the term 'government' and the term 'people' can be given more than one meaning. We raise two of the most fundamental problems of democracy in modern societies by the following questions:

- In what possible manner can so numerous a body as the people of a modern state rule?

- What meaning can be given to the term 'the people' when, as is always the case, there is no unanimous agreement about policies (either in general or in particular), and hence not one people but many peoples composed of overlapping groups based on occupation, gender, race, religion and beliefs about public policy?

The best place to start an investigation of what democracy involves is to ask what job it has been expected to do. For what kinds of reasons has it been recommended? What ends or benefits is democracy thought particularly well suited to achieve? What conceptions of politics, or of individuals, or of society lead so many to value democratic politics? If we know what democracy is expected to achieve or defend, we will be in a better position to determine what kind of thing it is itself, to assess the various accounts of it, and to judge its success by matching it to the claims made on its behalf.

The meanings of democracy

Whatever uncertainties there may be about it, democracy involves government by or in conformity with the wishes of the people, and most arguments in favour of it begin with statements or assumptions about the rights or interests of ordinary men and women. The starting place is with subjects or citizens rather than governments or rulers. Individuals are taken to possess rights in such a way that any government, and any politics, must be based on those rights, give expression to them, and acknowledge and defend them.

From this perspective, there are arguments for two kinds of democracy: one for *expressive* democracy, the other for *citizen* democracy. The first theory views democracy as a means of giving effect to our will or interests; the second sees it as the most important form of political activity, valuable in itself as an exercise and cultivation of freedom.[1]

Both views begin with the citizen, and see democracy as a means of achieving his or her objects. But whereas, for the first, democracy is a means to an end, for the second it is an end in itself. Both views involve an argument for democracy as liberty. The first sees it as a means of promoting or protecting liberty, both as the free expression and realization of the citizen's will and as the defence of the citizen against oppressive government. A democracy, as Jeremy Bentham put it, 'has for its characteristic object and effect, the securing its members against oppression and depredation at the hands of those functionaries which it employs for its defence' (*Constitutional Code*, quoted in MacPherson, 1977, p. 6). The second sees democratic citizen politics as in itself the essence of free activity. For expressive democracy, liberty is achieved in our social and economic relationships, both public and private. For citizen democracy, liberty is a way of conducting political life. In other words, expressive democracy defends or promotes liberty; but citizen democracy *is* liberty. As John Stuart Mill put it, 'to take an active interest in politics is, in modern times, the first thing which elevates the mind to large interests and contemplations' (*Thoughts on Parliamentary Reform*, quoted in Eccleshall, 1986, p. 163).

The definition of democracy as majority rule is inadequate for both expressive and citizen theories, and particularly so for the second:

- The first theory might concede that rule by the people leads to majority rule or to rule by the largest group ('plurality rule' as it is sometimes called). But that is because 'the people' is an abstraction. Even though majority rule might be acknowledged as an outcome, the justification of majority (or plurality) rule would still be simply that such a result aggregated the wishes of more sovereign individuals than any other. So, democracy could not consistently ignore the role of minorities, or assume that so long as most people's wills received expression, all its requirements had been met.

- For the second theory, mere recognition of majority opinion is not what democracy is about, because democracy is not achieved simply by the registration of opinions. That, after all, could occur in a benevolent despotism well kitted out with opinion polls. Registration of opinions does not give any place for the active politics of discussion and negotiation which constitute citizen democracy.

Expressive democracy

If democracy is a way for individuals to give collective political expression to their wills or interests, then it involves their agreeing on ways of collectively exer-

---

[1]   C. B. MacPherson (1977) has spoken of 'protective' and 'developmental' theories of democracy. I have departed from his usage a little because an expressive theory of democracy may be either protective or assertive, while a citizenship theory may see the activity of democratic politics as in itself the desired end, or as developing or cultivating the virtues of citizenship.

cising their rights. It constitutes an agreement among citizens to employ, and be bound by, particular procedures. This agreement has frequently been presented as if it were, or were like, a contract. If individuals are the owners of themselves, and if they (rather than society or the state) are the fundamental source and possessors of rights, then only by their agreement can any form of government be carried on.

But, depending on the size of the political community, such a political contract will be direct or indirect. It will be made either among the citizens or between the citizens and some form of governor. If the political community is small enough to allow direct participation by all citizens in the discussion and formation of policy (as it was only in the ancient Greek city-state or *polis*, or in the communes of eighteenth-century Switzerland), then the contract is with each other. Citizens agree to determine public policy by discussion and voting, and to accept the results of this procedure. There is no third party involved – merely the citizens acting individually and collectively. If the political community is too large for that – and all modern states are too large – then the contract is between citizens and a state which acts for them. The contract is given effect, in part, by elected representatives who mediate between state and citizen. This is 'representative' as opposed to 'direct' democracy.

Within a representative democracy a further distinction appears: between, on the one hand, the general rights of the state and the constitutional framework within which it will rule and, on the other hand, the particular acts and policies which it carries out. Through its constitutional arrangements, the state expresses the general will of those whom it represents. By expressing the fundamental consent or will of its subjects, it is legitimate: it constitutes not the will of a ruler or group of rulers, but the general will. It was in this sense that Rousseau, in *The Social Contract*, sought to justify a government which derived its right to rule from popular consent: the 'general will' of the sovereign people. But once consent is given, the day-to-day detail of the policy whereby the state governs is then a matter for its own best judgement. The citizens agree to a constitution, not a programme.

On the other hand, it is open to the citizens, while still accepting the constitutional contract, to judge programmes as well as the constitution on their merits. If the state is seen not just as the outcome of a general agreement about procedures, rights and duties, but as the expression – through representatives – of its subjects' will, then their wishes and interests should prevail in the day-to-day (or at least year-to-year) formation of public policy. Constitutional consent, in other words, *justifies* the state, but expressive representation *shapes* its actions.

It may be argued that a state whose general constitutional arrangements are popularly authorized does not, on that basis alone, qualify as democratic. It would be perfectly feasible for all or most of the population to agree to be governed by an absolute ruler. Although his or her authority might come from the people, this would not be government by the people but simply government by the consent of the people. Democracy clearly requires more than this: some continuing involvement by the people in the process of government, not simply a once-and-for-all act of creation. The democratic citizen is an active parent, not simply a legal progenitor. Thus it is no defence of the rule of Adolf Hitler (or any other despot who received popular acclaim on one occasion only) to say that he became German Chancellor as a result of an election. Democracy needs to be continuous.

But, once again, this active democratic politics may be conducted in either negative or positive ways. MacPherson (1977) aptly described the negative form of expressive democracy as 'defensive democracy'. Utilitarian liberals at the beginning of the nineteenth century, such as Jeremy Bentham or James Mill, saw individuals as the best judges of their own interests, and the maximization of happiness as arising from individuals' peaceful pursuit of their own chosen ends. But in order for this to happen, there must be a guarantee of the basic securities, the freedoms of the person, property and contract. Thus, government was necessary to facilitate the pursuit of individual goals by enforcing the rules of social interaction and competition. But although government was ideally a protector of its subjects' interests, given the character of human nature, it was also potentially an oppressor of them. Hence, it needed keeping in check, on the right lines, by those who had a direct interest in doing so. Democracy was the only way of doing this, and thus served to defend people against their defender.

A continuing liberal tradition of defensive democracy has evolved from these arguments. In their different ways, both A. V. Dicey at the start of the present century and F. A. Hayek in its middle, with neither unconditional commitment to nor any great enthusiasm for democracy, supported it because they viewed it as the system least likely to allow governments to get away with what they regarded as dangerous nonsense. For Dicey, the democratic citizen 'knows and feels' that the 'belief in formulas', which leads socialism to increase state power, is a delusion (Dicey, 1914, p. lxxviii). For Hayek, though democracy was 'by no means infallible' as a way of keeping the state in check, it was generally effective (Hayek, 1944, p. 52).

But the positive version of expressive democracy envisaged an altogether more active role for government. Such a theory, which might be either social-reform liberal[2] or social democratic, saw democracy as a means not simply of *protecting* but also of *furthering* the interests of citizens. Here the state is the application, in law and public policy, of the changing wishes of its subjects. The difference is both ideological and historical. At the beginning of the nineteenth century, it was easy to see the state in terms of a guardian who needed to be watched. But the growth of state involvement – both in social and economic regulation and in the provision of services, accompanied by a growth in citizens' expectations of the state – meant that such a view was increasingly challenged. People saw democracy not just as a means of protecting citizens against government, but as an instrument for employing government for their benefit. Social-reform liberals looked to social reform as a means of reducing inequalities in the life chances of citizens; social democrats viewed democratic socialism as a way of transcending capitalism.

Modern industrial and urban societies, however, pose problems and difficulties not just for the advocates of classical, direct democracy but for all forms of democracy. In such societies, the possibilities of arranging politics so that the

---

[2]   Late nineteenth-century tendency in English liberalism favouring state intervention, e.g. to promote education or health care. (NP)

people have any effective influence on, or control over, government appear thin and insecure. The greater the number of citizens, the less likely it is that even representative democracy can be an expression of their wills. The requirements of an active system of expressive democracy were always clear. The problems lay in finding organizational and institutional ways of achieving them. Political parties, which had at first appeared a means of channelling popular wishes into public policy, soon began to look like one more way in which a relatively small number of political professionals mobilized the people: not as active citizens but as malleable political raw material in the hands of contesting leaderships. The initiative, in such circumstances, was seen to pass to small groups of political activists, of which those in control of the state were both the most active and powerful.

This realization led Max Weber and the so-called 'élitist' theorists, in the last years of the nineteenth century and the first quarter of the present century, to argue that most of what had been thought of as democratic politics was little more than an appearance, either incidentally or deliberately deceptive. Not only did the people not rule, but the idea that actual democratic states were characterized by the domination of majority opinion was without historical foundation. The masses were largely the pliable foot soldiers in the armies of rival political leaders. While some of the masses' wishes might be pandered to, and others subtly distorted or manipulated, the initiative came from the active few, never from the democratic mass. Democracy, as Moisei Ostrogorski observed, had led not to the liberation of the people but to their organization (see Ostrogorski, 1902, and Barker and Howar-Johnstone, 1975).

One of Joseph Schumpeter's major contributions to the study of mid-twentieth-century democratic theory was his combination of this insight with an economic explanation, or at least analogy, of democratic politics. Schumpeter reinstated democratic politics as a means of giving expression to citizen preferences, but did so through a situation where élites, as the initiators of policies and programmes, supplied the voters' demands by competing in a political auction to offer what would be most attractive to the voters. In these circumstances, the initiating élites depended on popular support, but did not follow popular instructions. By setting the unavoidable fact of élite initiative in the context of popular approval, the democratic aspiration was fulfilled – though in a way which made the citizen largely a passive consumer of programmes and policies devised by others.

The result of this accommodation between the individualistic basis of democratic theory and the circumstances of populous modern states has been an incorporation of political parties into democratic theory. Parties offer the means for those citizens who wish to do so to engage in a limited amount of political activity. At the same time, the development of policies and programmes by parties in electoral competition provides a connection between government policy and the wishes of citizens, because the need to gain the support of voters, while it does not dictate policy, sets limits within which it must be constructed.

Citizen democracy

For the utilitarians Jeremy Bentham and James Mill, the purpose of democracy was expressive: essentially to protect the subject. For James Mill's son, John Stuart Mill, democracy had an altogether different purpose, being a form of free citizen activity to be valued for its own sake and, at the same time, a means of achieving the self-development of individual character. The freedom which for the utilitarians it was the function of democracy to *preserve*, was, for J. S. Mill, to be found in the active *development* of an individual's character in public political life. Freedom was free, self-developing activity, and participating in the political life of one's society was one of its principal forms. Democratic politics was to be a means to the 'advancement' of the community 'in intellect, in virtue, and in practical activity and efficiency' (Mill, 1861; 1977 edn, p. 404; quoted in MacPherson, 1977, p. 47). In this idea of democracy, unlike the expressive theory, 'Man is essentially not a consumer and appropriator ... but an exerter and developer and enjoyer of his capacities' (quoted in MacPherson, 1977, p. 48).

There are problems in justifying actual representative politics with such theories of citizenship democracy. Different conceptions of the purpose of democracy lead to different conceptions of what democracy is. It is much more important for a citizenship theory than for an expressive theory that people actually engage in political action of some kind, and participate in the discussion, evaluation and formation of public policy. For the expressive theory a passive representative democracy, of the kind portrayed by Schumpeter, may well provide a sufficient check on the ambitions of government. For the citizenship theory it cannot provide adequate opportunities for real citizen politics. Whereas in the world of the ancient Greek *polis* (idealized by modern writers such as Hannah Arendt, 1958) the political life of the citizen was a matter of frequent and sustained discussion, in the modern world it can be little more than the occasional casting of a vote. If politics is freedom, and if in representative democracy the only general form of politics is voting, then as Rousseau said of the English, the people 'are free only during the election of Members of Parliament' (Rousseau, 1762; 1968 edn, p. 141). C. B. MacPherson criticizes John Stuart Mill for just this reason. Rather a lot, he suggests, is claimed 'for a system of representative government in which the ordinary person's political activity is confined to voting every few years for members of Parliament, perhaps a little more often for local councillors, and perhaps actually holding some elective local office' (MacPherson, 1977, p. 52).

It is for this reason that there has been much recent talk of 'participatory democracy', by which is meant democratic government on a scale sufficiently small to approach close to, even if not to attain, the notion of democracy as self-government. The Swiss canton is often cited as an example of this. But for most people living in more populous nations, participatory democracy would have to be a matter not just of small scale but of specialized activities. In local community politics, in various forms of workplace democracy, and in the democratic management of local services such as schools, more people can become more directly involved in governing the circumstances surrounding their own lives than is possible with national, representative politics. As Carole Pateman argues, the 'notion of the participatory society requires that the scope of the term "political" is extended to cover spheres outside national government' (Pateman, 1970, p. 106). Alternatively, because the greater the numbers involved, the greater the dilution of any meaningful political activity, Benjamin Barber argues that the only way modern societies can approach democracy is by a representative system where citizens are involved in manageably small groups at every level. Democracy will still be representative, but the mass activity of voting will be supplemented by an upward flow of argument and information through a hierarchy of representative units (Barber, 1984). More involvement means less direct participation at the top.

Both advocates and critics of participatory democracy have perhaps relied too much on classical notions of direct democracy. Even if politics in a citizen democracy requires discussion and opinion formation, this does not necessarily have to take place between all citizens at once or in formally political situations. The reality of political power in democracy – however occasional its exercise – gives the arguments of citizens among themselves in all kinds of situations a relevance they would lack in a despotism. In other words, the democratic *culture* of a citizen democracy can be found around a breakfast table or in a bar as well as in a voting booth.

Any theory of citizen democracy involves an assumption about the autonomy or, at the very least, the distinctiveness of politics. Whereas in a theory of expressive democracy politics can, in the last resort, be a means to other ends and hence explicable in terms of them, this can never be so for a citizenship theory. Without necessarily implying that politics dominates all other forms of social relationship, or that it can operate without regard to them, there is an assumption that the important political distinctions between societies lie not in whether they are capitalist or socialist, secular or religious, but in the character of their political life and the extent to which free, democratic citizen politics is carried on. Thus for democrats in the 1930s the important distinction was not between communist Russia and capitalist Spain, but between free democracies like France or Britain and despotisms such as those of Stalin and Franco. At the present time, the relevant distinction is not between states with more or less of the economy under public control, but between democracies such as Italy or Czechoslovakia and semi-despotisms such as Turkey. The litmus test, in other words, is not the extent of state functions or the ownership of wealth, but the amount of active political freedom.

Democracy as a form of government

While the most familiar recommendations of democracy come from advocates of the rights and interests of citizens, there is a quite different perspective from which the system's virtues are defended from time to time. Democracy may be justified not from the point of view of the subject, but from that of government. In other words, democracy is desirable not for the benefits it confers on citizens and subjects, but for the ways it helps or makes possible stable government. One argument sees democracy as a means of organization, either in terms of the mobilization of citizens in the enterprises of the state, or in terms of the most efficient means of gathering information for the government. Another sees democracy as the most effective way of legitimizing government and hence of mobilizing citizens.

Democracy as a form of order or organization

As voting was slowly extended to the majority of at least the male part of the adult population in Europe, many commentators pointed out that, whatever the claims of democrats, the reality of democratic government was different. It served as a means of mobilizing the masses in the support of competing party leaders, and of enrolling them in the service of the common good. They argued this with particular force in relation to political parties, studied in Germany by Robert Michels and in the United Kingdom and the United States by the Russian political scientist Moisei Ostrogorski. Both argued that organized political life meant not an exercise of power *by* the masses, but an exercise of power *over* them. Michels spoke of the 'iron law of oligarchy', which frustrated the hopes of democrats.

But while, for such writers, the history of democratic politics was to some extent one of disappointed hopes, for others it was exactly the way things should have turned out. Fabian socialists like Beatrice and Sidney Webb in Britain viewed the ordinary citizen principally in terms of the contribution he or she could make to the national well-being. That meant democratic politics provided an essential information network for government, transmitting not so much the wishes of ordinary people, as their detailed knowledge of the day-to-day realities of the society upon which the state exercised its governmental skills. Although he took a pessimistic view of actually existing democracy, for Ostrogorski if the system were to work as it should, it would do so by subordinating the inferior judgement of the masses to the leadership of the few. W. H. Mallock neatly borrowed the arguments of emerging social science to clothe the preferences of old conservatism when he argued, from a reading of Michels, that democracy could function only through the 'directive ability' of political élites (Mallock, 1918, p. 378).

Democracy as a way of legitimizing government

One of the most important aspects of mobilizing the masses is legitimation, the willing acceptance by the governed of the rightfulness of the government which rules them. For Rousseau, the popular will was a means of *legitimizing* government rather than a means of *conducting* it. The question of legitimation is both a practical and a moral one. On the one hand, it is necessary to know how, in practice, systems of government are justified, what kinds of reason are in fact associated with obedience. On the other hand, it is also necessary to enquire what kinds of principles might, in theory, convince us that a system of rule is acceptable: the fact that some of their subjects willingly obey despotisms does not lead us to withdraw our criticism of them. But the two are linked, in that an enquiry into the actual character of legitimate government is an enquiry into the reasons which other people, the subjects, find for accepting a system of rule.

Max Weber made the principal contribution to the study and theory of legitimacy in the modern state. He has been much criticized for failing to include democracy as a means of legitimizing government. On the face of it, it is an odd omission considering the support which both the historical record of nineteenth-century European popular politics and the contribution of contract theory[3] give to the idea that governments are legitimated by the consent of the governed. Weber listed only three main forms of legitimacy: tradition, charisma and procedural propriety (see Weber, 1918, 1948 edn; also Barker, 1990). But he was correct. Democracy is a means of registering or expressing in quantitative terms legitimations of other kinds, such as belief in charismatic leaders or tradition. It does not itself provide the actual grounds for people's loyalty to the state. If a majority did not support a regime, that would be grounds for both criticizing it and predicting its demise. But the reasons behind that lack of support would not be found in the mere counting of votes. The reasons can be seen in the experience of nationalism and the nation state.

Nationalism and democracy

The problem for democracy in contemporary Europe is that the people – the *demos* – has developed within the nation state. Critics have pointed out the difficulty of 'fit' when democratic political institutions are set in class-divided societies. The political constitution assumes solidarity and equality while the social community, on which the political community must be based, is characterized by division. But the divisions of class are as nothing when compared with those of culture. And where the state governs a people divided into cultural, ethnic or national communities, it carries little weight with the smaller communities to be told that they have been duly outvoted by the members of the large community. The Sikhs are not greatly impressed by the assurance that the majority of the population of the Indian subcontinent opposes their claims to independent statehood. Nor do nationalists in Scotland, Ireland, Catalonia or the Basque country feel that their claim is neutralized by the fact that they are a minority within the territories of the states which govern them.

Democracy, in other words, seems acceptable as a manner of selecting, legitimizing and shaping government within states whose subjects are in some sense *homogeneous*. But once the formal democratic community lacks such homogeneity, dissident citizens assert democracy only within their own perceived community: as a means of determining the will of *that* community, not as a means of mediating between one community and another. Democracy has often been a powerful weapon in the hands of nationalism, and radical nationalists have always assumed that nationalism is a movement of the people and hence democratically legitimated (see Barker, 1990; also Nairn, 1977). But when democracy and nationalism come into conflict, it is democracy which gives way in the face of the nationalist demand that the state be reconstructed so the limits of the body of democratic citizens coincide with the limits of the national community. In other words, any conflict is met not by appealing to democratic majorities, but by reconstructing the democratic community within nationalist boundaries. The most dramatic instance

---

[3] The rise of contract theory is extensively discussed by A.-M. Rieu in this volume; see the section on 'A new philosophy of law and politics' in his essay. (NP)

Lithuanians show their nationalist colours in Vilnius, the Baltic state's capital, during a demonstration in favour of breaking away from the Soviet Union, March 1990 (credit: Associated Press).

of this is the fragmentation of the former Soviet Union once the democratic principle was introduced. Democracy for inhabitants of the Ukraine meant free elections and majority rule *within the Ukraine*. The USSR was an irrelevance to them. The disintegration of Yugoslavia after 1991 followed a similar course.

Criticisms of democracy

While democracy has achieved almost universal respectability in the twentieth century, it has not lacked critics. They have attacked it on three main grounds:

- that it is destructive of liberty, the criticism made on behalf of the individual

- that it is destructive of order, the criticism made on behalf of government

- that it produces bad policies or is not efficient, the criticism made on behalf of society and, in particular, the economic aspect of society.

Of the three, the first is perhaps the most familiar. The expressive and the citizen theories both see democracy in relation to liberty. But, for the first, democracy is a means of securing liberty, which is exercised in the private sphere and in civil society; for the second, the life of the active citizen is itself the most important form

93

of liberty, which is exercised principally in the political realm (that part of the public sphere which is political and governmental[4]). But if democracy is a form of political freedom, both the left and the right have criticized it as spurious. For the left, real freedom depends on social and economic capacities and powers which can never be accessible to the mass of people in a capitalist society. Rather similarly, the right often argues that democracy, far from ensuring real freedom (based on the autonomy of property and the household and the independence of the individual), sets up the despotism of the majority or of the state, which rests its despotism on the people's supposed sovereignty.

But while the criticism of democracy as a threat to freedom remains the most familiar, the criticisms of inefficiency and bad government have come increasingly to be voiced in the last quarter of the present century, especially (though not exclusively) from the political and academic right.

Conservative and liberal criticisms

The criticism of conservatives and some liberals is that democracy leads to despotism: either the ordered despotism of 'totalitarian democracy'[5] or the despotism of disorderly mob greed. Plato, the first of many conservatives to do so, voiced such views within the very heart of ancient democracy when he used a nautical metaphor to compare democracy in his native Athens to a ship where the crew voted for charlatans and demagogues. This belief in the unequal distribution of wisdom and public spirit underlay the conservative distaste for democracy, and the assumption that the people could only exercise power selfishly or foolishly, or both. It had been a firm conviction of all those European conservatives who reacted against the revolutionary impetus begun in France in 1789 that the general imperfections of humanity meant a firm and paternal hand was necessary to keep the people in check. In Britain, Sir Henry Maine used Plato's nautical metaphor to depict democracy extending the powers of the state in order to pillage the wealthy. The people would be like 'a mutinous crew, feasting on a ship's provisions, gorging themselves on the meat and intoxicating themselves with the liquors, but refusing to navigate the vessel to port' (Maine, 1885, pp. 45–6). The belief in human frailty and cupidity, which led defensive democrats to devise checks on government, led conservatives to devise checks on the people.

The most sustained criticism of democracy from a liberal perspective came from Alexis de Tocqueville in two studies, one of democracy in the United States, the other of the origins of the French Revolution of 1789 (de Tocqueville, 1835; 1968 edn; and 1856; 1947 edn). For de Tocqueville, democracy involved not only a

---

[4]   See H. J. Schmidt's essay in this volume for an extended discussion of the public sphere as an arena of debate, culture and mutual relations of which politics is only a part. (NP)

[5]   That is, totalitarian government legitimized by specious mass electoral support. The charge was coined in the title of Joseph Talmon's *The Origins of Totalitarian Democracy* (1952); for Talmon those origins lay primarily in the French Revolution.

The people demand power, 1848: a 'Chartist' meeting in support of democratic constitutional reform held in London, with the well-to-do looking on (credit: Mary Evans Picture Library).

method of selecting governments, but also an egalitarian sentiment throughout society as a whole. The authority of received opinion or of wisdom and experience was discounted, and everything was put up to the continual test of reason. Yet, paradoxically, because such an egalitarian rationalism was not possible in practice, what emerged in fact was a tyranny of public opinion. De Tocqueville saw these disadvantages of democracy as likely rather than inevitable, but he established a tradition of dismissing the claims of democrats to be promoting liberty with the charge that they were in fact subverting it: by centralizing state power, undermining alternative centres of authority and influence, and reducing everything to the domination of numerical majorities. In other words, far from being reciprocal, liberty and democracy might well be incompatible, unless exceptional care were taken or exceptional luck enjoyed. For liberty required diffusion of power, and democracy centralized it. What was therefore necessary was as much distribution as possible of governmental power and hence of political activity, especially to local bodies, and a cultivation of public activity in voluntary associations quite outside the ambit of the state.

The link between democracy and the destruction of liberty continued to be the principal theme in conservative and liberal attacks. For conservatives democracy was dangerous because the people could not be trusted; for liberals it was dangerous because the state could not be trusted. Either way, democracy was presented as involving a continual and unlimited extension of central state power legitimized by popular sovereignty. Since liberal freedoms had to be defended in large part against the state, democracy and liberty came into almost unavoidable conflict. Thus Jose Ortega y Gasset warned that 'sovereign Power of unlimited extension is characteristic of pure democracy' (*Obras Completas*, quoted in Dobson, 1989, p. 60).

Thus the conservative criticism is the very reverse of that set out by the so-called élitists. Michels, Pareto and Ostrogorski had argued that far from bringing the people to power, democracy had subordinated the people to the rule of organized minorities. Conservatives, on the other hand, complained that the proper elevation of minorities to positions of power and status had been destroyed by the levelling ideology of popular government.

Socio-economic criticisms

What the conservatives argued ought to *replace* democracy, the socio-economic critics, both Marxist and feminist, saw as the *reality* which had in fact always underlain the surface forms of representative government. Formal democracy was vitiated by the inequalities of the social structure, unequal control over economic resources, and the division of tasks and status by gender. Such a view is dissatisfied with a merely political or constitutional account of democracy. It is to that extent historical or contextual, and insists that visions of democracy can only be understood in the circumstances of their societies. It also returns, in a surprising way, to some of the observations on ancient democracy to be found in Aristotle. He stipulated that a public political life rested on a degree of economic independence. Male householders, precisely because they stood on the secure foundation of property and dependents, could act freely in the political arena. Their freedom from economic necessity arose from the labour of their households. The conservative use of that observation was to argue that the propertyless masses could not therefore be allowed full citizenship. The Marxist and feminist use of it was to argue that social and economic exploitation had be to brought to an end as a precondition of any true liberty in the political sphere.

Marxism

Marx stated his criticism of democracy in his 1843 essay, 'On the Jewish question' (reprinted in Marx, 1972). Since political rights confer only formal opportunities without affecting the economic world in which those opportunities must be realized, they were meaningless and could actually divert people's attention from their real problems. The answer lay in a revolutionary transformation which would raise society to a level where traditionally conceived liberal or democratic forms of politics were simply irrelevant. On this basis, he established a tradition of dismissing democracy as 'bourgeois democracy'. A view that political freedom in bourgeois societies was without content easily (but illogically) shifted to the assertion or assumption that political freedom *as such* was bourgeois, and hence worthless.

But twentieth-century thinkers have made two different uses of Marx's argument. On the one hand, some argued that the eastern European communist states as they were between 1945 and 1989, and the Soviet Union after 1917, were real democracies because the foundation of political liberty was economic and social power, which the people achieved in those systems in a way they never could under capitalism. On the other hand, without disregarding the value of traditional rights and freedoms such as free speech, others suggested that those freedoms were effectively hobbled in the western capitalist democracies. Whereas the earlier Marxist conclusion from this was simply dismissive, later arguments favoured radical social and economic reforms to give substance to the political liberties which democracy promised. C. B. MacPherson has argued not that democracy is meaningless *per se*, but that radical social and economic changes are needed to fulfil the expectations liberals have of it: 'a great reduction of the present social and economic inequality', since a restriction of democracy is needed to defend such inequalities (MacPherson, 1977, p. 100). The target of such democratic Marxist criticism has been the underlying inequalities which vitiate democracy: simple economic inequalities and their consequences for effective political organization, and the power exercised by capital through the control of the media of mass communication.

Feminism

Of the two socio-economic criticisms of existing democracy, Marxist and feminist, the feminist criticism has posed the most radical claims. This is because it presents serious difficulties not only for the expressive theory of democracy, but also for the theory of democracy as citizenship. The latter requires a public space where politics is carried on, and citizens with sufficient freedom from material necessity to participate. The sexual division of labour – whereby women conduct, under obligation, that very large part of a society's economic activity carried on in the household – places women under a unique and massive handicap when it comes to taking part in democratic citizen politics. The claims of the Marxist democrat could be met by a programme of common ownership of the public aspects of the economy (i.e. those outside the household which involve waged labour) or even, in a perverse way, by a successful capitalist property-owning democracy. But this would leave untouched the huge area of production which takes place *in* the household, and all those inequalities of status, power and wealth which are based on the assumed obligation of women to provide a vast range of services to men and children free of all remuneration. Because the classic democratic citizen was free only thanks to the services provided by a household of dependents, women in modern societies could never be politically free until that fundamental inequality, rooted in the household, was brought to an end.

From this perspective, simply to juggle with the proportions of women in the legislature or judiciary, while leaving untouched the systematic handicap of gender-divided household economies, would be to treat the symptoms rather than the disease. Thus writers such as Carole Pateman have been able to call into question the viability of the whole democratic tradition because of its dual character: blindness to gender division on the one hand, dependence on it on the other. 'For feminists, democracy has never existed; women have never been and still are not admitted as full and equal members and citizens in any country known as "democracy" ' (Pateman, 1989, p. 210).

Rational choice criticisms

Modern democratic theory began with utilitarianism, and 'rational' or 'public choice' critics have returned to that source. But whereas at the beginning of the nineteenth century utilitarian, liberal individualism provided the grounds for advocating democracy, by the last quarter of the twentieth century rational choice theorists are using it as the springboard for a double attack on democratic assumptions. They are questioning, on the one hand, the *possibility* of translating individual preferences into democratic decisions and, on the other, the very *desirability* of doing so.

The first criticism begins with the difficulty which lies at the heart of the attempt to apply to large modern societies political principles with their origin in a small Greek *polis*: whatever form of democracy is involved, it must now be indirect and representative, and face the problem of arriving at common policies for a large, varied and conflicting range of persons and opinions. This criticism calls into question the very possibility of representative democracy, and the sceptical view is capped by an argument (implied if not stated) suggesting a rationalist idea of concord, to the effect that since perfect agreement is not possible, no agreement is possible.

The origins of this analysis of democracy lie at the end of the eighteenth century and the beginnings of the modern political system: in the calculations of Jean-Charles de Borda[6] and the Marquis de Condorcet.[7] Both of them attempted to translate wishes into results for situations where, since more than two choices were available, there was no certainty that a simple majority would emerge. As Condorcet pointed out, there might be circumstances where no one person or policy was preferred against all others. Contemporary political scientists speak of the 'Ostrogorski paradox'. This is a situation where rational transference of individual choices into policy outcomes is impossible: given two parties, four groups of constituents and three issues, party X can be preferred by a majority of voters on each single issue, but party Y elected. His paradox can also be seen as a situation where some people's hostility to party X's policies carries more weight than the support for them from others. It shows there is no end to the games that can be played with the contradictions which can arise between one choice and another.

The observation that there are circumstances when given preferences cannot be translated into a democratic policy decision has received its most elaborate and sophisticated presentation in the work of Kenneth J. Arrow. In his 'impossibility theorem' Arrow has described a situation of cyclic majorities where, given three possible policies, each policy can be preferred in equal measure over one other

---

[6]   Jean-Charles de Borda, 1733–99, French mathematician and astronomer. (NP)

[7]   Jean-Antoine-Nicola Caritat, Marquis de Condorcet, 1743–94, French mathematician, philosopher and politician. (NP)

(Arrow, 1951). For example, higher taxes may be preferred to education cuts, reduced military expenditure to higher taxes, and education cuts to reduced military expenditure. This has led W. H. Riker effectively to a complete rejection of majority decisions because of their alleged flaws: 'the products of majority rule are probably seldom defensible as consistent or as the true choice of the voting body' (Riker, 1980, pp. 456–7; quoted in Offe, 1985, p. 292).

It is important to notice, at this point, what economic metaphors are doing to political choice. They are treating democracy as if it were an attempt to do what the market is alleged to do: register and put a price on preference, and determine outcomes from the various preferences of the citizens as consumers. Such a function is an important part of the theory of expressive democracy. But even the exponents of expressive democracy have seen it as more than an information system. Democratic politics *begins*, rather than ends, with the kinds of paradoxes identified by Arrow; both citizens and politicians engage in argument and negotiation to achieve workable results by persuasion and bargaining. In other words, the wishes of citizens are not frozen but are active and developing: the processes of democratic politics are the principal agency for that process.

There is a further weakness in rational choice criticisms of democracy. The more refined the analysis becomes, the clearer it is that what is being examined is not democratic politics – or anything that can be called politics – but simply the *registration* of opinions. In other words, the criticisms arise from an attempt to 'fix' a series of frozen wants or preferences. The difficulties identified may be real difficulties *of rational choice*, but it is less clear that they are real difficulties *of democracy*. Moreover, even if the difficulties are acknowledged, they are still no more than that. If democracy falls short of the claims frequently made for it, that does not disqualify it altogether, unless other forms of government (either in practice or in a theory which corresponds more or less exactly with practice) exhibit features which are preferable to those of 'imperfect' democracy. But any examination of other forms of government reveals just the same lack of fit between theory and practice. The criticism that undermines democracy undermines all forms of government.

If one wing of the rational choice assault questions the possibility of collective choices, the other questions their desirability. Democracy, they argue, is too expensive, as the process of bidding by parties for the support of an electorate spreads to the collectivity the costs of individual wants. Public choice theorists have described the process as 'moral hazard': a situation where voters are prepared to support policies whose cost will be shared, whereas they would not be prepared to pay directly for their individual needs.[8] But it is interesting that the examples used to identify 'moral hazard' are often ones where individual provision is a realistic alternative – preparing and serving a meal, for instance. It is less clear that 'moral hazard' applies in the case of goods and services which can only be provided by some form of collective effort – such as roads or public health. The criticism involves the assumption (sometimes stated, sometimes not) that the only things worth providing are those that markets provide.

---

[8]   A neat criticism of some of these arguments can be found in Barry (1989).

But that assumption, of course, does not criticize politics; it abolishes it. In seeing the market as providing a direct means of registering choices, and politics not as an activity worthwhile in itself but simply a means to the achievement of wants, rational choice theory shares with a heterogeneous collection of thinkers a belief that politics is a much overrated activity. It was the conservative Quintin Hogg who pronounced that, unlike socialists and others who enjoyed politics for its own sake, conservatives recognized it was only ever a means to those ends of life which were frequently private. Hence, for conservatives, although politics might be engaged in as an unfortunate necessity, 'the simplest among them prefer fox-hunting – the wisest religion' (Hogg, 1947, p. 10). Oscar Wilde made a similar point from a different part of the political spectrum when he complained the trouble with socialism was that it cut into your evenings so dreadfully.

But these arguments also point to the limitation of a rational choice criticism of democracy. For those who prefer politics to fox-hunting and do not regard it as an irksome erosion of their free time, numerical calculations about the relation between wishes and policies may be part of the raw material of politics, but they are neither its substance nor its conclusion. Since the purpose of politics is to engage in a particular kind of free and life-enhancing activity, it is enough that it be done. However, such activity generally is, and worse still necessarily must be, the activity of a minority, and this seriously qualifies its claim to be not so much a form of politics as a form of *democratic* politics.

Democracy and freedom

All the above criticisms – both of democracy's potential and of the failure adequately to achieve it – are more relevant in relation to expressive democracy. The opponents of democracy can make less headway against citizen democracy, and those who complain of the small achievements of actually existing democracy would be close to satisfied were citizenship democracy ever approached. For, if democracy is an active process of politics (involving discussion and the formation, changing and development of opinion), it assumes that the interests and wills of citizens are changing not fixed, and it depends upon a constitutional framework which acknowledges, defends and encourages this. For such a conception of democracy, one-party rule, democratic tyranny or the restriction of free expression would be a contradiction in terms. But so would the existence of social or economic conditions which systematically handicapped some and privileged others in the public life of politics.

Democracy in the European Community

Contemporary Europe provides great opportunities and demands serious and thoughtful responses from democrats. Both the recent revolutions in the East and the development of the European Community in the West mean that, whatever may be decided about the principles and purposes of democracy, they cannot simply be left to the continuance of tradition. Deliberate choices and principled judgements must be made in circumstances where change has occurred and is going to continue.

In the case of western Europe, the European Parliament provides a focus for both the hopes and frustrations of democrats. The problem here is that democracy and the nation state developed together. Democracy requires a people, and that is most readily provided by the nation state. In the case of the European Community, it is not clear whether the people of Europe provide an equivalent to the people of France, or of Italy, or of Britain. It may not be possible, and it has not yet proved possible, to translate democratic politics to a governmental system other than that of the nation state. Supporters of the idea of trans-European democracy through the European Parliament have assumed that the only opposition comes from the Commission and from national governments. But there is no reason to suppose that the people or the parties of France, Germany or the United Kingdom would be ready to accept the content, or acknowledge the authority, of a decision which went against them in a European assembly – any more than the people of Scotland or the Basque country would be ready to do so when faced by an analogous democratic 'tyranny' within existing national borders.

Of course, the problem is already faced within federal states and those states where, as well as national elections, there are elected local authorities. The evidence suggests that delimitation between central and provincial powers is possible, but that a mechanism for adjudication is probably necessary to achieve it. Centralization may be a response to the same problem. Moreover the comparison between the EC and, say, the electoral system in Germany is not appropriate. 'Germany', as a nation to which one may feel loyalty, is different from 'Europe'. In existing federal or quasi-federal systems there is an overriding national loyalty to a larger, federal community. But in the case of Europe, the reverse is true: national loyalties are given to the smaller, constituent parts, while the overarching European Community has to make do with an (as yet) far more cloudy sense of 'European-ness'.

The restatement of democracy?

The claim of eastern Europe to be democratic provides new opportunities for examining the nature of the democratic ideal and the possibilities of democratic politics. It also illustrates (if it should need illustrating) that, while calls for more democracy or the defence of democracy may continue to arouse more than they enlighten, the nature of democracy is as contentious, and the tradition of democratic political thought as alive and full of potential, as ever it was. The conception of democracy stated by the Civic Forum in Czechoslovakia revives a different tradition of citizen democracy. The Forum's 'Eight Rules of Dialogue' (reprinted in Bloomfield, 1991) is a recipe for democracy as an active intellectual engagement with the opinions of others, stressing both the need for views to be stated and the necessity of sympathetically understanding the contrary arguments of others. Such a dialogue is, of course, dynamic in comparison with the passive democracy of preference expression: it assumes that views will be not only expressed and challenged but also modified and developed.

But the claims of expressive democracy and of citizenship democracy frequently sustain one another. Expressive democracy requires the guaranteed independence of a political sphere. Citizenship democracy requires more than a formal political equality among citizens. This necessary 'double layer' of democratic theory has been a feature of recent discussion of democracy, whether from a libertarian socialist position (as with the work of democratic Marxist Norberto Bobbio, 1984, or with Claus Offe, 1985) or a feminist one (as with Carole Pateman, 1985 and 1989).

Both recent history and technology suggest new ways forward for democracy. Modern democracies depend on the written and broadcast word for the political communication which, in the ancient world, could be provided by the citizens debating together in the forum. And so the ordinary democratic citizen is doubly isolated. There is no face-to-face political community, and the political activity in which he or she does engage is either the isolation of the polling booth or the essentially solitary activity of reading or watching television. It has been suggested that computer technology can transform this atomization. But it may have the reverse effect. Technology cannot be guaranteed to be benign, and may do no more than accentuate the flaws of the existing system. If information technology does enhance democracy, it will do so not by increasing the flow of communication between citizen and government, but by easing the creation of an unpredictable series of networks among citizens. This occurred in the Soviet Union as fax machines circumvented the obstacles which still lie in the way of open publishing unconstrained by the government. The disadvantage of any such system is that once citizens communicate with each other electronically, they are vulnerable to espionage by the state.

We need to retain some scepticism. The experience of eastern Europe shows that large sections of the citizen body can maintain sustained political activity during a crisis. It does not show that they have much inclination or desire to do so in more normal times. The reason why élites can exercise so much power may lie, to some considerable extent, in the essentially private priorities of most people most of the time. If that is the case, then participatory democracy may not be a way to empower the people but simply a way to increase the number and diversity of empowered élites. Yet, as is so often the case in politics, this might end by empowering people in different and unexpected ways.

References

ARENDT, H. (1958) *The Human Condition*, Chicago, University of Chicago Press.

ARROW, K. J. (1951) *Social Choice and Individual Values*, New Haven, Yale University Press.

BARBER, B. (1984) *Strong Democracy: Participatory Politics for a New Age*, Berkeley, University of California Press.

BARKER, R. (1990) *Political Legitimacy and the State*, Oxford, Clarendon Press.

BARKER, R. and HOWAR-JOHNSTONE, K. (1975) 'The politics and political ideas of Moisei Ostragorski', *Political Studies*, December.

BARRY, B. (1989) 'Does democracy cause inflation?' in *Democracy, Power and Justice*, Oxford, Clarendon Press.

BLOOMFIELD, J. (1991) 'Citizen power in Prague' in G. Andrews (ed.) *Citizenship*, London, Lawrence & Wishart.

BOBBIO, N. (1984) *Il Futuro della democrazia*, Torino; trans. (1987) *The Future of Democracy*, Cambridge, Polity.

DICEY, A. V. (1914) *Lectures on the Relationship Between Law and Public Opinion in England during the Nineteenth Century*, London, Macmillan.

DOBSON, A. (1989) *An Introduction to the Politics and Philosophy of José Ortega y Gasset*, Cambridge, Cambridge University Press.

ECCLESHALL, R. (1986) *British Liberalism: Liberal Thought from the 1640s to 1980s*, Harlow, Longman.

HAYEK, F. A. (1944) *The Road to Serfdom*, London, George Routledge & Sons.

HOGG, Q. (1947) *The Case for Conservatism*, Harmondsworth, Penguin.

MACPHERSON, C. B. (1977) *The Life and Times of Liberal Democracy*, Oxford, Oxford University Press.

MAINE, H. (1885) *Popular Government*, London, John Murray.

MALLOCK, W. H. (1918) *The Limits of Pure Democracy*, London, Chapman & Hall.

MARX, K. (1843; 1972 edn) 'On the Jewish question' in *Early Texts*, ed. D. McLellan, Oxford, Blackwell.

MICHELS, R. (1949) *Political Parties*, Glencoe, Illinois, Free Press of Glencoe.

MILL, J. S. (1861; 1977 edn), *Consideration on Representative Government* in *Collected Works*, vol. xix, Toronto, University of Toronto Press.

NAIRN, T. (1977) *The Break-up of Britain*, London, Verso.

OFFE, C. (1985) *Disorganized Capitalism: Contemporary Transformations of Work and Politics*, Cambridge, Polity.

OSTROGORSKI, M. (1902) *Democracy and the Organization of Political Parties*, London, Macmillan.

PATEMAN, C. (1970) *Participation and Democratic Theory*, Cambridge, Cambridge University Press.

PATEMAN, C. (1985) *The Sexual Contract*, Cambridge, Cambridge University Press.

PATEMAN, C. (1989) *The Disorder of Women*, Cambridge, Cambridge University Press.

RIKER, W. H. (1980) 'Implications for the disequilibrium of majority rule for the study of institutions', *American Political Science Review*, vol. 74.

ROUSSEAU, J.-J. (1762; 1968 edn) *The Social Contract*, trans. M. Cranston, Harmondsworth, Penguin.

TALMON, J. (1952) *The Origins of Totalitarian Democracy*, Harmondsworth, Penguin.

DE TOCQUEVILLE, A. (1835, 1840; 1968 edn) *Democracy in America*, London, Collins.

DE TOCQUEVILLE, A. (1856; 1947 edn) *The Ancien Regime*, Oxford, Blackwell.

WEBER, M. (1918; 1948 edn) 'Politics as a vocation' in *From Max Weber: Essays in Sociology*, ed. H. C. Gerth and C. W. Mills, London, Routledge & Kegan Paul.

Essay 4
The state under the rule of Law

Prepared for the Course Team by
Francesco D'Agostino
Lecturer in the Faculty of Jurisprudence in the
University of Rome 'Tor Vergata'
Translated by Darren Skeats and Noël Parker

The Idea of the state under the rule of Law

The concept of the 'state under the rule of Law'[1] originated in nineteenth-century German jurisprudence (philosophy of law), where it was developed as part of the broader 'doctrine of the state'.[2] Thanks to its prestige in Germany, the doctrine of the state spread to all European countries except Britain, which has retained its own distinct notion of 'government'.

The state under the rule of Law began as a jurisprudential idea but has since become a basis of juridical and political values in its own right, emerging as one of the key ideas of our time.

The importance of the concept of the state under the rule of Law lies in two areas:

(i) it encapsulates the most characteristic feature of the modern state as a form of social organization: freedom from the personal exercise of sovereignty by individuals;

(ii) it underlies our widespread aspirations for a strong commitment to democracy, respect for human rights, and opposition to totalitarianism.

The importance of the state under the rule of Law owes more, in fact, to the political implications of the concept than to its specifically jurisprudential origins. As a result, debate on the state under the rule of Law has become too important to be

---

[1]   The phrase 'state under the rule of Law' is used in this essay to translate the German word *Rechtsstaat* (literally, 'law state' or 'justice state'), the French and Italian equivalents of which are *état de droit* and *stato di diritto*. The word *Rechtsstaat* was coined by nineteenth-century Prussian jurists in opposition to the *Polizeistaat* (police state). Rudolf von Gneist (1872) attributes the first use of the word *Rechtsstaat* to the German jurist Robert von Mohl (1799–1875).

[2]   German, *allgemeine Staatslehre* (universal theory of the state).

left to jurisprudence and has become the province of politicians and political thinkers.

In this essay I do not wish to deny that the state under the rule of Law is a political construct. But I shall argue that it is a political matter only because it is *primarily* a juridical one. From the juridical standpoint, the issue that the concept of the state under the rule of Law embodies can be rigorously formulated. It is the question of the sovereign authority of Law, which is embodied in the English expression 'the rule of Law', about which I shall have more to say later.

Limits to the authority of the state

Much of the responsibility for the mistaken view that the state under the rule of Law is primarily a political construct lies with the jurists themselves. Particularly responsible are those who, attracted by the myth of statism,[3] have reduced jurisprudence's notion of 'right' to something established by convention, which they then identify with whatever has been enacted in law.

One such jurist was the German constitutional lawyer Georg Jellinek (1851–1911), whose celebrated theory of personal or 'subjective' public right (that is, rights that belong to the citizen rather than to the state; Jellinek, 1892) suffers from this fundamental flaw. In Jellinek's view, such rights can only have substance if the state limits itself. In consequence, the principle of the state under the rule of Law is undeniably weakened. What 'self-limitation' amounts to is that the state is 'under the rule of Law' in the sense that it exercises power through the laws it enacts. Rather than limiting the exercise of power, the law simply acts as a vehicle for the expression of power. Though theorists of the state would not intend it, starting from this theory it is possible to arrive at what can only be termed legalized despotism (Matteucci, 1966, p. 266).

Let us likewise consider the doctrine of one of the greatest jurists of this century, the Austrian-American legal philosopher Hans Kelsen (1881–1973). Though a committed democrat, Kelsen considers democracy to be a mere 'ideological' value, rather any part of the jurisprudential notion of right. To Kelsen, Law appears to be an implicit, formal dimension of human experience, compatible with any actual system of government. Objectively speaking, therefore, the expression 'under the rule of Law' (understood as values, in the way I have emphasized) is superfluous to our understanding of the state. Given jurisprudence's understanding of the phenomenon of the state, any state, simply by virtue of being a state, would count as a legal order. Kelsen writes:

> ... the state only exists in acts of state, and these are performed by individuals and attributed to the state as a juristic person.[4] Such attribution is possible only on the basis of legal norms which specifically determine

---

[3] That is, the belief that the state is the foundation of all social existence. (NP)

[4] i.e. an entity with no existence outside its legal form. (NP)

these acts.[5] That the state creates the law merely means that individuals, whose acts, on the basis of law, are attributed to the state, create the law. But this means that the law regulates its own creation. It does not happen, and never can happen, that the state, which in its existence precedes the law, creates the law and then submits itself to it. It is not the state which submits itself to the law, but it is the law which regulates the behaviour of men and, particularly, their behaviour directed at the creation of law, and which thereby subjects these men to law.

(Kelsen, 1960, p. 315; 1967, pp. 312–13)

If the expression 'under the rule of Law' is superfluous, how can we explain the historic impact of the idea of a 'theory of the state' (German, *Staatslehre*)? For Kelsen, the answer lies in its 'ideological' force. A 'state under the rule of Law' does not consist of anything scientifically objective and analysable, but is merely a particular, historically identifiable type of state. Its characteristic features do not concern the jurist, since in the last analysis its *political* values are in no way related to the *formal* dimensions of human experience formulated in law. These values, according to Kelsen, are the sole basis for objective debate:

A *Rechtsstaat* in this specific sense is a relatively centralized legal order according to which jurisdiction and administration are bound by general legal norms – norms created by a parliament elected by the people; the courts are independent; and certain civil liberties of the citizens, especially freedom of religion and freedom of speech, are guaranteed.

(Kelsen, 1967)

In this description of the characteristics of the state under the rule of Law, Kelsen specifies precisely all the possible contingent, *technical* aspects of public organization characteristic of the modern state. The accuracy of Kelsen's technical specification of the *Rechtsstaat* as the characteristic form of the modern state is not in doubt. But the perspective in which he presents it undermines all understanding of the meaning of 'state under the rule of Law'. Contrary to what Kelsen believes, this is a meaning that is essential for the science of Law, since the status of jurisprudence itself depends on it.

My key point here is that the 'state under the rule of Law' is an essential ethical notion that guides our reflection on the state. It is so, but not because of its intrinsic complexity as an idea. (Its meanings, historically, have been very variable.) It is so because the concept of the state under the rule of Law unambiguously entails the principle that *Law*[6] *must have primacy over politics*. One may, therefore, correctly define as a 'state under the rule of Law' *every* historical instance where a state has been emancipated from the primacy of the political sphere, and where the general, juridical principle of liberty has found proper room for expression. Clearly, in this type of state, all the structures identified as belonging to the political sphere are not abolished. But they undergo a profound transformation when transposed into jurisprudence's notion of 'right'.

---

[5]   i.e. specify what actions are allowed and what form they may take. (NP)

[6]   See note 24 below. (NP)

The connection which the theory of the state usually makes – that between the *modern* state and the state under the rule of Law – must therefore be rethought. In modern history, states under the rule of Law have multiplied. But at the theoretical level, one must question whether the *principle* of the state under the rule of Law is necessarily modern, and whether there is any necessary correlation between modernity and this particular juridical structure of the state.[7] Pursuing this line of thought from a theoretical, historical or sociological point of view, it would be more correct to claim that twentieth-century totalitarianism (rather than the state under the rule of Law) has a uniquely modern character.

In any discussion of the state under the rule of Law there is an implicit debate about what is specific to the sphere of the law, as opposed to politics. And this discussion turns on fundamental dimensions of human experience, rather than on merely historical, contingent ones. If this point is not grasped, comparisons between the state under the rule of Law and other possible forms of political organization are extremely misleading. In making such a comparison, the state under the rule of Law appears to be a political model of organization. The principles of the state under the rule of Law derive, however, not from any *political* dimension of social organization, but from a strictly *juridical* one. To justify this assertion fully, it is useful to go back over the traditional 'doctrine of the state', and show how it is sustained by the force of the principle of Law.

The essential elements in the doctrine of the state

The modern doctrine of the state, following the teachings of Jellinek,[8] generally lists three essential elements for an adequate theoretical definition of the state form: the people, territory and sovereignty. These elements, however, are not separate, but mutually integrated. The *synthesis* between them properly characterizes the state as something more than the sum of its parts. Taking this proposition as a starting point (and avoiding, for the time being, the question of the essence of the state) we can extrapolate various implications from it.

The people

In terms of the doctrine of the state, the people can be a totality made up of individuals bound not by arbitrary links but by some principle of objective, shared identification. This principle can be ethnic (determined by race, language or cus-

---

[7] According to the great Italian political scientist G. Miglio, to insist on the originality of modern constitutionalism by comparison with the political doctrines of the ancients is a serious historiographical error, in view of the 'fundamental unity of development in the Western political experience', founded on the 'continuing aspiration for the depersonalization of authority' (Miglio, 1988, p. 330).

[8] Particularly his *Allgemeine Staatslehre*, Berlin, 1914.

*Marcus Tullius Cicero (106–43 BC), Roman lawyer
and statesman (credit: Alinari).*

toms); religious; or even ideological. In all cases, the principle can be rendered objective in juridical terms, and is not arbitrary or grounded in individualism. With this principle in mind, the Roman philosopher and statesman Cicero eloquently defined the *res publica* not just as any assemblage of human beings, but as a union founded on respect for Law and on the common good.[9]

In other words (as Max Weber has shown), a people can be identified by the fact that what unites the individuals composing it is *not* the mere pursuit of limited interests, albeit shared ones. This could be said of any association, public or private, which is identified by the particular aims it sets itself. For Weber, a people is distinguished by the fact that all the possible interests of an individual member can, in principle, be located within the higher, common interest. Here lies the root of the dimension of organic totality (the organicist model, to which I shall return) that is inherent in the people as a body of individuals organized into a state.

The state under the rule of Law defines the people via the category of citizenship. However often it has been twisted for narrowly political purposes, a strictly juridi-

---

[9]   'Not just any assembly of the mass of the people, but a union based on respect for law and community of interest'(*De Re Publica*, Bk. I, ch. 25, para 39).

cal principle is expressed through this idea. Even if belonging to the given political group can be made dependent on historical or material factors (be they national, ethnic, ideological or religious), for Law the status of citizen has a single ultimate reference point: belonging to the human race. There is no person who cannot, in principle, be recognized as a citizen. Law, unlike politics, is never founded upon exclusion. The supra-national ideal of cosmopolitanism[10] neither implies nor advocates abolition of the diversity that has appeared in the world throughout history. This would be unrealizable in fact, as well as undesirable in principle. But what cosmopolitanism does advocate is the subordination of diversity to the universal principle that is implied in the recognition of persons by the Law.

Territory

Territory can be as extensive as an empire or as limited as the ancient Greek *polis* (city-state), but it must figure as the site of the people's historical roots.[11] A state cannot be said to exist where territory is not in principle necessary to the identification and constitution of the people. This is the case, for example, with the great monotheistic religions, which certainly have a people but which cannot be likened to a state – and, for the most part, do not wish to be. They maintain a radical distinction in principle on this matter, even if this is sometimes problematic. (One thinks of the difficulty posed for the unity of the Islamic world by the recognition of different states within it). This stipulation applies even more plainly to bodies such as the UN, the EC, the Holy See, the Order of Malta, etc. They exist under international law and are granted an individual sovereign identity in law, but not statehood as such. This explains two things: why a people deprived of its territorial roots cannot survive as a state (the people of Israel is a famous, albeit not unique historical example); and why, conversely, a government-in-exile cannot continue to represent its own people, except in the short term (see Schmitt, 1974).

In the relationship between the people and its territory, the state under the rule of Law recognizes one of the essential supports not only of the state's own identity, but also of the subjective identity of the individual citizens, who are seen as 'owners' of the soil of 'their land'. In the long-standing dispute over the 'natural', and hence 'absolute' character of the right of property, the final reference point is not so much different economic ideologies as different anthropologies. To support the right of the individual to a form of property that is historically appropriate to the time and place does not, in principle, endorse *capitalist* social organization. It simply recognizes that the individual is a person living not only in time, but also in space; and that, for such persons, living in space entails a link to material things, which they consider as theirs.

---

[10]   i.e. the idea, formed in the eighteenth-century Enlightenment, of people as citizens of the world, or of the human race. (NP)

[11]   In some primitive forms of organization it can even change according to the seasons, as happens with nomadic peoples. This does not make it impossible to identify a state, provided that the periodic migrations do not stand in the way of a deep-seated relationship between the given people and the given area of land – even if this relationship is not a long-term one.

Furthermore, the principle of Law is beneficial in the context of these disputes, which if left to the logic of politics are bound to lead to absurd conclusions. Because the law is a form of human experience grounded in people's experience of each other, it is incapable of construing property as merely a relationship between humans and things, such as could be defined solely in terms of the power one has over the other. Rather, the law thinks of a relationship between human and human, mediated by things and defined (in quite distinct forms) by the mutual boundary that is implicit in any inter-subjective relationship. It follows that the juridical defence of the right to *property* can never deny the higher requirement of juridical recognition for *people*. This is the reason why slavery is not truly a juridical condition, but a political one.

The political meaning of sovereignty

Sovereignty is amongst the most complex and controversial concepts of the modern doctrine of the state. It is also one of the most ambiguous, having a double sense, a hybrid of juridical and political meanings.

The political aspect of the concept of sovereignty refers to the existence of an autonomous, transcendent source of supreme power: a power that *creates* values and meanings – making it, in Hobbes' suggestive images, a 'mortal god', a 'Leviathan' (*Leviathan*, 1651, ch. 17). It is a source of power, which, according to Rousseau, 'by the mere fact that it is, is always all that it ought to be' (Rousseau (1968), book 1, ch. 7, p. 63). In the final analysis, however, it is a power grounded in *myth*, and hence one that is false in itself.

The concept of sovereignty as a secularized theology first developed when absolute monarchies were establishing themselves in Europe, and found its full theoretical elaboration in Hobbes. We must reject one inevitable implication of the *strong* concept of sovereignty: the subordination, at the very core of the state, of Law to politics. We must do so, not out of fear that such power can be deployed autocratically by small, privileged élites, but for reasons of principle.

Rousseau sought to purify Hobbes' concept, democratizing it by transferring sovereignty to the totality of the people. But that transfer of mythical, autonomous, transcendent power did not rectify the fundamental flaw in the concept. Paradoxically, it compounded the theoretical difficulties. Hobbes' sovereign was at least specifiable in some kind of material terms: it was identifiable either as an individual (a monarch) or an oligarchy. Rousseau's sovereign seems so much more concrete: it corresponds, to an apparently quantifiable reality, namely the people. But it is unidentifiable in material terms. What Rousseau calls the 'general will' – the will that sustains the state and creates Law – has nothing to do with the will of the majority of citizens. The general will is fundamentally singular, superior and indivisible; it emanates from the people as a single totality and consequently is always in the right.[12] The general will's

---

[12]   Rousseau (1968), book 2, ch. 3. Consequently, according to Rousseau, 'When a law is proposed to the people's assembly, what is asked of them is not precisely whether they approve of the proposition or reject it, but whether it is in conformity with the general will which is theirs... When, therefore, the opinion contrary to my own prevails, this proves only that I have made a mistake...' (book 4, ch. 2).

absolute claim to be *right* reveals an impressive (if not unprecedented) nostalgia for theological absolutes. It also makes Rousseau both the most coherent theorist of modern democracy and the one who most systematically subverts not only the state under the rule of Law, but also Law itself.

The juridical meaning of sovereignty: the legal order in a state under the rule of Law

If we examine the concept of sovereignty in a strictly juridical sense it yields fundamental insights.

First of all, sovereignty can serve as an ultimate criterion to recognize the *specific character* of the legal order in a state under the rule of Law.

Until such time as the human race establishes a universal, cosmopolitan order,[13] it will be forced to recognize the continued existence of a plurality of legal orders. Each of these can be characterized by 'sovereignty' in a juridical sense. This kind of sovereignty has nothing to do with the state's pretensions to embody an autonomous, transcendent power, as in the political concept of sovereignty. It merely reflects, on the juridical level, the fragmentation into groups, ethnic or otherwise, that is characteristic of human history. Such groups are sovereign in the sense that they answer only to themselves. A *non-sovereign* order would not be an authentic order at all.[14]

But sovereignty in this juridical sense also conveys something much more important: the recognition that, to merit the term 'juridical', an order must answer to the logic of Law, rather than to the arbitrary will of whoever holds political power. An authentic sovereign order, therefore (that is, one that does not recognize any superior authority[15]) does not permit non-juridical categories (from politics, ethics, sociology, theology, etc.) to intrude and alter its character.

A system that is sovereign in the juridical sense will therefore contain its own, internal rules to make possible a change of rulers without recourse to violence.[16] In the absence of such rules, the juridical order would not be sovereign, but a slave to whoever happened to hold power. These rules have normally found their formal, technical framework in two celebrated principles: the *primacy of Law* and the *separation of powers*.[17]

---

[13]   Thus realizing the aspirations not only of Kant, but, more generally, of all those who have at heart the primacy of Law over politics.

[14]   That is, unless it was, in the language of jurisprudence, *secundum quid*, i.e. operating within limits accorded it by an order superior to itself.

[15]   In the language of jurisprudence it is *superiorem non recognoscens*.

[16]   This principle is skilfully defended by Popper (1945; 1966) and Hayek (1979).

[17]   The influence of the separation of powers is discussed in Pierre Avril's essay in this book. (NP)

The primacy of Law must apply directly to the activities of government. This essentially means two things: the government must function in accordance with *existing* law (*sub leges*[18]) and also through the *general, abstract*[19] norms of Law (*per leges*). The doctrine of the primacy of Law is very ancient.[20] What is modern is for it to be elaborated in a range of judicial powers providing for checks on public administration.

For this modern development of the doctrine of the primacy of Law we are chiefly indebted to the nineteenth-century Prussian jurists' polemic against the *Polizeistaat* (police state) and in support of the *Rechtsstaat* (state under the rule of Law). The description of Prussia as a 'bureaucratic-military' state (see, for example, Schlangen, 1973, p. 135), though formally correct, is essentially an historical and sociological description. Such a description should not obscure the link made, in the Prussian state type, between the principle of sovereignty and the necessity for power to be impersonal. In the Prussian *Rechtsstaat* no limits were placed upon sovereignty (in keeping with the eighteenth-century principles of enlightened despotism). But, according to this model, neither the king nor the people was truly sovereign. The state alone was sovereign: the king was regarded as the chief among its servants. The state was an absolutely impersonal body, which found its two most typical expressions in the bureaucracy and the military. But, precisely because it was impersonal, the state could not act except through the Law; that is to say, through a will bound up with absolutely general norms and with procedures given concrete form in the Law.[21] By comparison with those of the state, citizens' rights were not properly recognized. Nevertheless, citizens enjoyed absolute guarantees of freedom (in a juridical sense) because the state would never act towards them in a capricious or arbitrary way.[22] To this end, the state had to ensure that a rigorous distinction was maintained between the legislative power and the executive, which was required to operate through decrees and was subject to precise controls over what it could do legitimately.

[18]   According to the principle *lex facit regem*, authoritatively exemplified by Bracton (1968), vol. II, p. 33.

[19]   One of the clearest principles of the Twelve Tables [i.e. the first code of Roman law, formulated, under the Republic, in 451–50 BC (NP)] is the requirement that one must not legislate to grant privileges *(privilegia ne inroganto)*, but by general and abstract laws.

[20]   It is found as early as Hesiod, in the eighth century BC, when he admonishes sovereigns not to rule arbitrarily, but to respect received justice (the *Dike*) (*Works and Days*, lines 202 ff.). In the *Supplicant Women* (lines 433–4), Euripides (*c.*480–406 BC), has Theseus say: 'when the laws are written down, rich and poor have the same justice'.

[21]   In fact, the Prussian state managed internal politics through the bureaucracy, and external politics through the army. In either case, it was a *rule-bound* government, in which personal or class interests could find no place. It is an historic tragedy that the Prussian state, the definitive embodiment of pure reason of state *(reine Staatsvernunft)*, tied its reputation and its historical destiny to coercion, and met its nemesis in formal abolition on 25 February 1947 at the hands of the Allied Control Commission.

[22]   Robert von Mohl goes so far as to state that the freedom of the citizen is the entire foundation of the state under the rule of Law (cf. von Mohl, 1844, vol. I, pp. 16–17).

Throughout the nineteenth century there was a growing debate as to the ultimate purpose of the controls over the executive. In the end Rudolf von Gneist's doctrine prevailed (von Mohl, 1966), giving victory to the requirement of absolute independence for the administrative courts that supervised the activities of state functionaries. By the same token a further principle was affirmed: that the purpose of controls over public administration is not to make one power of the state (the executive) subordinate to another (the legislature), but to make *both* faithful to Law itself. The Prussian model of the state under the rule of Law thus reached its zenith in the work of von Gneist.

The rights of man tradition

Though the principle of the separation of powers plays a very important role within the juridical model of sovereignty, it is ultimately subordinate to the higher principle of the unity of the state. The principle of separation of powers has operated in a different way in the another great tradition of continental Europe, that generally said to stem from Montesquieu. The profound, moral character implicit in Montesquieu's doctrine is apparent in one of the most powerful and lucid formulas for the specific nature of the state under the rule of Law. In Article 16 of the *Declaration of the Rights of Man and of the Citizen*,[23] we read the famous statement: 'Any society where there is no guarantee of rights or of the separation of powers is without a constitution'. Formally, 'to have a constitution' means to separate the powers of the state. But in essence to have a constitution means to guarantee oneself against tyranny, against government by men (especially by one man), as distinct from government by Law. The emphasis we find in Article 16 helps us to understand how the separation of powers is not a mere technicality, but a principle to be embodied in legal norms. It is the bridle that Law places on government, a bridle with which (incredible as it may seem) government has – at least in many cases – allowed itself to be curbed.

The rule of Law and the continental tradition of jurisprudence

Once we recognize that the primacy of Law is the central value of the theory of the separation of powers, we can understand the common ground between this theory and the Anglo-Saxon principle of 'the rule of Law'. This common ground is not visible in constitutional provisions, but at the profounder level of aspirations and intentions. The English expression 'the rule of Law' cannot be directly translated into other languages – a fact which demonstrates how deep-rooted it is in the English constitutional tradition. It does not have the breadth of meaning of the expression 'state under the rule of Law',[24] which comes from the continental tradition of jurisprudence.

---

[23]   The formal declaration of human rights and legitimate limitations on those rights, inserted at the head of the first post-Revolution French constitution in 1791. (NP)

[24]   The term 'Law' (with a capital 'l', and without an article) is used throughout this essay to convey something of the continental *Recht, droit*, etc., with their connotation of a meta-legal sphere above and beyond the positive law of particular states. (NP)

The expression 'the rule of Law' is essentially ambiguous. Does it mean government 'by the Law' or government 'by the principles of right'? The ambiguity can only be removed if we recognize that there can be no conflict of substance between Law and right. This is extremely difficult for the continental tradition to recognize, because this tradition is accustomed to viewing the law (in the sense of formal expressions of the will of the legislature) as the only possible act that creates justice (or right). It does not see Law as the concrete, operationalized form of tangible justice, which ought to constitute the very core of human juridical experience.

Throughout the last century, the continental tradition of jurisprudence remained crushed under the weight of the principle laid down by the famous Article 6 of the *Declaration of the Rights of Man and of the Citizen*: 'The law is the expression of the General Will'. On the one hand, this principle seems to place the power of the state within a legal framework, and hence to *limit* it, for the general will can only be expressed through the law, that is juridically. On the other hand, the principle also *expands* state power to the utmost limit. For it does not recognize any right that can be counterposed to the will of the people as expressed in the general will.[25]

The theoreticians of the nineteenth-century liberal state – who achieved remarkable results for the history of political thought[26] – focussed on this difficulty. The French legal theoretician Carré de Malberg (1861–1935[27]) argued that to take the state under the rule of Law as a point of reference introduces a mediating element between the sovereignty of the people and the sovereignty of Law. As the interpreter of national sovereignty, the state has regard to the sovereignty of political institutions, thus setting a limit to revolutionary demands on behalf of the sovereign people. On the other hand, the state also has regard to the sovereignty of positive right, setting a limit to the arbitrary exercise of power by those who actually hold power, even if they have acquired democratic legitimacy. The concept of national sovereignty is essentially doctrinaire, a hybrid concept that cannot claim to have a crystal-clear theoretical foundation. But it does have an explicitly modern, or rather an *impersonal, objective* character.

Carré de Malberg's insistence on this point is of great importance (Carré de Malberg, 1920–22, book II, p. 197). This impersonal, objective character clearly runs through the concept of national sovereignty, distinguishing it from the 'ancient' criterion of sovereignty that Carré de Malberg notes in both the monarchical power of the *ancien régime*, and the popular power of the revolutionary period. These two very different forms were analogous in the personal, subjective way that they exercised sovereignty.

---

[25]   Least of all did it recognize laws by custom and tradition, such as rights that had been held under the *ancien régime*, which were not regarded as expressions of will at all.

[26]   On this point, see most recently Fioravanti (1991).

[27]   Amongst R. Carré de Malberg's works we should note *Contribution à la théorie générale de l'Etat* (1920–22) and *La loi, expression de la volonté générale* (1931).

Lithograph of the Declaration of the Rights of Man, 1789. On the left the figure of France breaks her chains. On the right Law points downwards to the Rights of Man and upwards with her sceptre to the eye of Reason, which is dispersing the clouds of error and obscurantism.

In the final analysis, then, the liberal state under the rule of Law as it developed in the nineteenth century revolves around the principle of objectivity. This objectivity is both a criterion to guide the activities of state agencies operating within society at large, and a limit to narrow, sectarian demands arising from the body of society. Through this development, the continental doctrine of the state rediscovered independently the fundamental principles of the Anglo-Saxon tradition of the rule of Law.

The meaning and significance of the rule of Law

I now want to explain more fully the principle behind the Anglo-Saxon rule of Law, which is so important to this discussion. (There is no exhaustive, formally exact and universally recognized definition of the rule of Law, however, and I shall identify its meaning inductively. Although this leaves the definition incomplete and imprecise, it does have the benefit of flexibility.)

I shall begin by following Wade, who indicates at least four fundamental meanings of the rule of Law as it relates to actions of the state (Wade, 1961, 1968, pp. 23–25; cf. Paulson, 1992, pp. 251 ff.).

(i)   Wade's first meaning is that of 'legality': 'everything must be done according to law'. In other words, an act of government can be considered legal if (and only if) it is envisaged by the law.

(ii) The second meaning of the rule of Law is that the activity of the government must 'be conducted within a framework of recognized rules and principles which restrict discretionary power'. This meaning contains something missing from the first, with which it is closely linked. The first meaning recognizes the sovereignty of Law, but in some way leaves open the question of whether 'Law' refers to something beyond, and different from, the legal system in force. Thus, the second meaning introduces two new categories: 'rules' and 'recognized principles'. The state must move within the ambit marked out by these categories. Since they are not part of the existing law, these two dimensions belong to a sphere beyond the given, positive law of the state.

(iii) From the second meaning, however, it is not possible to determine with certainty how the specific sphere of the law should be identified – especially if it is related to meta-legal principles. To this end, it is essential to introduce a third meaning: 'that disputes as to the legality of acts of government are to be decided by judges wholly independent of the executive'.

(iv) Finally, it remains to determine the criterion by which judges should decide the law. The fourth and final meaning of the rule of Law does this by establishing that 'the law should be even-handed between government and citizen'. To put it another way, the state 'should not enjoy unnecessary privileges or exemptions from the ordinary law'. As a consequence, a judge can reject as illegal any rules that do not respect this principle.

As I have already said, it is not possible to reduce the practice of the rule of Law to just these four meanings, important though they are. We know, for example, that in the Anglo-Saxon tradition the principle of the rule of Law translates, in practice, into the primacy of common law over statute law.[28, 29] A full discussion of it would require some reflections on history, which might imply that the rule of Law is a significant principle only within a specific historical experience (such as that of the Anglo-Saxon world) and cannot be generalized.[30] It would be misleading to suggest that the principle of the rule of Law should be adopted by the institutions of other systems. Rather, it is an example that should be absorbed into the broader theorization of Law.

The great significance of the rule of Law is its reluctance to unify the state and the Law, which has been the error of much of continental juridical science. The conceptual gain that the rule of Law perspective offers the continental jurist is that of 'government': the range of political, administrative and institutional processes ordering society. The concept includes all three of the traditional functions of the state, or, at least, those of the executive and the legislature. According to the English rule of Law, government has always been held subordinate, in principle, to the authority of the law. The consequences of this principle are extremely important and well-known, the primary one being the equality, before ordinary law courts, of citizens and the government.

But in the present context, I want to underline another principle, which is much in evidence in *Introduction to the Study of the Law of the Constitution* (1885) by Albert Dicey (1835–1922), the great theoretician of the rule of Law. The unwritten norms of the English constitution are not the source of the personal rights of the citizen – as a continental jurist trained in the doctrine of the *Rechtsstaat* might be led to think. The norms of the constitution contain the *consequences* of those rights. Law does not derive from the constitution: it is the constitution that derives from Law.[31] There is still debate in the Anglo-Saxon world as to whether this principle should be given more than superficial respect, and whether it is compatible with the needs of social-welfare states[32] in the second half of the twentieth century. But its value as a principle of legal behaviour seems absolutely unquestionable.

[28]   This explains the enormous difficulty of applying it in advanced societies, like the contemporary Anglo-Saxon ones. But this is obviously a problem of sociology, rather than of the theory of right.

[29]   Common law is that developed over many centuries through decisions of judges in particular cases; statute law is that laid down by Act of Parliament. (NP)

[30]   As M. Barberis has perceptively observed: 'Thus the adoption of English institutions which was brought about in France by liberal constitutionalism (in particular, during the Restoration) always takes the form of their retrieval, which is both partial and problematic within the different tradition, because it is marked from the start by popular sovereignty and by the principle of equality between citizens' (Barberis, 1991, p. 357).

[31]   See Dicey (1915), pp. *cvl* ff. Dicey distinguishes 'conventions of the constitution' from the general run of the 'laws' (i.e. the juridical norms which, written or unwritten, are always positive). Rather than deriving their legal significance from positive legal application, these conventions constitute the fundamental framework of positive constitutional norms.

[32]   That is, states primarily devoted to ensuring the material welfare of their populations. (NP)

The character and foundation of the modern state

There is a widely-held view that the birth of the modern concept of the state (or even of the concept 'state' itself) depended on the rise of the political conception of sovereignty. Ancient and medieval vocabulary lacked the term 'the state', which was coined by the Italian political philosopher Niccolò Machiavelli (1469–1527). The significance of Machiavelli's coinage is not just lexicographical, but is part of an essentially theoretical problem. Machiavelli initiated not only the word (in its political sense), but also the process of debate about the reality of a form of collective organization that was unknown to antiquity and the Middle Ages.

The German sociologist Max Weber (1864–1920) developed the thesis of a discontinuity between the *res publica* of antiquity and the state of modern times. In his view, only the modern state (through processes of formal rationalization and concentration of power) comes to possess a complete form of sovereignty. It achieves this in two ways:

(i) undisputed dominance of its own norms over other, traditional sources of law (that is, the supremacy of *its* law over common law, natural law, etc.);

(ii) monopolization of the services essential to the maintenance of public order.[33]

The lucidity of this analysis must not, however, mask the fact that its scope is exclusively historical and sociological. The great point in favour of the opposing theory (that is, of the historical *continuity* of the state form) remains the affinity between the state and the law. This affinity, within limits, can characterize the system of internal organization of *any* state-like community, and itself provides the terms for the crucial problem of what lies at the foundation of such a community.[34]

The problem of the foundation of the state, emerging from Weber's theories, is a problem of the philosophy of law, rather than of its sociology. From the very beginning, Western juridical and political thought has tried to resolve this problem by constructing two antithetical models, which will be described briefly here and in greater depth in the following sections.

(i) In the *individualist* (or *contractualist*) model only the individual is real. In consequence, the state and the law which defines its rights and powers ('public law') have no intrinsic legitimacy, only a legitimacy dependent on convention. Legitimacy can be conferred solely by individuals, through what are, strictly speaking, *political* acts of decision. (According to the prevalent version, 'public' law has its roots in the social contract, that is, in the 'private' rights of the individual.)

[33] One thinks of monopolies over fiscal, jurisdictional, military and police functions. But in fact almost all public services, from education to health and transport, are nowadays controlled, if not actually monopolized by, the state.

[34] According to Weber's analyses, that affinity has expanded in the modern epoch.

(ii) According to the *organicist* model, the state and the law do not need any political legitimation. Given that human nature is in principle social, the state and the law do not require an origin in acts by (non-social) individuals. State and Law possess an inherent reality of their own. Only those who *represent* the state, therefore, and act in the name of the law, need legitimation.

The individualist model of the state

According to the individualist model, the state is an artificial body created by *convention*, typically a contract between the citizens. Consequently, public law assumes a single function: defending the citizens' innate rights, which, in a society without a state, are left precariously for people themselves to defend. It is difficult to determine in concrete terms what such rights are. For Hobbes they amounted only to a right to self-preservation. For others in the liberal tradition there is a great patchwork of fundamental rights, centred for the most part on the principle of liberty. The individualist model of the state, with its contractualist theory, supplies incontrovertible (if rarefied) logical criteria for limiting the public power of the state. Born to safeguard private rights, the state cannot (without logical contradiction) become an instrument for their suppression. Looked at in this way, the historical merits of individualism are no doubt incalculable. Despite its merits, however, it has a specific historical failing: it has made the state the *mere product of political will*, a product of the will of the citizens who draw up the social contract. In this way it has opened the way to the *politicization* of Law.

The limitations of the individualist model become clear as soon as we consider how it touches on the foundation of the duty to obey the state – that is, on 'political obligation' (see Green, 1895, vol. II). Deriving political obligation, as it does, from a voluntary, contractual commitment, individualism cannot give proper reasons for the specific powers that the state exercises over its citizens. In other words, it cannot find adequate grounds for the monopoly of the use of force that has been the state's jealously-guarded possession at all times in its history. Consequently (according to the individualist view) the state exists in a dimension that is fundamentally alien to its citizens. Just as they have wished it into existence as something *other* than them, so in principle they could reject it, precisely because it is 'other' than them. This incurable 'otherness' lies at the root not only of all the classic anarchist positions, but also of all those anarchic attitudes of rebellion which have distinguished the decades since 1968.

The organicist model of the state

The organicist model is sounder in speculative terms, but also more despised – unjustly, I believe. It boasts an uninterrupted line of European theorists running from Aristotle to Hegel, who saw the state as having what he called an 'ethical' role in human development. The idea of the state playing an ethical role has been denigrated, and needs to be reconsidered. It does not mean that the state is the

G. W. F. Hegel (1770–1831) (credit: Mansell Collection).

source of individual morality – as in the usual right-wing understanding of the state-form, which has led to the distressing consequences of fascism and Nazism. Rather, it means that the state exists only when (and because) it exists in the consciousness of its citizens. The law of the state ('public' law) is not therefore an artificial derivative of some other, 'natural' law ('private law'); in its own way, it is as 'natural' as the private law, because the social nature of humans is every bit as primary as their pure, innate individualism.[35]

From the organicist perspective it is not possible to understand the state as the *product* of a *convention* between human beings (as in the individualist model), for the simple reason that such a convention already presupposes a reciprocal recognition amongst those who agree it. That is to say, it presupposes an

[35]   In the light of this, we can readily understand the irony with which Hegel treated the question, 'Who is to frame the constitution?' To the philosopher, the query seemed naïve, because it presupposed a time when there was no constitution. This is to say, it supposed that there could be an historical period when humans did not live as humans, but as an agglomeration of isolated atoms. It evidently showed a total incomprehension of the specific character of a constitution, which is a *principle,* not a *product.* (How, out of a mere agglomeration, could one breathe life into a constitution?). See Hegel's *The Philosophy of Right* (1821) in Hegel (1952), para. 273.

The Apotheosis of St Thomas Aquinas (1224–1274) by Francesco Traini (credit: Mansell Collection).

inter-subjective bond of mutual trust in which the essence of what we must characterize as the state is already present. In other words, the 'whole' which is the state cannot be formed by juxtaposing its individual parts (the citizens), as if the sum of the individual wills could produce the general will. The opposite is the case: the whole precedes the parts – not in ontological status (as I hope is clear), but structurally.[36] The citizens exist because their individual being does not detract from their natural sociability; because they live in communities; because, in short, the state exists, or (if one prefers) because they have a 'homeland'.

By cleansing the term 'homeland' of any nationalistic overtones, we are left with the healthy core of its meaning. Besides being the children of their parents, humans are also the children of their homelands; that is, of that complex of traditions, institutions, powers and shared feelings that reach maturity in the state, and only in the state. Looking at the state in this way calls into play the category of 'totality'. Here we return to the dimension of organic totality in the people (see the section on 'The people' above). But this category of totality should *not* be understood in a totalitarian way, as though it implied a levelling-off and the violent and brutal identification of all the citizens under the yoke of cruel and despotic power. The totality invoked in the organicist theory of the state is that which presupposes in fellow citizens a *common good*, which, in so far as it is common, is the interest and the concern of all. The principle of political organicism is that the state should set itself the task of promoting the common good, precisely because no *real* community exists except in the form of a state. Because this (and only this) embraces all human functions, it follows that the legitimacy of the state is greater than that of any other form of collective organization. In short, the political sphere (as Aristotle and Thomas Aquinas[37] maintained) must be allowed primacy among the different forms of human experience. But it is a primacy not of *force*, but of *service* for human good.

Liberal-democratic critics of organicism

Liberal-democratic thinking, and the thinking of advocates of the state under the rule of Law, is hostile towards the organicist conception of the state. This hostility is well-founded if the state is taken to have sovereignty in the political sense. If, on the other hand, the state's sovereignty is understood as a juridical sovereignty, a sovereignty of *service*, the reasons for this hostility are less justified.

Critics of organicism generally focus on the defence of human rights: is it possible, within the organicist perspective, for the individual to have *absolute* rights that command respect even *against* the state? For political organicism such rights simply cannot exist. Critics then conclude – *incorrectly* – that the upshot of organicism can only be the theory (and the practice) of 'reason of state': that is, the claim that the state, having a 'reason' different from, and superior to that of individual citizens, is free to pursue its aims unconstrained by the ethical scruples and hindrances that guide the actions of an individual. In more modern terms, this is called totalitarianism.

---

[36]   That is, the state does not have a solider, more significant or fundamental existence than the individual citizen. But it is a necessary structural condition of the citizens being citizens. (NP)

[37]   ' ... since one man is a part of that perfect whole that is the community, it follows that the law must have as its proper object the well-being of the community.' St Thomas Aquinas, *Summa Theologica*, Question 90, article 2 (Aquinas, 1970, p. 11).

The idea of the common good

Between the correct premise and the incorrect conclusion that critics derive from it is to be found the principle of *common good*. This is the true 'reason of state'. But the common good is also the reason for the existence of public law; and the reason for the existence of the social body itself. One can even say that the common good is the reason for the existence of every human being – understanding human beings, not in the individualist, atomistic sense, but as members necessary to the community (just as the community is necessary to the individuals).

If the state is understood as the very structure of that collective life, which, via the law, is orientated towards the common good – and if, furthermore, it is maintained that the common good can be objectively determined – there can only be one conclusion. No citizen has absolute rights – rights that the state can never set aside – *vis-à-vis* the state. The citizen has no absolute claim on property, freedom, or even life itself when the common good (but only this!) requires that they be sacrificed. Property can be expropriated by reason of the general interest; freedom can be limited, not only by reason of crime, but for reasons of public health; finally, the state may ask its citizens to risk their lives for reasons of national security. But in all this, there is no danger of totalitarianism, as long as the priority of the state over the individual rights of citizens is understood within the logic of *objectively understood common good*.

One of the great errors of much of modern political philosophy and jurisprudence is its misinterpretation of the concept of the common good. It has been interpreted as though it coincided only with the interests of the state, and not also with those of the individual citizens – as though the state had a reality apart from that of being the community of all citizens. Expressed in more modern terms, the concept of the common good has been understood *politically*. Deprived of all objective meaning, the common good has tacitly been reduced to the good of just one part of the social body: to that of the class in power, or of a small oligarchy, or of the monarch alone. If this is so, the state does indeed degenerate into a tyrannical or totalitarian state: but only owing to this erroneous premise. The sacrifice of individual rights that it claims no longer has any *objective* justification, only an *ideological* one – that is, one based effectively on more or less concealed violence. But this degradation of the state is brought about not because it is considered in organicist terms, but because of the political deformation of the concept of the common good, which the state is called upon to promote and defend.

Correctly understood, therefore, the organicist perspective accounts for the dynamic of state power much better than the individualist one. According to the latter, the optimal state should be the 'minimal state': one which limits the exercise of its power as much as possible, and exists only to guarantee the minimal conditions of coexistence between the citizens.[38] The sphere of citizens' rights should remain entrusted to debate and decision by civil society alone. In one sense, this is

---

[38]   The most recent (and brilliant) defence of the 'minimal state' is that by Nozick (1974).

an abstract theory; for it does not account for the continual expansion of activity by the state, which in the modern world has become a maximal, rather than minimal state. The contractualist theory is also dangerously defenceless when it comes to the delicate issue of the internal functioning of the state. A state that is not dedicated to the promotion of the common good can transform itself into the most consistent and impersonal of totalitarian states. A technocratic state that merely pursues the smooth running of public administration from a technical point of view is one where the absolute rationality of the ends, and the complete abandonment of any consideration of values, can preclude all judgement over the *means* used to reach those ends. Here lie the roots of the legitimation crisis of the modern state. It is a crisis that has become more acute since the collapse of the communist regimes made clear the urgency of re-integrating Law as the fundamental system of social values.

The objective basis of the common good

The theory of the common good as the objective basis of Law in the state requires further clarification. In the first place, the common good must be *objective*: that is to say, not determined on a voluntary basis, or according to people's inclinations. The quest for objectivity is clearly difficult for those who insist on searching from within strictly *political* parameters. Take Carl Schmitt's definition that politics belongs to an essentially dualistic sphere, marked by the juxtaposition of friends and foes. According to this definition, no objective criterion can ever define the common good. What is considered good by one group will of necessity be seen as bad by an opposing group. An objective definition of the common good, therefore, can only exist in a perspective that deliberately places itself outside the political sphere: that is, within a *strictly juridical* perspective.

Kant's thinking on the nature of the pursuit of happiness is relevant to the search for the basis of the common good. Kant does not deny the legitimacy of people's pursuit of happiness. He does, however, deny that the yearning for happiness can have anything to do with the purposes of the state or of public law. As regards happiness, Kant observes:

> Men have different views on ... what it consists of, so that as far as
> happiness is concerned, their will cannot be brought under ... any
> external law harmonizing with the freedom of everyone.
> ('*Über den Gemeinspruch: Das mag in der Theorie richtig sein, taugt
> aber nicht für die Praxis*' *[On the common saying: 'This may be true in
> theory, but it does not apply in practice'] (1793);
> see Kant, 1900– ; 1971, pp. 73–4.)*

In other words, happiness is a *psychological* aim and, as such, arbitrary and subjective. A state or a system of justice which set itself the goal of making its fellow citizens happy, believing that in this way it could achieve the common good, would enter an endless spiral of contradictions. It could never find a fixed point on which to base its own activity. The purpose of Law, Kant teaches us, is not to make people happy, but to put them in a condition to become so. Law does not promote happiness, even if, indirectly, it can make it possible (this being in itself an extremely desirable aim).

The common good consists, therefore, in the possibility of living communally, of being a community. Law alone can guarantee this possibility, in so far as it is its own central principle. That is to say, Law can be a protection against the perpetual risk of distortions and degenerations in communal life. In this sense, therefore, Law can never be the product of an act of will. Of necessity, it must be the boundary to which the will of any individual must conform in order to be compatible with the will of others. The juridical way of laying down how we are to live in society is a general system for mutual compatibility. Like Kant, we can avoid the basic error of Rousseau's theory of power: namely, that making the common good the product of the general will does not provide a rational basis for the concrete content of the general will. The general will, ending up without any 'good' as its yardstick, becomes no more or less than an arbitrary, subjective will, dangerously open to mystification.

Kant's thinking also allows us to resolve the other great paradox inherent in all the theories defining democracy in terms of formal procedures, which make the common good merely the product of popular will. According to these theories, there is nothing in principle to prevent the general will from denying itself and handing over all power to an individual will. Taking such formalistic theories to their logical conclusion, then, does not succeed in giving democracy a guarantee against self-destruction. Popular referenda can be seen as examples of Rousseau's democratic model, but have sometimes given power to a dictator, abolishing the principle of democracy in the process.[39] The essence of democracy (and thus of the state under the rule of Law) does not lie in the formalism of elections by universal suffrage. (Such elections are essential, but only as a means to an end.) It lies in the common feeling of the citizens that there is a good which objectively unites them, and that, being for the good of everyone, it must be maintained and guaranteed for all.

The argument for liberty and personal rights, therefore, can be sustained, not through an abstract, *a priori* opposition between individuals and the state, but by the recognition that liberty and personal rights are the good of each and every person, and in everyone's interest to defend, within the framework of the common good. The freedom of the citizen, therefore, is not understood as a mere 'freedom in principle', and thus empty of meaning. (The futile recognition of freedoms in the abstract that cannot be realized in practice is wide open to criticism.) In contrast, the freedom of the citizen consists of freedoms woven into the social fabric,

---

[39] Kant was well aware of this hypothesis, not least because it formed part of the criticisms that Justen Möser had made of the essay 'On the Common Saying ...'. Kant replied by observing that the problem 'is not that of knowing how the people *will* choose so as to satisfy their changing inclinations, but how they *must* choose absolutely, regardless of whether the choice will, or will not, be of benefit to them' ('Erster Brief an Herrn F. Nicolai' [First letter to Herr F. Nicolai]), *Über die Buchmacherei* (On the making of books), in Kant, 1900–, p. 434).

and therefore dynamically related to the social and civic growth of the citizens. Law provides the very basis for co-existence under justice: that is, in the recognition of equality between humans and within their mutual relations. Thus Law resumes its proper place as a full and integral part of the common good. It thus becomes possible to maintain that the organic state is truly a state under the rule of Law in the full sense.

The limits of the state and the common good of humanity

One final observation. Once it is anchored to the common good, the organicist theory of the state allows us to perceive exactly the limits of the state form. If one recognizes the existence of a common good of (and within) the political community, by the same token one must recognize the parallel existence of a broader common good. This is the common good of humanity as a whole, or the entire 'human family'. There is a widespread awareness today that real solutions for our grave social and political problems can only be found at the international level. The common good of the planet provides objective grounds for individual nations to limit their sovereignty in order to establish a supra-national human community. What was once referred to as the 'sacred egoism of nations' today seems an increasingly empty expression. We have come to understand that when states recognize the primacy of international co-operation over the interests of their particular political community, they do not betray themselves. Rather, they are pursuing more fully and coherently their vocation to promote the common good. This good is not truly common unless, as is coming to be true in our own era, it embraces humanity as a whole.

Let me repeat that the objectivist (and therefore juridical) conception of the common good produces benefits on another level as well. Saint Augustine, one of the fathers of Western culture (not only in a religious, but in a political sense), alluded to this duality of levels when, in *The City of God*, he contrasted two cities: that is, two dimensions of human life. The earthly city and the city of God are both perfect: but the former is destined to play itself out in the relativity of historical experience, whereas the latter finds its fulfilment in eternity. Obviously, in this context, reference to Saint Augustine does not have a religious significance, but it helps us to understand how human social experience will not survive being turned in upon itself: if it does not wish to suffocate in shallow formalism, it needs always to look up to a transcendent horizon.

This does not require – as is often incorrectly believed – that one dimension of human experience (the spiritual, for example) be opposed to another (the earthly dimension, as found in the state). It demands that all humans beings attempt to integrate the two dimensions, which share the same space for self-expression, though not the same source. The state that regulates social relations and whose chief attribute is the monopoly of force cannot truly be itself unless it has its foundation in human consciousness – where, without freely-given consent, no force can really impose itself. But no state can penetrate the inner consciousness of its citizens unless it respects that consciousness, and recognizes its uniqueness. In sum, no state can be grounded in human consciousness unless it recognizes that there is no common human good except one born from a fundamental recognition of the common humanity of every individual, and that equality between humans is always the dialectical product of the meeting and the clash of their differences. Given this final perspective, organicism, with regard to the state, is as different from the monolith of collectivism as a dynamic process of birth and integration is from the rigidity of a lifeless body.

References

AQUINAS, T. (1970) *Selected Political Writings*, ed. A. Passerin D'Entrèves, Oxford, Blackwell.

BARBERIS, M. (1991) 'Progetto per la voce "costituzione" di una enciclopedia' (Plan for an encyclopedia entry on 'constitution'), in *Teoria politica*, no. 5.

BRACTON, H. (1968) *De legibus et consuetudinibus Angliae* (Concerning British laws and customs), 2 vols, ed. G. E. Woodbine, Cambridge (Mass.), Harvard University Press, vol II.

CARRÉ DE MALBERG, R. (1920–22) *Contribution à la théorie générale de l'État* (Contribution to the general theory of the state), 2 vols, Paris, Librairie du Receuil Sirey.

CARRÉ DE MALBERG, R. (1931) *La loi, expression de la volonté générale* (The law, expression of the general will), Paris, Librairie du Receuil Sirey.

DICEY, A. V. (1885; 1915) *Introduction to the Study of the Law of the Constitution*, London, Macmillan (reprinted Indianapolis, 1982).

FIORAVANTI, M. (1991) *Appunti di storia delle costituzioni moderne* (Notes on the history of modern constitutions), Turin.

GNEIST, R. VON (1872) *Der Rechtsstaat und die Verwaltungsgerichte in Deutschland* (The state under the rule of Law and the administrative jurisdiction of Germany), Berlin, J. Springer.

GREEN, T. H. (1895) 'Lectures on the principles of political obligation', reprinted in *Works*, vol. II, 1885–1891, London, Longman.

HAYEK, F. VON (1979) *The Political Order of a Free People*, London, Routledge.

HEGEL, G. (1821) *Hegel's Philosophy of Right*, trans T. M. Knox, Oxford, Clarendon Press, 1952.

JELLINEK, G. (1892; 1905 edn) *System der subjektiven öffentlichen Rechte* (System of subjective public laws), Freiburg im Breisgau. Reprinted 1905, Tübingen, Mohr; 1979, Aalen.

KANT, I. (1900–) *Gesammelte Schriften* (Collected writings), vol. VIII, Deutsche Akademie der Wissenschaften (German Academy of Science), Berlin, Cassirer.

KANT, I. (1971) *Kant's Political Writings*, ed. H. Reiss, Cambridge, Cambridge University Press.

KELSEN, H. (1934; 1960 edn) *Reine Rechtslehre*, Wien, Dueticke; trans. (1967) *Pure Theory of Law*, Max Knight, Los Angeles, University of California Press.

MATTEUCCI, G. (1966) Entry on 'Costituzionalismo' (Constitutionalism), in *Dizionario di Politica* (Dictionary of politics), N. Bobbio and G. Matteucci eds., Turin.

MIGLIO, G. (1988) *Le regolarità della politica* (The regulation of politics), Milan.

MOHL, ROBERT VON (1844; 1872; 1966) *Die Polizei-Wissenschaft nach den Grundsätze des Rechtsstaates* (The science of regulation according to the foundations of the state under the rule of Law), Tübingen, H. Laupp; reprinted 1966, Darmstadt.

NOZICK, R. (1974) *Anarchy, State and Utopia,* New York, Basic Books, Oxford Basil Blackwell, 1975.

PAULSON, S. L. (1992) 'Teoria giuridiche e "Rule of Law"' (Juridical theories and 'Rule of Law'), in *Analisi e diritto.*

POLIN, R. (1971) *L'Obligation politique* (Political obligation) Paris, Presses Universitaires de France.

POPPER, K. (1945; 1966 edn) *The Open Society and Its Enemies*, 2 vols, London, Routledge.

ROUSSEAU, J. (1968) *The Social Contract*, trans. M. Cranston, Harmondsworth, Penguin Books.

SCHLANGEN, W. (1973) *Demokratie und bürgeliche Gesellschaft: Einführung in die Grundlagen der bürgerlichen Demokratie,* (Democracy and civil society: an introduction to the foundations of civil democracy), Stuttgart, Kohlhammer; Italian translation (1979) *Democrazia e società borghese*, Bologna, II Mulino.

SCHMITT, C. (1950; 1974 edn) *Der Nomos der Erde im Völkerrecht des Jus Publicum Europaeum* (The rule of the land in the law of nations according to European public law), Berlin, Duncker and Humblot.

WADE, H. W. R. (1961; 1988 edn) *Administrative Law*, Oxford, Clarendon Press.

Bibliography

AVINERI, S. (1972) *Hegel's Theory of the Modern State,* Cambridge, Cambridge University Press.

BENDIX, R. (ed.) (1968) *State and Society: A Reader in Comparative Political Sociology*, Boston, Little Brown.

BOBBIO, N. (1976) *La teoria delle forme di governo nella storia del pensiero politico* (The theory of forms of government in the history of political thought), Turin, Giapichelli.

BOBBIO, N. (1985) *Stato, governo, società* (State, government, society), Turin, Einaudi.

BOBBIO, N. (1989) *Democracy and Dictatorship*, trans. Peter Kennealy, Cambridge, Polity Press.

BOCKENFOERDE, E.W. (ed.) (1976) *Staat, Gesellschaft, Freiheit* (State, society, freedom), Frankfurt am Main, Suhrkamp.

BAURMANN, M. AND KLIEMT, H. (eds.) (1990) *Die moderne Gesellschaft im Rechtsstaat* (Modern society in the state under the rule of Law), Freiburg, Munich, Alber.

FORSTHOFF, E. (1964) *Rechtsstaat im Wandel* (The state under the rule of Law in transition), Stuttgart, Kohlhammer.

FORSTHOFF, E. (ed.) (1968) *Rechtsstaatlichkeit und Sozialstaatlichte* (The idea of the state under the rule of Law in a social welfare state), Darmstadt, Wissenschaftliche Buchgesellschaft.

GOUGH, J. W. (1955) *Fundamental Law in English Constitutional History,* Oxford, Clarendon Press.

GRIMM, D. (1987) *Recht und Staat der bürgerlichen Gesellschaft* (Right and state in civil society), Frankfurt am Main, Suhrkamp.

HELLER, H. (1930) *Rechtsstaat oder Diktatur?* (State under the rule of Law or dictatorship?), Tübingen, Mohr.

KAUFMANN, A. (1986) *Gerechtigkeit, der vergessene Weg sum Frieden* (Justice, the forgotten way to peace), Munich-Zürich, Piper.

KELSEN, H. (1928) *Der soziologische und der juristischer Staatsbegriff* (The social and judicial concepts of the state), Tübingen, Mohr.

KOJEVE, A. (1981) *Esquisse d'une phénoménologie du droit* (Sketch for an epistemology of right), Paris, Gallimard.

KOSLOWSKI, P. (1982) *Gesellschaft und Staat* (Society and state), Stuttgart, Klett-Cotta.

KRIELE, M. (1987) *Die demokratische Weltrevolution* (The democratic world revolution), Munich, Zürich, Piper.

KRIELE, M. (1990) *Einführung in die Staatslehre* (Introduction to the theory of the state), Opladen, Westdeutscher Verlag.

KUHN, H. (1967) *Der Staat: Eine philosophische Darstellung* (The state: a philosophical approach), Munich, Kösel.

MARITAIN, J. (1951) *Man and the State*, Chicago, University of Chicago Press.

MACILWAIN, C. H. (1940, 1947) *Constitutionalism Ancient and Modern*, Ithaca, Cornell University Press.

MEINECKE, F. (1924) *Die Idee der Staatsräson in der neueren Geschichte* (The idea of the reason of the state in recent history), Munich, Berlin, Oldenbourg.

NEUMANN, F. (1980) *Die Herrschaft des Gesetzes* (The dominion of law), Frankfurt am Main, Suhrkamp.

PASSERIN D'ENTRÈVES, A. (1962) *La Dottrina dello Stato*, Turin, Giapichelli; trans. (1967) *The Notion of the State*, Oxford, Clarendon Press.

PIEPER, J. (1987) *Grundformen sozialer Spielregeln* (The foundations of the rules of social conduct), Munich, Kösel.

QUARITSCH, H. (1970) *Staat und Souveränität* (State and sovereignty), Frankfurt am Main, Athenäum.

ROMMEN, H. (1935) *Der Staat in der katholischen Gedankenwelt*, Paderborn, Bonifacius-druckerei; trans. (1945) *The State in Catholic Thought: A Treatise in Political Philosophy*, St. Louis and London, B. Herder.

SCHMITT, C. (1928) *Verfassungslehre* (Constitutional theory), Munich, Leipzig, Duncker and Humblot.

STRAUSS, L. (1968) *Liberalism Ancient and Modern*, New York, Basic Books.

VILLEY, M. (1975) *La formation de la pensée juridique moderne* (The formation of modern juridical thought) Paris, Montchrétien.

ZIPPELIUS, R. (1980) *Allgemeine Staatslehre* (The universal theory of the state), Munich, Beck.

Part III
Public opinion and the role of criticism

Introduction to Part III

Prepared for the Course Team by Gérard Duprat
Translated by Noël Parker

This introduction sets out the main subjects of the two essays in Part III and looks at some of the connections with Part IV.

Hans-Joachim Schmidt's essay considers the relations between democracy and public opinion, while my own essay focuses on the relations a democratic society maintains with its political institutions. Both essays are broadly based, placing democracy in relation to fundamental political ideas such as those dealt with by Barker and D'Agostino, and building on what has been covered so far. What has already been said regarding the relationship of democracy to issues of knowledge, liberty, Law and society is particularly relevant for a clarification of the role of public opinion in the democratic system. The central concern of Part III is to define 'public' opinion, and to establish its place in a state under the rule of Law that claims to be democratic.

One fundamental question about public opinion originates in Rousseau's concept of 'the general will' as the source of legislation in a republic. In this perspective, democracy is only one of the possible forms of government for the 'republican' state.[1] For democratic government (as for non-democratic forms), there is a distinction between the general will (the expression of the sovereign body politic) and the will of all (the product of aggregating the wills of individuals). Sovereignty is regarded as exclusively the creation of the general will, which alone can be just and lawful. This 'democracy of will', however, is incompatible with another kind of democracy, which, since it accords public opinion some value as a form of reason, we may call 'democracy of opinion'. Democracy of opinion presupposes that government can be effective and legitimate only if opinion is represented in all its diversity. If these two concepts of democracy are contrary to each other, the question remains: How is it that in practice each is realized simultaneously in democratic states' own interpretation of their political practices?

Principles that are drawn up hastily and on too schematic a knowledge of theories of democracy or of public opinion are liable to contain contradictions. Since the

---

[1] The government is only one component of the state, in the wider sense of public and semi-public institutions managing the activities of society. Hence, different 'forms of government' can be envisaged for any one form of state. For example, it is perfectly conceivable that a republican state in the sense being used here – namely, a state explicitly organized around the notion of a *res publica*, of common public concerns – might be governed on a non-elective basis. The question that then arises is whether democracy is only one form of government or is also, under a different guise, more intimately connected with the very nature of society. In Essay 1, Alain-Marc Rieu defended the latter view. (NP)

law has to be general, the theory of the general will devalues the opinions of individuals in the formation of the law. Yet the theory of the general will does not ignore public opinion, and does not underestimate the problems that forming, informing and educating citizens pose for a republic. The *political culture* of the citizens, therefore, determines the quality of the laws they make as legislators in the sovereign body politic. Since the task of the government is to apply laws to particular cases, it has to take account of this political culture if its decisions are to be acceptable to the citizens affected. Thus Rousseau, when first drawing up this model of politics, did not manage to stay within the confines of his conception of the different forms of government. He considered democracy *both* as one form of government among others *and* as the underlying form of all republics.

'Democracy of opinion' has to come to terms with the problem of decisions and the means of measuring how democratic they are – in particular, how representative they are of the 'general interest' of the body politic.[2] Accounts of this 'general interest' may introduce a contradiction between the value placed on public opinion and that placed on the action of the government, which is the sole practical expression of any general interest. From the point of view of a 'representative' government, public opinion is viewed ambivalently: either as a significant range of distinct ideologies that sustain the different groups within the body politic, or as the insignificant product of adding up individual or collective opinions of the moment.

The general theories of public opinion considered by Hans-Joachim Schmidt cannot confine themselves to either of the views adopted by government. A purely sociological focus prevents them taking the expression 'public' seriously. Nor can they merely study the available techniques for measuring opinions and for modifying them through political persuasion. Theories of public opinion have to confront the issues posed by the pursuit of a specifically democratic *public life*. These issues are not contained merely within the individual obligation to make a reasoned contribution to public debate (a feature of all states under the rule of Law), nor within the technical problems which the 'free market in opinion' poses for governments that wish to arrange a good reception for their policies and to be re-elected. In short, theories of public opinion have to formulate a concept of the 'public'. Habermas is the model of this line of thought.

The conclusions of Schmidt's essay will be taken as read when in my own essay I consider the political apparatus in a democratic society. Though concerns very close to the issue of public opinion do appear, they are pursued from a different perspective. The particular objective of my essay is to illuminate the specific relationship which a democratic society maintains with the political apparatus, and the reasons why that relationship is necessarily 'critical' in character.

My essay reflects on what the state and the government are, and goes on to define the different levels on which criticism is practised *vis-à-vis* these two major components of the political apparatus. It concludes that no single account of their respective functions (and of their relationship to the apparatus) can be satisfactory.

---

[2]   See Pierre Favre (1976) *La Décision majoritaire*, Paris, Presses FNSP.

For democratic states and governments – and hence democracy itself – are viewed in different ways if one chooses to judge them by the criteria of functional effectiveness (so-called 'governmentability'[3]) or according to more fundamental and exacting aspirations that touch the very foundation of political life.

Public opinion plays a crucial role in the institutions of accountable government in a 'republic'. It constitutes a form of criticism that is practised in all states where freedom of opinion is regarded as fundamental. In western countries since the Enlightenment (despite periods of regression), liberty of thought and subsequently the liberty to express thought (individually or collectively) have been gradually added to the 'sacred' liberty of opinion.

But in addition to public opinion, we must recognize the parts played by ideology, law, and belief. Last, but not least, we must take account of the plurality of discourses that can be pursued about politics. That leads us back to the general theory of knowledge and of its different forms. The questions which this raises are closely linked to those which political theory confronts in distinguishing the different forms of domination. Quite apart from scientific debates and the technical problems of the methods used nowadays to measure (or construct) public opinion, the problems raised by public opinion are incomprehensible without some reference to theories of knowledge, to political theory, and to their mutual links. These theories take us back to the deepest level of the logic that has formed Western politics, and to its historical origins in the foundation and democratic development of the Greek city in the fifth century BC.

Historically, democratic politics was the creation of people who, if they were to govern each other in a fashion that made them all into citizens, had only the usual means available to human beings: the methods of reason and law. For the Athenians of the fifth century BC, politics and democracy could only be attributed to a domain where knowledge was called 'opinion', in order to distinguish it from science, myth and divine revelation. For these latter were all forms of knowledge which, within the political processes of the city, were not subject to challenge or debate. On that logical level and hence at that historical moment, politics and democracy first addressed the question of political organization and explored the limits of its relationship with rationality. In sum, politics and democracy had to be regarded as a branch of rational thinking.

What emerges from all this is the necessity, in democracy alone, of keeping the rationale of the political apparatus constantly in view within all public debate. As a result, the political institutions of a democracy are nothing like as clear or 'transparent' to public opinion as political professionals often suggest in their publicity or their programmes for government. The various anti-democratic traditions from Plato to today base their opposition to democracy on the uncertainty that it casts over the state and the questioning it encourages about political life. But we cannot conclude, with those traditions, that democracy is purely a 'theoretical' ideal that

---

[3]   This concept simply addresses the way in which, within a given society, the government successfully functions to control society and the extent to which society is susceptible to being controlled by government. It therefore takes no account of whether the given society could be said to be truly democratic, just, good, etc. (NP)

offers an incurably ungovernable version of politics. What democracy does do is to make 'the citizen' (rather than the state, the government, or the law) the primary institution of political life.

It is, then, quite logical for the treaty concluded by the EC member states at Maastricht to put the creation of *European citizenship* before all the other provisions covering the political institutions of the union which is its objective. At several points, the essays below touch on the details of this issue of citizenship. Two aspects of the Treaty are entirely in step with the concerns I have raised. On the one hand, when it comes to institutional apparatus, the Treaty leaves several principles in competition: the preamble declares its respect for the 'principles of democracy', but equally it stipulates that the principle of 'efficiency' must be satisfied. On the other hand, European union (and hence the citizenship it establishes and the institutions that constitute it politically) finds its fulfilment in the creation of a 'European identity', manifested in a 'European awareness' which, for practical purposes, is expressed in the 'political will' of the citizens.[4] This raises many questions which confront Europe as a political entity at the moment of its birth, and which the member states' experience in democracy allows it to address.

[4]   Maastricht Treaty, Article. G (Title II [provisions amending the Treaty of Rome]), new article 138a, on European political parties.

Essay 5
The role and the realities of public opinion

Prepared for the Course Team by Hans-Joachim Schmidt
Lecturer in philosophy at the FernUniversität, Hagen
Translated by Ulrike Hill and Noël Parker

Public opinion: the current situation and issues

It is evident that public opinion, or what Habermas calls a 'public capable of functioning politically'[1], is vital to an understanding of democracies based on the rule of Law. Hard-won human and civil rights guarantee that public opinion can exist and can be expressed: freedom of thought, opinion and speech; freedom to associate and to demonstrate; and, finally, freedom of the press. In so far as it is open to all to contribute to public opinion, these freedoms also lend it a basic democratic aura. In marked contrast to the act of voting, which the individual undertakes in isolation, public opinion seems designed to offer a permanent guarantee of the active sovereignty of the people, of its will to control and to participate in politics.

In accordance with the overall theme of European democratic culture, I will be looking at public opinion from a theoretical perspective that relates it to democracy and embraces political philosophy and political science. Pursuing an interest in both concept and reality, this essay aims to explain the origin, the present role, and the future prospects of public opinion, as well as commenting critically on possible alternatives for its development and role in the democratic state under the rule of Law. It will do this on the basis of findings in various disciplines.

The socialist view of public opinion

The end of East–West rivalry also marks the end of a distinct type of public opinion associated with Eastern Bloc socialist states. Because public opinion, as I have just characterized it, was a central concept of the *bourgeois* understanding of

---

[1]   See Habermas (1989a), esp. ch. 13; also note 18 below and the section below on 'Recent controversies' for further explanation. Habermas argues that, in the eighteenth century, the 'public' formed by assembling self-interested private property-holders was given a particular political function. (NP)

democracy, the Eastern Bloc socialist view had to take it (i.e. public opinion in the West) as a reference point in demonstrating its own superiority.[2] The specific socialist type of public opinion only ever made sense through opposition to (and ideological denunciations of) the liberal-democratic version.

The socialist view denies that public opinion in a bourgeois democracy can ever express a general interest. Within a class society, it is said, public opinion has always been synonymous with class opinion: 'determined by the class interest of whatever class has the ruling power – that is, the class which by virtue of its dominant material power is also society's intellectually dominant power' (Reimann, 1971, p. 818). Thanks to skilful manipulation, mainly on the part of the mass media, the opinions of the public are transformed into the opinion of the people as such, or into the universally valid general perspective. It is preserved in this form by impeding alternative channels of information, instruction and education. Opinion polls are thought of as part of this system of manipulation and suppression. Under the guise of scientific objectivity, they stabilize the system, producing results compatible with the established pattern of domination, and infusing them with an illusory general validity.

By contrast, under socialism there exist, according to this view, the 'objective conditions for the development of a uniform public opinion to reflect the interests of the working class and all its allied classes and social strata'.[3] The function of public opinion is not to air issues of the development and tensions confronting socialism. Rather, it is to disseminate and deepen an appropriate socialist consciousness. Diverse opinions get in the way, but are undermined or pushed aside.

This type of eastern European Marxism, intransigent and intellectually weak, was debased to the level of an ideology serving merely to legitimize the ruling bureaucracies. The consequences in practice were remarkable: a depoliticization and apathy amongst the population, a willingness to obey, a fixation on authority and an intellectual modesty affecting even middle- and lower-party executives and other representatives of the system. These are precisely the kind of social conditions and psychological dispositions which a lively public opinion in the traditional sense ought to counteract. It is encouraging, then, that a non-manipulated public is coming into being in the former people's democracies and intervening in public affairs in the form of public opinion.

---

[2]   See, for example, Reimann (1971) pp. 818–26; and also any Marxist–Leninist dictionary of politics of sociology, such as Heinrich (1969) or Rückmann (1969).

[3]   *Kleines politisches Wörterbuch* (i.e. Smaller Political Dictionary), (1973) East Berlin, p. 607. According to the socialist view, there are differences of opinion amongst cadres or the representatives of the masses in the state, the party and society at large. Rather than public discussion, however, these call for internal decisions which are fed, as appropriate, to public opinion. Since the ruling class is the working class and all antagonisms have been dealt with, the mass media restores to the working class and its allies the harmonious ideas and feelings that reflect socialist conditions of production. The wheel has thus come full circle: Marxist ideological criticism and 'scientific socialism' confirm each other. The polyphony of the bourgeois public becomes the sign of error in public opinion: the unity under socialism becomes the sign of truth.

However, one should not simply regard these developments as the victory of a clearly superior, western conception of public opinion. The real experience of a socialist alternative poses important challenges to the way public opinion is understood and actually operates in bourgeois democracies. Even allowing for obvious simplification and an element of self-apology, these challenges are well-founded.

The problem of public opinion

The Gulf War of 1991 showed that the institutions of free expression of opinion and free flow of news are also precarious in the West.[4] Military censorship and restrictions on news resulted, in the last analysis, from the fear of public opinion. In their different ways, the governments of both Iraq and the United States were affected. Their reactions can be taken as evidence of the potential weight and influence of public opinion. Yet the fact that this censorship operated not just nationally, but throughout the world, also demonstrates the dangers that rapid technological development hold in store for an effective public opinion.

At a more fundamental level, however, there is a problem in the very nature of public opinion; it contains a paradox. The idea of an effective public opinion is an essential part of the heritage from which western democracies derive legitimacy. Yet, in spite of countless theoretical and empirical studies of public opinion, there is no agreement as to its structure; how it arises and changes; its real place in the democratic system; how (if at all) it can be authoritatively identified; and to what extent it possesses force as a legitimation. Davison succinctly describes the state of research worldwide: 'In spite of voluminous discussions on the subject, scholars still do not agree on a definition of public opinion' (Davison, 1985, p. 353). This can be stated more radically: 'In all of the social sciences, there is hardly a concept that has been used with so much variation across different epochs, cultures and intellectual disciplines' (Kleinsteuber, 1985, p. 623).

This verdict crystallizes the ever-present tension over the concept. The focus and significance attributed to public opinion, indeed, the very idea of the public and public opinion, derive from a quite specific historico-cultural context: namely, the development, within the European and Anglo-Saxon traditions, of the first constitutional, liberal (or later democratic) states under the rule of Law. This concept of public opinion cannot, therefore, be transferred casually to other times and places such as our own. When it comes to research on public opinion, the subject belongs not only in the social sciences (sociology, political science, social psychology, media studies), but also in jurisprudence and the humanities, not least philosophy. Each of these uses its own methods and approaches, and brings distinct research interests to its investigations.

If the multifaceted object of our investigation is not to be lost, we need to be clear from the start about our objectives. Public opinion (*öffentliche Meinung*) is used here exclusively in its political sense. This embraces three ideas:

---

[4]   See Dossier (1991), which brings the fundamental concepts of media analysis to bear on concrete instances.

- a *principle* of so-called 'publicity'[5] (*Publizität*) which contains the values necessary to the proper, objective consideration of shared, public concerns;

- an *arena* of debate or 'public sphere'[6] (*Öffentlichkeit*), including a bearer of the role required in that sphere: 'the Public' or 'audience' (*Publikum*);

- an *object* of attention which public opinion considers; namely, the state and the political system.

The historical origin of public opinion and its evolution

Like their cognates in other European languages (the German 'öffentliche Meinung', French 'opinion publique' and 'publicité'),[7] the concepts of public opinion and the public sphere are tied to the socio-economic rise and the political emancipation of the bourgeoisie in western Europe during the Enlightenment period. It is true that processes were recognized still earlier whereby public opinion was formed and expressed its will. However, it was only with those social foundations and political processes that the 'age of public opinion' (to use von Holtzendorff's expression from 1879) overturned late absolutism's pretensions to represent the public interest.[8] Still today, public opinion underpins a constitutionally guaranteed duty to engage in the critique of authority.

[5]   i.e. the 'postulate of publicity as a principle' following the usage which Habermas defines from the following passage in Kant: 'The public use of one's reason must always be free, and it alone can bring about enlightenment among men' (Kant, 1784, 'What is Enlightenment?', quoted in Habermas, 1989, p. 106).

[6]   Again following Habermas's usage in *The Structural Transformation of the Public Sphere* (1989). (NP)

[7]   The expression 'public opinion' is one of a number of group nouns in grammatically singular form which demonstrate, in Lucian Hölscher's words, an 'interchange between the European nations most affected by Enlightenment philosophy'. They 'contributed considerably to the emergence of a new set of concepts, shared by many nationalities. These concepts established the cornerstones of the politico-social language of our age, as used in countries far beyond Europe' (Hölscher, 1979, p. 106).

[8]   In their dealings with the public sphere, the absolute rulers – be they spiritual or worldly – manifest their own superiority, power and higher dignity. Thus they have a relationship to public opinion, even though they cannot be its representatives.

The emergence of public opinion and the classical-liberal view of it

Our casual use of the concept makes it easy to forget that public opinion is a relatively recent institution in history.[9] It is the economy that is the motive force behind the modern age. Initially, by trading in goods over long distances, capitalism upset the processes of social reproduction in static feudal-agrarian western societies. However, a qualitatively different mode of production only became apparent once financial and commercial capital (already influential since the sixteenth and seventeenth centuries) had subjugated urban small-goods production; once the feudal mode of agricultural production had collapsed from within; and, finally, as wage labour was becoming an established part of production. At first, capitalism was completely dependent on the protection and privileges given by monarchs. But the subsequent development of capitalist sectors created a kind of mutual dependence between state power and bourgeois economic interests. The bourgeoisie needed legal security, protection for internal and external markets, and a better infrastructure; the monarchs needed money for a standing army and a professional administration.

Analysed in the light of those historical processes, the growing distinction between the 'state' and the 'court' did not simply introduce the specifically modern process of making power-relations impersonal. It also permitted, indeed required, monarchs deliberately to include commoners within existing power-structures. It contributed decisively, therefore, to the disintegration and eventual removal from power of feudal institutions such as the church and the ranks of the aristocratic hierarchy. These processes gradually developed a bourgeois society, whose members derived their status from property or education and who increasingly adopted a critical attitude towards the state.

Rising education and literacy, increasing acquaintance with art and high culture, and improved communications, all enhanced the prospects and heightened the need for expression felt by the new urban élite of civil servants, intellectuals, clerics, army officers, bankers and manufacturers. The coffee house in England, the salon in France and the 'Tischgesellschaft' or 'Lesegesellschaft' in Germany, all gave people the opportunity to exchange information and engage in intensive debate – fed, from the eighteenth century on, by an expanding press. A public sphere took shape in the world of letters: in the opening of theatres and concert halls; in the professionalization of literature, journalism and art criticism; in the foundation of book-clubs, public and subscription libraries; and in lively discussion around society periodicals and scientific or political journals.

---

[9]   The seminal literature for this section is Hölscher's historical studies of the formation of concepts (Hölscher, 1978, 1979, 1980, 1984) and Habermas's writings in history proper and intellectual history (Habermas, 1989, 1990); Otto (1966) and Speier (1950) are also useful.

A German coffee house at the beginning of the eighteenth century (illustration: Mary Evans Picture Library).

The 'principle of publicity'

From this audience – small in number, but in theory open to all – developed a public and a literary public sphere, formed in the private sphere of the bourgeois family.[10] Socialization in this urban, bourgeois culture taught the first version of 'publicity': the value of humanity, that is, of rising above personal ties and considerations of status. Through lived experience, socialization lent plausibility to the civic values of equality and freedom. And it consolidated the standing of rational judgement, which, in the end, would only be satisfied when allowed the right to embrace political and legal issues. Since the eighteenth century, therefore, the public sphere has been no longer merely 'the area of government control'; it is also the *political* public sphere: 'the intellectual and social arena from which government willingly receives both legitimacy and criticism' (Hölscher, 1978, p. 438). The concept of public opinion validates the political claims of this public of reasoning, private (and also male), individuals to criticize, control and participate in the state.

Although it was initially a controversial concept, following the French Revolution, *öffentliche Meinung* ('public opinion'), soon became the trademark of political lib-

[10]   Habermas calls the psychological make-up of this bourgeois individual (male and female) 'privateness orientated towards an audience' (Habermas, 1989, pp. 43ff; 1990, p. 114).

eralism in Germany. The French equivalent, *opinion publique*, had itself only very recently lost its pejorative slant. England was undoubtedly ahead in these matters. There, the capitalist mode of production was already far advanced. The Glorious Revolution of 1688 created favourable conditions for the representation of a public interest. In 1695, censorship (prior to publication) was abolished. And parliamentary opposition (partly by documenting and discussing parliamentary debates) gave rise to a political press that exhibited the distinctive, if contested, English 'freedom of the press'.[11]

Amongst philosophers, John Locke and David Hume were important in preparing the way for public opinion.[12] The former's *Essay Concerning Human Understanding* (1690) introduced the 'law of opinion'. Although not part of legislation, the law of opinion provided a third source of independent judgement (alongside the laws of God and of the state), which sustained the citizen's legitimacy as a competent member of society. Whilst Hobbes still held that the maintenance of property and just social conditions could be entrusted entirely to the irresistible ruler's will and judgement, Locke made a plea on behalf of consensus in public opinion (though not yet named as such). Hume also followed in the wake of the Glorious Revolution of 1688. He maintained that 'It is...on opinion only that government is founded',[13] undercutting the claims of Church and Crown in favour of the moral and political principles of bourgeois society.

Hume's influence on the French discussion was particularly marked. Yet decades later, Rousseau, in initiating the expression *opinion publique*, described it with deep ambivalence. He separated the search for truth by discussion, on the one hand, from the 'general will', on the other. (The latter is a manifestation of public opinion enjoying unreserved approval.) So it fell to the Physiocrats[14] and to a politician, the finance minister Necker, to be the real protagonists of a public opinion which 'proved its mettle as a check on government', to the point that 'the sphere of a public that eventually also engaged in critical debate of political issues now became the sphere in which civil society reflected on and expounded its interests' (Habermas, 1989a, p. 69). The assumptions underlying Necker's politics exemplify the connection between the rise of public opinion and the bourgeoisie's struggle for control over the state's budget.[15]

[11]   In spite of these advances, according to Habermas (1990, p. 168), the term 'public opinion', in the sense of 'public spirit' and 'general opinion', is not found in the literature before 1781.

[12]   Hölscher (1979) Ch. 3.3, and Habermas (1989) Chs 7 and 12, provide penetrating commentary on the intellectual setting of the philosophical concept of public opinion in western Europe.

[13]   'On the First Principles of Government' (1742) in *Hume: Theory of Politics*, ed. F. Walkins (1951) London & Edinburgh, Nelson; p. 148.

[14]   A pre-revolutionary group of French liberal philosophers and economists, notably de Quesnay (1694–1774) and Mirabeau the elder (1715–1789). (NP)

[15]   Speier (1950), pp. 379ff., warns against underestimating the 'close connection between public finance and public opinion'.

The French Revolution set the standard and brought together what had been torn apart: criticism, control of the state and the formulation of laws. Revolution not only creates the institutions of the political public sphere (the press, an arena for public debate, parliamentary groupings and the precursors of political parties), it also establishes the constitutional status of these things and, for the future, an explicit awareness of the functions (both actual and potential) of a political public opinion.[16]

The new political public of the French Revolution: citizens of the new Republic assembled in Paris in 1790 to celebrate and swear an oath of loyalty (illustration: Mansell Collection).

However, the Revolution also provoked other, more intellectual developments. There were the connotations given to the concept of public opinion by Condorcet in his philosophy of history. And there was Bentham, for whom opinion has a 'dual role, as the controlling authority behind Parliament, and as a public forum where public opinion [should] take shape, with the help of the press and of parlia-

[16]   This last, historically significant point is emphasized by Habermas (1990) p. 119.

mentary debates' (Hölscher, 1980, p. 1026). There is a direct line to Guizot, who linked the concept to the rehabilitation of public opinion after the 1833 July Revolution in France, with its classical-liberal assumptions:

> It is, moreover, the character of that system, which nowhere admits the legitimacy of absolute power, to compel the whole body of citizens incessantly, and on every occasion, to seek after reason, justice, and truth, which should ever regulate actual power. The representative system does this, (1) by discussion, which compels existing powers to seek after truth in common; (2) by publicity, which places these powers when occupied in this search, under the eyes of the citizens; and (3) by the liberty of the press, which stimulates the citizens themselves to seek after truth, and to tell it to those in power.
>
> *(Guizot, 1852, p. 264; quoted in Habermas, 1989a, p. 101)*

The adoption of the idea of public opinion in German language philosophy was less clear-cut and unified. Even though the 1789 Revolution had revealed the complex of social-psychological processes which brought a new type of 'public opinion' to power, Christian Garve asserted (in 1795) that there was 'agreement amongst the great majority of citizens in any given state on judgements which they had reached as individuals, each through his own reflections or his own experience of the matter at issue'.[17] This rationalist view of public opinion is supported, in his way, by Kant. Without referring either to the concept or the institutions of public opinion, he nonetheless takes the freedom of the public to apply reason in all matters to be a sufficient condition of Enlightenment. Moreover, he justifies publicity as a 'transcendental', bridging principle between politics and morality.[18]

Hegel's no less influential position remains ambivalent. His *Philosophy of Right* acknowledges public opinion's common-sense insight into the foundations and tasks of the state, but also complains about its individualistic, subjective distortions (Hegel, 1821, paragraphs 314ff). All the same, Hegel does help to establish that public opinion has a 'moral authority above or close to that of governments' and 'a hitherto unknown type of legitimacy...[rightly] acknowledged by its opponents ... irrespective of the question whether it was right or wrong' (Hölscher, 1979, p. 112).

---

[17]   From Christian Garve, 'Uber die öffentliche Meinung', ('On Public Opinion'), in *Versuch über verschiedene Gegenstände der Moral, der Literatur und des geselligen Lebens* ('Essay relating to various issues of morality, literature and social life'), No. 5. 1802, quoted in Hölscher (1980), p. 1027.

[18]   According to Habermas (1989a, 1990; Ch. 13), Kant, epitomizing the problems of Enlightenment thought, gave the sphere of public debate a demanding, metaphysical task: to ensure that the political order of society obeyed the higher-level morality of law. But that function straddled a paradox: self-centred 'private' persons were required to enter public debate with an implausible, rational disinterestedness and an autonomy *vis-à-vis* their private interests. Given the inveterate difficulty of achieving that state of mind, the perpetual 'content of politics' became the effort to subsume politics under morality (see Habermas, 1989a, pp. 111–12). (NP)

Although its revolutionary French connotations were missing from the German concept, the Revolution had brought an end to the total disregard of public opinion; henceforth, rulers could not disregard it (ibid., *cf.* also Hölscher, 1978, p. 452). Its final recognition in German politics came about through the success of the liberal opposition. Under the banner of public opinion, the movement brought together the German nation's demands to do away with secretive aristocratic politics and to see human rights respected. Though unable, or unwilling, to see formal safeguards for the supremacy of public opinion, it did establish the framework: open, published parliamentary debates; public court hearings; freedom of opinion and of the press. Thus, following the examples of England (with its 'government by public opinion') and of post-revolutionary France, by the middle of the nineteenth century, the political public sphere in the state under the rule of Law was also recognized in Germany – even if without a democratic foundation.[19]

The break-up and delegitimation of public opinion

In retrospect, public opinion turns out to be a key concept by which feudal-absolutist society (with its politics founded on estates of the realm[20]) could be replaced by the bourgeois, class society of the nineteenth century (with its parliamentary politics). This explains why the hour of its triumph coincides with the beginning of its decline. Today, faced by the hegemony of parliaments, it is disputed as an inalienable basis for the legitimation of government. As an authoritative index of the views of the people, it appears the creature of manipulation and ideology. How is it that, since the second half of the nineteenth century, this change of view has come about?

Even before the turn of the century, the growing effects of a capitalist economy brought into question the so-called 'democratic' perspective of early liberalism. Liberalism had presupposed that, by acquiring independence, all members of society could exercise the same right to contribute to public opinion. As class inequalities and social polarization developed, this turned into nothing more than empty ideology. Those adversely affected by inequality refused to come to terms with it. Taking advantage of increased opportunities to participate and to articulate their views, they sought to accomplish through the state what they were unable to gain through the market: a secure material existence, a share in the surplus product of capital and broad social equality.

In the course of these struggles and debates, the notion of a united public opinion disintegrated. An old problem presented itself with new force: how to distinguish true from false public opinion, or to establish, in the event of dispute, what can be called the true voice of public opinion. Consequently, 'truth retreats into the back-

[19]   For further discussion of the legal framework of the nineteenth-century German state, see Essay 4, 'The legal order in a state under the rule of Law'. (NP)

[20]   That is, distinct status groups and institutions (the nobility, the Church, the town corporations) formally granted privileges and the right to be consulted by the monarch. (NP)

New manifestations of public opinion: a mass meeting for electoral reform in London's Hyde Park in 1867 (illustration: Mary Evans Picture Library).

ground'; public opinion appears to be merely the creature of ideological forces (Hölscher, 1979, p. 109 n.16, and pp. 112ff). Suspicions of ideology are all the more pressing to the extent that an increasing proportion of the population, equating public opinion with the general will, declare it to be beyond question. Criticism is voiced from two sides, from liberals and socialists alike.

Liberals such as J. S. Mill and de Tocqueville called for public opinion to be contained by the political system, preferring it to be articulated by a public educated on aristocratic lines. In excluding the political and economic claims made by other groups in the population, this version of liberalism was not only at odds with its own tradition but, more important, was also the target of criticism from the socialists. The latter understood, correctly, the relationship between public opinion and social class:

> In nineteenth-century Europe, public opinion was a synonym for opinions expressed by the political representatives of the electorate, by newspapers and by prominent members or organizations of the middle class.[21]
>
> *(Speier, 1950, p. 385)*

---

[21]   Compare Speier's description of public opinion as a 'phenomenon of middle-class civilization'.

Certainly, socialist criticisms arose in reaction to the increasing power of private interests, such as powerful newspaper publishers. In a context where freedom of opinion and of the press is guaranteed, such power undermines the rights of individuals. Socialist criticisms generated a negative attitude towards public opinion and its potential. This only changed once the socialist movement came to be more integrated in the state and played a part in forming public opinion, through its own associations and political parties.

Even the limited social and political advances of the workers' movements in the nineteenth and twentieth centuries (such as mustering a wider, politically involved and self-aware public) did have a price. To have gone further, to have taken a mass population, deprived of power and treated unequally, and turned it into the protected clientele of a socialist state (where the public arena would be swamped by mass culture) would probably have driven many into political apathy. It would have been incompatible, that is to say, with a self-confident and effective public opinion. It is undeniable, therefore, that if one simply diverts the liberal state under the rule of Law in a social-welfare direction, one irrevocably undermines the social basis of public opinion as envisaged by liberalism.

For some time now, a blurring of the boundaries has been observed between state and society. Society abandons collective responsibilities to the competence of institutions acting under the authority of the state, which intervene to organize the economy and the social order. They do this:

> without any political intrusion by reasoning private individuals. The Public is largely relieved of these tasks by other institutions: on the one hand, associations in which private interests are organized for political purposes; on the other hand, political parties which merge with public bodies and place themselves above the Public, whose instrument they once were.
>
> *(Habermas, 1990, p. 268)*

These new organizations do not usually make their decisions publicly, or even control their own internal decision-making properly. Rather, they try to win public support, or toleration, for the decisions they make and for their position in society. At best, they seek to tailor public opinion to their own purposes, by their visibility, by manipulation, or by force of argument.

For this, these organizations need the press, which, once it is tied into publishing in the contemporary capitalist market, alters the character of public opinion considerably. The press changes from what it was under the liberal ethos and liberal market of the nineteenth and early twentieth centuries. This change turns news and opinions into commodities, renders the editorial section dependent on advertising and makes the press as a whole the 'entrance through which privileged private interests gain access to the public arena' (Habermas, 1990, p. 280). The influence of such interests in structuring capital and political power can be seen indirectly from the way that the independence of the new electronic mass media in the western European democracies is supposedly being guaranteed by the power of the state. The state was going to put these new media into public or semi-public corporations (an idea that would have been perverse in classical-liberal terms). In the event, however, it was prevented from doing this by the burgeoning sellers' market for these media in the private sector.

The capitalist form of growth requires the mass media to be the motor of consumerism and cultivates the public solely as its passive target. This is true not only for the non-political public sphere. Everything can be advertised. The new profession of public relations promotes political interests and organizations as well as commercial products and manufacturers. Politics and politicians trade in a thriving market for their own kind of consumer goods, cultivating the political public sphere through the use of those social-psychological mechanisms (such as the acceptance of role-models), that suit it. Surveying these developments, Habermas concludes that the public and public opinion now appear remote anachronisms:

> The public sphere – first shaped and then governed by the mass media – has become an arena where the power of the public is diffused. The topics and the contributions in public debates are simply objects of a competition for influence. The flow of information is carefully managed by competing forces, which, while influencing public behaviour, keep secret their true strategies and intentions.
>
> *(Habermas, 1990, p. 28)*

Two aspects of these developments are particularly noteworthy. In the first place, once public debate no longer offers the appropriate information and discussion for public opinion to develop, the task of criticizing, as enshrined in the principle of publicity, is lost. In fact, the principle is turned on its head: public decision comes to mean selling decisions already arrived at in secret, and legitimizing the positions of influence held by various powerful political and social forces. The public, at one time the enemy of the secretive politics of absolutism, is converted into the instrument of a new version. In the second place, there is a clear, long-term tendency for the mass media, political parties and other associations to be concerned less with articulating public opinion than with creating or manipulating synthetic 'opinions'. At worst, the public becomes a mere instrument, and public opinion nothing but a medium for use by others. At best, the principle of conducting a public discussion so as to establish the truth and arrive at consensus or compromise, retreats into the background. In different terms, this process of distortion also affects parliament – which was originally the 'public' face-to-face with government. Over the long term, a change can be observed in the character of parliaments: from true debating bodies into institutions conveying legitimacy to prior decisions. This constitutes a loss of power *vis-à-vis* the administration on one side, and political parties and associations on the other.

These social and political tendencies explain the decline of public opinion over the last century. Once the creation of shared efforts to discuss, regulate and guide the exercise of power, it has now become an increasingly passive authority, formed by the mass media. This trend also explains why, over a period of a century and a half, the concept of public opinion has become less precise and its institutions have lost much of their force as legitimations.

It is possible that the old paradigm of a unified public opinion could be reconstructed around a spectrum of competing 'public opinions'. Yet, that approach disposes of only one aspect of the radical transformation that has taken place. Class struggle, and the ideological use of public opinion as a device to impose agreement in a political system already exhibiting totalitarian potential, suggest that we should loosen, or even completely abandon, the connection formerly made between public opinion and the principles of the state under the rule of Law.

Indeed, from the late nineteenth century on, the practice of treating public opinion as a phenomenon to be analysed (using concepts for mass psychology developed by social psychology and sociology[22]) has been undermining that connection. Falling political participation and passive consumerism join forces with a political life staged for the consumer. Together they reinforce the now dominant scientific positivism[23] and affirm its concealed outcome: to deprive public opinion of both its significance as knowledge and its claim to authority in moral and political matters. 'Opinions', then, come to mean no more than views that can be totted up on any topic of general interest. In due course, opinions are assimilated to other attitudes or forms of behaviour, which can be measured without ever being put into words. A 'public' opinion is then reduced merely to a view held in common by a social group of a given number.[24] The results of this type of public-opinion polling are anything but value-free, for such polls are constructed in the first place out of an interest, which is not always conscious, in their use as the instruments of those with political and socio-economic power.[25]

Public opinion in contemporary democracy

By the early 1950s, Hans Speier thought the old belief in a strong public opinion that would establish rational and humane conditions amongst nations was finished. 'The hope that public opinion will be able to solve the problems of international

[22]   Herd instinct and mob psychology, for example. (The work in these fields is exemplified by works such as Tard (1901), Bauer (1914, 1930) or Doob (1948). See also Otto (1966), pp. 110ff. and Habermas (1990), pp. 347ff.)

[23]   The view which limits valid knowledge to that obtained by following the objective investigative procedures epitomized in the physical sciences, and holds, in consequence, that knowledge proper is 'value-free', i.e. indifferent, and irrelevant to questions of value. (NP)

[24]   Otto (1966, p. 111) compares the classical conception of public opinion (namely, a view formed through discussion in a public of educated and morally or politically concerned people) with a standard definition from positivist political science: 'people's attitudes when they are members of the same social group' (Doob, 1948).

[25]   A contemporary example is the instant public opinion survey (the so-called 'lightning survey', or *Blitzumfragen*), in which one collects unconsidered views that would traditionally not have been called 'public', and tots them up to make a 'public opinion' tailored to one's needs. 'Public opinion' in this sense is deemed to create, or substantiate public opinion in the fuller sense of a widely shared opinion with political weight.

policy has waned' (Speier, 1950, p. 387). However, over the subsequent decades, from the Vietnam War to the appearance of *glasnost*, public opinion has successfully gained an international hearing for the causes of peace, disarmament and co-operation. It may be that 'belief in the perfectibility of man' has been replaced by a common interest in the global preservation of the species (ibid.). However that may be, we can now qualify Speier's pessimistic assessment. In 1981, the MacBride Commission identified a range of topics around which a regenerated, 'world public opinion' was forming. Those opposed to the moral and political demands made in these fields had to face a collective, world-wide opinion.[26] The example of this change should teach us not to assume irreversible trends in the development of public opinion.

In the last section, I outlined an historic change brought about by media manipulation, which undermined the public's capacity for critical reasoning. The public of the past has been turned into the basis and agent of a qualitatively different type of public opinion. Rather than attempting to reflect reality accurately, my outline applied an ideal type to public opinion. Yet the historical digression has its positive side. It may help us to differentiate between the reality of public opinion and the situation that is claimed, or assumed for it. It could help to prompt research into what would be required to reduce the awkward gap between socio-political reality and the aspirations inherent in the concept of public opinion.

The contested and intangible reality of public opinion

Such aspirations are widespread and are recognized at the highest level of the state. Members of social movements and constitutional judges agree: a public which is critical of established power can guarantee individual freedom and promote political participation. Here is a social and political fact which contradicts the prospect that public opinion might be totally overwhelmed or turned into the instrument of power.

Furthermore, at least for the democratic state under the rule of Law, belief in the value of an open political public sphere and an unconstrained public opinion to guarantee freedom, are important elements of political culture. Such beliefs, imprinted on the political behaviour of large sections of a heterogeneous population, do not simply dissolve under the onslaught of massive social and political changes. As is confirmed by Almond and Verba's debate on the 'Civic Culture Concept' (see Almond, 1988, p. 183), while political culture does not determine political (or social) structure, it is more than a merely dependent variable.

---

[26] 'World public opinion wants peace preserved through international agreement…is opposed to torture and inhumane treatment, as well as to the persecution of those who hold minority beliefs… [It] is opposed to privilege or domination on the basis of race or colour. [It] demands action taken against poverty, hunger and backwardness, which are the lot of most of the human race' (S. MacBride, E. Abel *et al.*, 1984, *Many Voices, One World* (The MacBride Report), abridged edn of the Report of the International Commission for the Study of Communication Problems, Paris, Unesco, p. 154).

During recent decades, eventually even in the states of middle and eastern Europe, more and more citizens have been organized by others or have come together spontaneously. They have got the better of the mass media, or forced a reaction within the political parties and the agenda of parliament. Their chosen means – from sit-ins to readers' letters, from silent demonstrations to discussions in schools or parish meetings – show that public opinion does not have to depend on the written or printed word. On the other hand, these experiences clearly confirm the importance of the mass media. For, without the intervention of the media, the public sphere actually available to the citizens and their political impact would have been minimal.

It is, therefore, rather rash to take the problems of public opinion to be solely the problems of the mass media. Public opinion, in other words, is not the same thing as *published* opinion. Within the highly differentiated system of public life in western democracies, constitutionally guaranteed processes survive, below the level of mass communication, which (regardless of the mass media) form, modify and articulate public opinion. In the theory of democracy, the political conversation in the smallest of small groups is no less important than the public occasion for sharing information, for electioneering, or for making a protest.[27]

This section adopts, from sociology and social psychology, the more descriptive approach needed to grasp the link between public opinion and mass media. The pressure exercised by the media explains why even those critics who consider public opinion immune to scientific treatment do not dispute the influence of public opinion on politics and politicians. As a rule, public opinion will not directly influence the actions of people in government; but it will set certain limits.[28] As Davison explains:

> Public officials will usually seek to satisfy a widespread demand, or will
> at least take it into account in their deliberations, and they will also try
> to avoid decisions that they believe will fly in the face of popular
> opinion.
>
> *(Davison, 1985, p. 355; see also Luhmann, 1975, p. 20)*

Public opinion and the mass media

In a democracy, the various channels of the mass media (the periodical and non-periodical press; the audio media such as radio or records; the visual media which carry pictures and data; and the audio-visual media of TV, film etc.) fulfil three functions:

---

[27]   Gerhards and Neidhardt (1990) emphasize the many levels of existence of the public (*cf.* also Rodney Barker's concept of 'citizen democracy' in Essay 3).

[28]   This is less true for that 'public opinion' which, though influential, does not achieve dominance. It is rare, of course, for public opinion on a given topic to speak with one voice. So, in the processes of forming public opinion, one variant comes to dominate, and is considered, by the political actors it is aimed at, to be *the* voice of public opinion. Though this pragmatic definition of public opinion cannot count on universal acceptance, it is the basis of the analyses in this essay.

- they inform;

- they control and criticize government;

- they form public opinion.

In describing a set-up where its members seek to understand the political system, entertainment channels could be ignored were it not for the fact that, for producers and recipients alike, they pose an almost insoluble problem: how to distinguish between informing, developing and entertaining the public? One of the best-tried means of manipulating opinion, indeed, is to merge those different functions.

1   Informing the public

Technical advances and the appearance of new media have multiplied the already impressive capacity (first shown by the press in the early part of this century) to provide information. A network of news agencies, supported by a high-technology infrastructure, provides comprehensive, worldwide news coverage with an immediacy that is hard to better. At the same time, formal agreements and guarantees secure the free flow of information and the freedom of journalistic investigation. Behind these positive tendencies, however, are hidden far-reaching problems in respect of democracy's theoretical requirement for 'objective' information: that is, for information which is not distorted by hidden, private interests.

Since the nineteenth century, centralization of decision-making and a concentration of capital have overtaken the information sector's technical infrastructure. The immediate consequences have been a loss of editorial independence and marked limitations on access to publicity. Where the media are under direct legal control, these difficulties have been displaced but not overcome.

This problem has an international dimension. The selection of news is predominantly made by western (largely Anglo-Saxon) news agencies (AP, UPI, Reuters, Agence France Presse, etc.), judging 'news value' according to the criteria of Anglo-Saxon journalism. The technology of the future, in computing and information-relay, is dominated by the USA (see Schulz, 1988, pp. 141ff. and *passim*). The principle of 'the free flow of information' between the First and the Third Worlds is realized, almost exclusively, in one direction. With this in mind, the MacBride Commission criticized the international system of communication for 'inequalities between developed and developing countries', as well as for 'asymmetrical communication processes, orientated from top to bottom and from centre to periphery' which 'distort the contents of communication' and 'threaten the national and cultural identity of many countries' (as summarized by Schulz, 1988, p. 150).

Finally, the sheer volume of information and the selectivity of individuals' interests limit the degree to which the majority of the public feels able to check the truth of the information it receives. Only skilled and trained users can make appropriate use of the multiplicity of sources. H. Meyn, following the views of Schulz, observes that:

> The theory of democracy prompted the hope that, by increasing
> knowledge and making the population better informed, more widely

Politics and the media today: press and broadcasting reporters swamp Dutch party leaders after negotiations to form a coalition government at The Hague in October 1989 (photo: Roel Rozenberg/Hollandse Hoogte).

> available media, especially new radio and TV channels, would lead to more active participation in politics. That hope has not been realized.
> *(Meyn, 1988, p. 317)*

What Schulz himself adds is hardly less disquieting:

> …concern, interest in politics and a *feeling of being well-informed* have all increased. At any given time, most people can name the issues and events of the moment. But it is clear that this rather diffuse knowledge of affairs – of crises and catastrophes, of controversies and problems – shadows quite closely the *prioritization of topics* made by the media.
> *(Schulz, 1988, p. 139 – author's emphasis)*

2   The criticism and control of government

The media make an indispensable contribution to the criticism and control (albeit inadequate) exercised over those in government. Granted, there are grotesque differences between the capacity of different publishers and broadcasting stations. But only the mass media have the personnel, the technical and financial resources, and the institutional security needed to pursue this function on a long-term basis. None the less, under the prevailing conditions of concentration and competition, we have to be wary of media bias – and not just in general terms. Specifically, there is the effect of professional information management and public relations, which, conducted for the benefit of organized private interests and government, counters the investigation and monitoring conducted by the press (*cf.* Baerns, 1985).

3   The formation of public opinion

Plainly, it is not only through explicit commentary and leading articles in the press that the mass media form the opinions of individuals and the public at large. They also do it through the control of information. Headed by a small number of élite papers and political magazines of international repute, the political press and media of most western democracies present an apparently varied landscape: offering space for diverse interests and traditions, and genuine alternatives for those who are politically aware.

The public shows little concern about a conflict of interest that touches the media themselves: their dependence on the economic framework provided by the private sector and the legal framework provided by government, political parties and other associations. The public, on the other hand, is concerned by reductions in the range of publications and by concentration of control within the media. A very small number of firms often dominate the landscape of the national press, and divide private-sector media markets between them.[29] Yet, the more citizens' time and attention is absorbed by all-encompassing media, the more direct can be the media's influence in the processes that form opinion.[30]

It follows that research into the effects of the media is particularly important for the survival and development of democracies under the rule of Law. At the moment, however, research seems more preoccupied with pursuing out-worn issues and disproving old hypotheses than with establishing reliable knowledge of the empirical processes. Yet, there are some more challenging approaches, which, with modification, can prove useful.

Amongst these are the study of 'agenda-setting' and the hypothesis of a 'knowledge gap'. The former shows how the media, by their selection and treatment of topics and issues, influence media-users' perception of reality. Whatever the media emphasize will count as important in people's thinking. The hypothesis of a knowledge gap suggests that, because it benefits those higher up the social scale, an increased flow of unequally distributed information is deepening the gap between higher and lower social strata.

---

[29]   In this context, a number of questions pose themselves, requiring different answers for different countries: What increases or (more usually) decreases the number of firms in publishing? How many firms dominate the market of the national dailies? Which multi-media firms dominate the international TV market? Impressive, disquieting figures can be found in the appendix to Meyn, 1988, pp. 319–34).

[30]   Citizens of the Federal Republic of Germany devote about five hours per weekday to watching TV, listening to the radio, or reading the paper (Schulz, 1988, p. 139). Though figures vary for different western countries, time spent on one or other product of the media is the third largest element (after work and sleep) in daily time use.

More recent research suggests that both these hypotheses require modification (*cf.* Schenk, 1987b. See also the critical survey in Merten, 1991b, pp. 58ff.). On the one hand, the processes of agenda-setting are subject to intervening variables from interpersonal communication (Schenk, 1987b, pp. 3 and 14ff.). On the other hand, it appears that the knowledge gap is more strongly influenced by individual motivation and interests than by levels of education or membership of social strata. Yet, the methodologies and concepts developed within these lines of thought are now well-established and accepted as fundamental to research on the public sphere. They show how much progress has been made in investigating the effects of the media, compared to the early days of simple measurement procedures and undeveloped concepts about those effects.

The simplistic 'stimulus–response' approach, which concentrated on one variable and assumed clear causal relations and measurable effects, has been strongly criticized, and is now seldom used even in the USA (see Schenk, 1987b, p. 3). Indeed, the idea of strong and direct media effects was put in doubt long ago by Lazarsfeld's observation of a 'two-step flow' in communication[31] (see Lazarsfeld *et al.*, 1944). Merten summarizes the stimulus–response account as follows:

> Recipients of the mass media use it as their prime source of information;…some views are needed about the importance and accuracy of the information available. These operate as a meta-statement to evaluate information on offer and facilitate a decision on what to accept.
>
> *(Merten, 1991b, p. 61)*

The recipient obtains this meta-statement either from opinion leaders of his/her acquaintance, or from reputedly trustworthy, 'virtuoso' opinion leaders in the media, or from discussions in the media and in private. Hence, as the supply of mass media increases their 'opinion-forming function and thereby [their] general impact are increasing'.

The social-psychological theory of the 'spiral of silence' has attracted attention because it postulates close connections between election results and publications in the media.[32] In general, people notice the opinions (including the election preferences) of those around them. Those who perceive their opinions to be dominant are more likely to voice them; whilst those who feel in a minority tend to remain silent, out of fear of isolation. The upshot is that opinions at first merely thought dominant actually become so in reality. The mass media fulfil a politically dubious function in this process, when their publication of the apparent distribution and trend of opinion points the way for the behaviour of individuals.

This hypothesis has often been empirically tested, but it remains more or less unsubstantiated. Though research into the effects of the mass media has produced

---

[31]   Whereby the mass-media message was mediated through other social processes. (NP)

[32]   See Noelle-Neumann (1982), and also the contributions by W. A. Jöhr and E. Katz in Baier *et al.* (1981).

important insights, little certain knowledge has so far been gained regarding the consequences for the formation of opinion amongst individuals and the public at large. If we proved that the media are not omnipotent over their users, that would still leave open the possibility that they have a significant influence in the formation of opinion. But that influence is more likely to be found over long periods of time, as *indirect* effects which are difficult to prove. It is to be expected that such effects will increase in the future, as the media come to influence, or even oust, those personal factors (i.e. the individual's circumstances, knowledge, preferences, and social situation) which have up to now sustained users' relative independence.[33]

Quite apart from the actual content of the mass media in influencing individuals, the form which the process takes seems objectionable in terms of democratic theory. Mass communication is essentially a one-way process, which must be viewed as both intellectually and socially negative: the person exposed to its influence may withdraw from it, but cannot shape it.

The achievements and inadequacies of opinion research

Opinion polls on political issues are an important part of the media's pool of news. They have also become an indispensable source of enlightenment for political representatives and managers of the political system. They are a device drawn from opinion research, a form of investigation which first arose in market research and uses scientifically based representative surveys to ascertain people's attitudes, common patterns of behaviour, opinions and interests.

Sampling is a key element in the correct conduct of a survey of opinion.[34] The sample selected has to represent the total of the population under investigation. Still more important is the way that results are obtained from the sample. The form and wording of the questions, the layout of the questionnaire, the interviewers' behaviour and, of course, the interpretation of data collected, can all influence the outcome. Data are never self-explanatory. To offset unsatisfactory results or controversial interpretations, we may use refined statistical tests, or alternative forms of question.[35]

---

[33]   I am therefore surprised by Davison's statement that: 'The press, radio and television are usually less important than the immediate social environment when it comes to the formation of attitudes, but they are still significant' (Davison, 1985, p. 354).

[34]   There is a great deal of literature on this. For Germany, see, for example, Friedrichs (1985) or Karmasin (1977). For Britain and the USA, see Hoinville *et al.* (1988) and Fowler and Floyd (1984).

[35]   Or we might resort to altogether different, deeper investigative procedures, which permit more revealing interpretations: e.g. the non-structured interview, or activity-based methods such as the Rorschach test.

It is polls at election time that attract most interest in western democracies. Now, although we may think of elections primarily as expressions of public opinion, we have also to understand their other aspects. For one thing, tradition and unthinking affection often prompt people's opinions. Furthermore, in electoral expressions of opinion, the representative system forces individual voters to lose part of themselves to the group. To make a choice implies an underlying alienation of oneself, brought about by consenting to the organized 'opinions' decided on by the person or the party voted for.

Surveys after an election may help to clarify how the will of the electors might be implemented. But surveys before elections seem primarily to provide politicians and political parties with the opportunity to change their tactics and their presentation, giving altered weight to different topics and voter preferences. For this reason, the political critique of opinion polls is most heated when it comes to election-time polls and reports of them in the media. They are said to provoke copy-cat or bandwagon effects – intentionally or otherwise – as voters switch to what they perceive to be the stronger camp. (This process is suggested by the theory of the spiral of silence.) They are held to narrow down the spectrum of topics and candidates, and produce an atmosphere more akin to a sporting contest than a process of political choice. Finally, they are said to encourage opportunistic trimming on the part of politicians to the fluctuating opinions of the people – or rather to the opinions of the majority. This last reproach, in particular, is often levelled at opinion polls on political issues. Though far from proven, it carries great weight, particularly amongst adherents of the conservative-élitist picture of democracy and the public sphere.

However, it is perfectly possible that a properly conducted investigation of the distribution of opinions and preferences within the population (particularly after lengthy public discussion) could increase the involvement of the governed in the democratic formulation of the people's will. Investigations into opinions are always helpful when they uncover those opinions, needs and fears that are not otherwise articulated, or are not capable of articulation. Likewise, polling might enhance public discussion: by a differentiation of the range of opinions and reasons for holding them which matches the complexity of the topic.

Yet the reality is usually quite different. The formation of public opinion is adversely influenced by surveys whose conduct and interpretation are orientated around altogether narrower interests. The approach and the results of a survey are almost invariably presented in a highly selective form. Accordingly, the population is unable to interpret and evaluate it. This makes opinion polls particularly susceptible to manipulation and misuse in politics and the mass media, turning public opinion itself into an instrument of others.

Finally, public opinion is further delegitimized simply by opinion research's grip on the idea of it. For, under the investigative procedure of opinion research, the growth and the rationale behind anyone's 'opinions' are deemed unimportant. And the shared, active character of public opinion is only acknowledged as a trivial adjunct to attitudes and behaviour already ascertained by survey. Hence, there are no concepts with which to identify the inadequacy of the much-loved 'lightning survey'[36] as a way of placing public opinion on the throne of power.

Recent controversies and new conceptions of public opinion

The view of Critical Theory

It was the Frankfurt School,[37] in particular Theodor Adorno, who drew attention both to the decline of a properly informed, rational-critical public opinion, and to how indispensable it is in terms of democratic theory.[38] In the early 1960s, Adorno wrote that:

> If public opinion is going legitimately to fulfil the function of control over government – which, since Locke, the theory of democratic society has assigned to it – then it must be capable of monitoring for itself its own grasp of the truth. As things are, public opinion can be monitored only as the statistical average of individual opinions.

On the other hand:

> ...to eliminate the concept of public opinion, to relinquish it completely, would mean the loss of an impulse which is capable of preventing the worst, even in an antagonistic society – as long as it has not turned totalitarian.
>
> *(Adorno, 1961/62, pp. 24ff., quoted in Hölscher, 1978, p. 467)*

This is the point of departure, not only for the study by Negt and Kluge (1972), but also for Jürgen Habermas's *Structural Transformation of the Public Sphere*, which attempts to demonstrate the importance – indeed the necessity – of a democratic development of public opinion and of its grasp on truth.

Outlining the rise of the bourgeois–liberal state under the rule of Law, Habermas's multidisciplinary analysis traces both the first emergence of the public political

---

[36] See note 25 above.

[37] The intellectual current formed in the early 1930s at the Institut für Socialforschung in Frankfurt. Its leading members – Max Horkheimer, Herbert Marcuse and Theodor Adorno – moved their activities to New York in 1933–34. Building on their central, Marxist-inspired idea that modern capitalist society was turning human beings and their social life into inhuman, impersonal things (what they called 'reification'), they developed a so-called 'Critical Theory' to expose oppressive concepts and delusions, which, they argued, were systematically embedded within many aspects of contemporary culture and society. In the early 1950s, the Institute was re-established in Frankfurt and spawned a second generation, notably Jürgen Habermas. (NP)

[38] In reaction to the adverse treatment given to the institutions of public opinion and public sphere in the first half of the century, i.e. by Schmitt (1923), Tönnies (1963) and Heidegger (1927). At the time that Adorno was writing, these views were enjoying a rehabilitation, along élitist lines, at the hands of Wilhelm Hennis (1957).

sphere in bourgeois society, and the change of its political function in the wake of western societies' transformation into mass social-welfare democracies.[39] In the course of these fundamental changes, the public has ceased to be 'culture-debating' and has become passive: 'culture-consuming'. The principle of 'publicity' no longer serves as a basis for the public's rational-critical function, but rather as a means to manage social integration. There is no longer room for political debate that simply seeks the truth. Rather than opinion generated from within the public, the arena of debate is shaped from above, by organized private interests in mutual competition. The arguments of committed private individuals are lost almost without trace. There could hardly be a wider gap between, on one side, the value that public opinion is supposed to have for the democratic state and, on the other side, the day-to-day practice of politics and the current disintegration of the idea of public opinion within the social sciences.

But why should we stick in the first place to these assumptions, founded on supposed continuities with the earlier liberal state under the rule of Law? Habermas is convinced that established power can only be rationally controlled via discussion that is 'public' in liberal terms: accessible to all, directed towards the general interest and amenable to the force of argument. For him, these are the only terms which can provide a guarantee that, under a representative government, the sovereignty of the people will be realized in practice. Yet, Habermas himself identifies other bodies which, under the changed historical conditions, might pursue the principle of rational-critical publicity; namely, parties and associations whose internal decision-making is democratic and subject to open public scrutiny. He considers that these are now alone in functioning, as 'in effect, a network of public communication which still has a capacity for regeneration' (Habermas, 1990, p. 32), and in supporting other impulses in the direction of democratic transformation. It is because Habermas himself retains the prospect of a socialist democracy, grounded on a revitalized public opinion, that he addresses the issue of whether 'from the unresolved plurality of competing interests...a general interest could ever emerge and be taken as a yardstick by public opinion' (ibid., p. 340).

The response of Systems Theory

Niklas Luhmann, Habermas's interlocutor from Systems Theory,[40] articulated this difficulty more forcefully and even elaborated a solution:

> The concept of public opinion cannot simply be re-cycled for use in the context of activities internal to an organization. For, characteristically,

---

[39]   That is to say, representative democracies with a mass electorate where the state, in return for popular support, is ostensibly devoted to ensuring the material welfare of its citizens. (NP)

[40]   Systems Theory, developed initially in the USA after the Second World War, seeks to describe society as a set of interlocking systems and subsystems: the economy, the family, the state, political parties, the media, etc., etc. These systems and subsystems combine together to sustain a self-contained whole. Typically, therefore, Systems Theory asks of any given system within the whole: How does it sustain itself? How does it function to sustain society as a whole? (NP)

organizations are founded on a compartmentalization of awareness amongst their members. Therefore, neither the structural premises nor the related experiences required for a critical public opinion can arise within the organization.

Systems Theory, in any case, is less interested in the character of public opinion as an evolving *outcome*, than in its function as an *instrument* of selection and control for the political subsystem of complex societies. Like any system threatened by the extreme complexity of its environment, the political system is in need of help to reduce the complexity.

> The extended range of political and legal possibilities...needs to be reduced through opinions tempered in discussion.
>
> *(Luhmann, 1975, p. 12)*

In the final analysis, to the Systems Theorist, it is not the content or the truth of the opinions circulating amongst the public that are important. What matters is the range of topics entering the process of opinion-forming. Once there exists what Luhmann calls a functional 'topic-structure for the process of political communication', public opinion takes on:

> ...the function of a steering mechanism within the political system, which does not determine how power is exercised and opinions formed, but does lay down the parameters of what is feasible under the given circumstances.
>
> *(Ibid., p. 20)*

Although the Systems Theorists do not entirely lose sight of the basic problem of the liberal concept of public opinion, it has to be borne in mind that, from their point of view, it is of secondary importance that power be constrained or made to operate more rationally by public opinion. So this description of a kind of practical truth arising from public opinion cannot really address the issue.

There are other Systems Theorists who, like Habermas, complain about the low value placed, throughout the social sciences, on the public sphere and public opinion. But they view the systematic historical work in which Habermas addressed the issue as a limited success. Gerhards and Neidhardt, for example, state that Habermas did not serve social sciences well when he conflated 'the empirical and the normative elements' in his concept of the formation of public opinion, and overloaded it with issues from philosophical theories of truth and judgement (Gerhards and Niedhardt, 1990, p. 5). For them, public opinion is an 'intermediate system...to mediate between, on the one hand, the political system, and, on the other hand, citizens and the demands arising from other subsystems of society' (ibid., p. 12). If the function of the political system is taken, as here, to be 'the production of collective, binding decisions' (ibid., p. 8), then the system is being given a quite particular meaning: as the channel, or addressee for unresolved problems (arising in the other systems of society), and as the possessor of a unique, binding right to shape them all (ibid., p. 9).

To contain centrifugal tendencies, which would endanger the whole system, does indeed require a critical public. The function of public opinion is to control politics and relate it back to the opinions and needs of the citizens. By generalizing component interests within the system, the public sphere produces shared, 'public' opinions. If the system of political power disregards them, that may be registered by that same public, which can then re-inforce them through the institutional feedback of competition between political parties and of changes in government. Exaggerating somewhat, we could say that democracy comes to the aid of the system: the public sphere and public opinion impact on the political subsystem to sustain the flexibility of the system as a whole. In effect, Gerhards and Neidhardt admit processes making the established power operate rationally and permitting democratic change in society – though only as underlying and, in the final analysis, a contingent feature of the system.

What is not admitted into Systems Theory, however, is the democratic political thrust of socialism (as in the work of Oskar Negt and Alexander Kluge), and feminism (represented here by Carole Pateman), two perspectives intended to make an historical intervention in the system.

Socialist perspectives

Negt and Kluge develop the concept of a special 'proletarian' public: in their view, an idea that is uniquely able to identify, explore and give due social weight to the lived experience of working people. For, under capitalism, the world as the lived experience of the working class construes it (what is known as the *Lebenswelt*, or 'life-world') is diffused and re-cast by external forces. Evolving dialectically, the proletarian public takes the bourgeois historical experience as its starting point. Both bourgeois and proletarian publics 'lay claim to the public sphere, securing their political power, and developing a channel for demands arising from the deficiencies they experience as outsiders' (Stamm, 1988, p. 278).[41]

It follows that the older, bourgeois public has now to be seen as an instrument of repression, rather than as a medium for emancipation. The proletarian public is the sole medium to define, promote and realize the interests of the proletariat. A point of conflict with Habermas arises in the contention that the proletarian public is not a variant of the bourgeois public (as Habermas would see it – *cf.* Habermas, 1990, p. 52), but a 'completely different all-embracing view of society' (Negt and Kluge, 1972, p. 8, note 1) which emerged as far back as the French Revolution. Since that time, its members have seen through the ideological veneer of bourgeois universalism and no longer pursue liberal enlightenment and joint discussion: 'Only the counter-products of a proletarian public can be of use against the output of bourgeois public discussion: idea against idea, output against output' (ibid., p. 143).

For Negt and Kluge, this proletarian public is essentially 'a matter for the future' (ibid., note 39). Up to now, it has only been realized at certain 'historic moments

---

[41]   According to Stamm, the two versions of the public (bourgeois and proletarian) would develop different, and competing, channels for putting forward their demands. The bourgeoisie might write letters to *The Times*, for example, whereas the working class might stage a lightning strike and demonstrate in the street. Clearly, each class will be uneasy, or even hostile, to the other's medium for putting its case. Furthermore, if the public sphere is confined too narrowly (by, for example, bans on street marches), this can be oppressive to those less able to employ the remaining channels. (NP)

of breakdown', such as war, revolution or military capitulation (ibid., p. 7). However, they point systematically to contradictions within the bourgeois public which might encourage possible alternatives to emerge. For example, the bourgeois public 'claims to represent the whole of society' (ibid., p. 11); but, by concentrating attention elsewhere, it tucks away out of sight substantial areas of social life, such as the private company and socialization within the family.

Ways of dealing with this contradiction, both in theory and in practical politics, are suggested by two other writers who could be thought of as taking a socialist line somewhere between that of Negt/Kluge and that of Habermas.

Leo Kissler introduces the concept of an 'autonomous public within the production-process' (Kissler, 1984, 1989). Though supported by precise analyses of the regulations governing industrial relations and working conditions, Kissler's concepts (like Negt and Kluge's) take the basic principles of democracy as their point of departure. His aim is a fundamental change in the processes of production and of work in general. He distinguishes three models of the public within the production-process, according to the type and level of participation by the workforce. In the 'secretive model' the workforce is subject to top–down production decisions. In the 'integration' or 'modernizing model', asymmetrical forms of communication are instituted to promote acceptance and motivation amongst employees. The 'emancipation' or 'autonomy model':

> ...assumes that the validity of production decisions is derived from discussion and, therefore, from the proper participation of all concerned... [Its version of the publicity principle] makes possible real participation in the decision-making process by publics located inside or outside a company, on the basis of largely symmetrical communications which are potentially free from domination. The subordinate is up-graded to 'citizen of the company'...
>
> *(Kissler, 1989, p. 62)*

However, people are not simply appointed 'citizens of the company'; they have to develop themselves to achieve that. An autonomous public within the production-process is not established merely by arranging discussions which assume that all employees are equally competent communicators. For the necessary learning process to take place, there are both objective preconditions (such as internal openness in the company and communication at the level of the workplace), and subjective ones (such as the capacity for change and the motivation to participate). And some of these preconditions have to be fought for; they cannot all be handed down from above (see Kissler, 1989, pp. 158ff).

Like Habermas, Kissler takes public opinion to be a well-grounded principle of democratic society. He then extends its application into society's basic economic units. What distinguishes his conception from the liberal model of the public is that it does not depend on conditions which are unlikely to be fulfilled (such as personal independence), but on competence in communication and on learning processes to achieve that. Although his conception of the public is aimed at the democratization of individual companies, were such practices to become widespread, this would no doubt impinge considerably on the structure and motivation of the public, as well as on the range of topics dealt with in the critical public sphere.

Karl-Heinz Stamm points to the current 're-politicization' and 'revitalization' of the bourgeois public sphere which has resulted from the appearance, within the so-called 'new social movements', of an 'authentic public' (see Stamm, 1988, pp. 15, 266, 272 and *passim*). These 'alternative' groups, such as the women's movement, the Greens, the peace movement and the 'citizens' initiative' (*Bürgerinitiative*) have been able to convey important topics to the broader public, and bring pressure to bear on the political system (ibid., p. 278). This new public is formed from intermediate strata of the population, who are likely to place greater value on conducting dialogue and on human solidarity, than on power, status or achievement (ibid., p. 267). What is more, though it does embrace the world of work and production, this public is more concerned with an everyday, personal level of experience, which is closer to people. By a critical confrontation with the limits of what is given as 'possible' within society, that which is authentic within the private sphere enters into the public one.

This form of public has features of the bourgeois version (an orientation around reason and consensus), as well as of the proletarian one (theoretical reflection on collective experience and an impulse to reclaim areas of life excluded from human control). And yet, it is also quite different: notably, in its treatment of the bourgeois division between public and private. Furthermore,

> ...it has overcome the fixation with the working class as an agent [of social change]...for its protest is fired by conflicts which cannot be defined in terms of the production process and its associated property relations. It arises instead at the 'interface between the system and the life-world'...[42]
>
> *(Ibid., p. 276)*

Kissler's idea of an 'autonomous, production-process public' and Stamm's of an 'authentic public' both illustrate what Habermas has referred to as the 'paradigm shift from a work-society to a communications-society' (quoted in Stamm, 1988, p. 283).[43] Rather than being objections to the bourgeois model of a critical public,

---

[42] The phrase in quotation marks is taken from Habermas. The insertion in square brackets is added to the text: the expression in the original German (*proletarisches Klassensubjekt*) also refers to the Lukácsian Marxist idea (much in evidence in the thinking of the Frankfurt School) that the working class might be a 'historical subject'; that is to say, an agent capable of bringing about a future transformation, in much the same way as the bourgeoisie is held to have transformed society in the historical past. Stamm's contention is, then, that the new 'authentic' public has left behind that kind of thinking about the working class. The reference to 'life-world' echoes Habermas's belief in a 'colonization of the life-world', discussed below. (NP)

[43] Habermas's claim is that, whereas, at one time, society was founded on mechanisms to impose work on people, it is now organized around complex networks of communication, which coordinate the different groups, levels and individuals. The logic inherent in the process of communication can engender shared perceptions and values, a 'communicatively achieved consensus' (Habermas, 1984, p. 179). According to Schmidt, the authentic public and the production-process public are outcomes of society's new dependence on communication. (NP)

these ideas would supplement it in ways adapted to needs of the present. They do not, then, overturn the influence of Habermas. Not so Carole Pateman, whose new critical reading of the mainstream history of ideas and of institutions shakes the normative foundation of Habermas's conception of the democratic public (see Pateman, 1986, 1988, 1989).

A feminist perspective

Pateman points to the continuing sources of modern, liberal-democratic ideas on government and the public: contract theory linked to the rationalist theory of the basis of law. To be sure, these ousted the paternal figure which had legitimized explicit political patriarchalism. But they themselves constituted a new 'fraternal' patriarchalism: 'Patriarchalism has two dimensions: the paternal (father/son) and the masculine (husband/wife)' (Pateman, 1989, p. 37). The 'fraternal social contract' is patriarchal in so far as it begins a taken-for-granted division of the social order into public and private, which is constitutive of politics. Civil society is conceived (!) from a contract between private spheres, where wife and family, love and strong feeling are ruled over by men or husbands. It is governed by rational calculations of interest, and populated by ostensibly genderless 'individuals', whose character we have to call non-, or even anti-feminine. However, no state can rest on reason alone. Hence, the creation of a 'brotherhood' between citizens, which is not merely a linguistic aberration, compromising the universalism implicit in ideas of human and civil rights. Rather, it is the indispensable emotional foundation for economic and political reasoning and the natural complement to the militaristic drive. Moreover, it has ensured the exclusion of women from citizenship.

For philosophers from Kant to Rawls,[44] universalism can be grounded not only in reason, but also in the reality of history as it has been experienced over recent centuries. Since ideas of a critical public are founded on universalism, they therefore conceal an inherited power relationship.

> The social contract is a modern patriarchal pact that establishes men's sex right over women, and the civil individual has been constructed in opposition to women and all that [women's] bodies symbolize...
>
> *(Ibid., p. 52)*

If open access to political activity and to employment is not to demand of women that they voluntarily relinquish their femininity once and for all, it will be necessary to delineate theoretically a completely new set of gender-specific human and civic rights. Likewise, it will be necessary to rethink entirely the relationship between the public sphere and the private.

---

[44] John Rawls: American political philosopher, whose *Theory of Justice* (1971) derived comprehensive principles of social justice from reasoning claimed to be appropriate to rational human beings in the 'original position'; that is, rational thinking as it might be pursued in the absence of social relations. (NP)

Habermas revisited

We should round off this discussion of explicit and implicit debates over Habermas's 'structural transformation' of the public with his own current view. In the preface to the eighteenth edition (1990) of his 1962 classic, Habermas has presented a self-critique, which takes account of numerous views from various countries, and which is impressive in its power of synthesis. Habermas feels that the historical elements of his exposition have been substantially confirmed. Likewise, his revisions to the systematic elements owe very little to his critics.[45] But he has accepted the distinctiveness of the plebeian public, and the claim that the liberal model systematically suppressed women. He considers both to be justifiable objections against idealizing the bourgeois public: the 'tensions that are erupting have to be recognized more clearly as a source of potential self-transformation' (Habermas, 1990, p. 21). In the meantime, Habermas considers his thesis of a steady development 'from culture-debating to culture-consuming public' too extreme. He had underestimated, he says, 'the potential for resistance and...critical capacity of...a highly differentiated mass public'.

However, Habermas distances himself from his earlier central claim that the internal public of democratized parties and associations could become the focus of a regenerated critical public. Only a further development of his overall theory, Habermas believes, has answered the fundamental problem of how a general interest serving as a standard for public opinion could emerge from the plurality of interests and antagonisms found in bourgeois democracies. The liberal model of the public lost its exclusive normative significance in history once the theory of communicative action had discovered a 'self-conscious potential for rationality inherent in everyday communicative action' (ibid., p. 34), and allowed it to take its proper place in democratic political practice.[46]

However, Habermas himself considerably reduced the scope for this rationality when he turned away from the Hegelian–Marxian 'concept of society as a self-organizing totality', and re-admitted a dichotomy between the social system and lived experience, or the life-world.

> I now consider the economy and the state apparatus as systemically integrated areas of activity, which could no longer be changed democratically from the inside...without their identity for the system being damaged and their capacity to function disrupted.

[45]   Though the distinction he acknowledges between system and life-world, which was always central to his 'theory of communicative action', could be regarded as a concession to Systems Theory.

[46]   Habermas is referring to his own, seminal theory, which contends that ordinary language-users develop a common understanding of and adherence to criteria for evaluating communication made by themselves and by others: namely, norms of truth, truthfulness, intelligibility and correctness. It is these norms, rather than any particular social experience (such as that of the bourgeoisie), which ensure rational cooperation between social actors. See Habermas (1981/1984). (NP)

> Colonization of the life-world[47] by an encroaching capitalist economy
> and a bureaucratic power system has to be countered by the demands on
> behalf of the life-world that are generated through solidarity amongst
> competent communicators.
>
> *(ibid., pp. 35ff).*

Habermas takes it for granted that social conflict and antagonism between interests can be considered rationally, and resolved. The ethics of discourse that he and a fellow theorist, Karl-Otto Apel, have developed set out the essential pre-conditions for such rational debate. For him, therefore, it is plausible to believe that the 'political public' will revive and progress to become the 'basic concept of normative democratic theory' (ibid., p. 38). Theory ought to advocate that procedures which are grounded in the ethics of discourse should be incorporated into the institutions of the democratic state under the rule of Law. These procedures would develop a 'cooperative search for truth', where public opinion, solving problems and nurturing its own values, would promote informed debate and the growth of a common purpose. Thus a form of popular sovereignty that has been articulated procedurally can be realized within the framework of the democratic state under the rule of Law. The public and its common purpose develop through evolving opinion and unconstrained debate.

Habermas's attempted revisions show a logical continuity over the course of his philosophical work. Their political and philosophical foundations are impressively supported by other components of his thought not discussed here.[48] I do not wish to deny that an informed, committed, critical public is indispensable in terms of democratic theory. Nor do I find misplaced the programme to render political power more legitimate, and subject it to the constraints of rational discussion procedures. But I should like to conclude this essay with some critical comments. Their declaratory tone is due to lack of space; perhaps their inclusion will prompt readers to further, independent inquiry.

Habermas seems to outflank the radical critique (in particular, the feminist critique) that something is suppressed within the liberal model of the public, and to re-assert the public's 'potential for self-transformation'. He does this by adopting and re-interpreting ideas found in Negt, Kluge and Pateman. Yet universalism and individualism grounded on rational law, to which Habermas also subscribes, remain vulnerable to a fundamental criticism: they have to be paid for by excising the feminine element from our concept of the human species. Pateman's diagnosis cannot be circumvented by an updated theory of democracy. Individuality fails us because, at bottom, it is 'not a unitary abstraction but an embodied and sexually differentiated expression of the unity of humankind' (Pateman, 1986, p. 9).

---

[47]   That is, developments through which the requirements of other social subsystems intrude into lived values, especially those acquired in communicative action. See Habermas (1981/1984). (NP)

[48]   Examples are his theory of consensus as 'rationally motivated agreement' formed in the 'ideal speech situation'; his justification of discursive norms through 'universal pragmatics'; and his account of the ethical-social development.

The limitations that Habermas thus imposes on his own theory are apparent in the way that democracy becomes merely a 'sort of security fence between the system and the life-world' (Dubiel, 1988, p. 117). It is all the more surprising for Habermas to argue that the economic and political systems cannot be further democratized 'without their role in the system being damaged and their capacity to function disrupted'! Habermas's theory of democracy is ostensibly motivated by an interest in social and political emancipation and the wish to see world-wide injustice, hunger and dependency reduced. How, then, is it possible that it should select as its highest values the capitalist economies' capacity to function efficiently (see Habermas, 1990, p. 27) and the 'system identity' of state bureaucracies?

Similarly questionable is the emphasis on truth in the formation of public opinion as Habermas has described it. There are good philosophical and historical reasons to argue that public discussion and opinion formation do *not* result in any widely shared truths. They have instead to foster such procedures and agreements as allow people and groups to live together without hostility, *in spite of* a plurality of truth claims and heterogeneous notions of truth. The problems of a democratic theory based on the ethics of discourse are further compounded if simple-majority decisions (which, on the face of it, would constitute democracy of this kind) are granted the high status implicit in the philosophical concept of practical truth. For it would then only be possible to establish consensus, and also the criterion of truth, empirically; that is, on a basis that could be revoked from one moment to the next. Conversely, in the reality of political life, it is likely that this reified 'truth' would reinforce even the flimsiest of pluralisms: by rejecting, as 'undemocratic' and 'out-of-place', any well-thought-out position which happened to transcend the given ethics of discourse, break with established procedures for discussion, or undermine the advantages of the existing consensus.

Finally, given Habermas's roots in Marxist materialism, it is strange that the analysis of so subtle and well-informed a thinker is hardly at all geared to the technological dimension or to the development of relevant forces of production. Indeed, the philosophical problems raised by the changing technological relationship between the public and the media remain unexamined. Yet, are we not threatened with apathy and passivity merely by the technical power of the media's high-technology structures – regardless of increasing transmission speeds and the pressures of ceaselessly up-dated news – which block our attempts to acquire an understanding that would be capable of putting forward political demands founded on morally responsible grounds? Should not the question of the technical restructuring of the existing and future media be a matter of primary concern to any up-to-date critical theory of the public and of public opinion?

References

Fundamental studies

HABERMAS, J. (1990 18th edn; 1st edn 1962) *Strukturwandel der Öffentlichkeit. Untersuchungen zu einer Kategorie der bürgerlichen Gesellschaft*, Frankfurt, Suhrkamp Verlag. Jürgen Habermas (1989a): *The Structural Transformation of the Public Sphere: an inquiry into a category of bourgeois society*; translated by Thomas Burger, Polity Press, Cambridge.

HÖLSCHER, L. (1979) *Öffentlichkeit und Geheimnis. Eine begriffsgeschichtliche Untersuchung zur Entstehung der Öffentlichkeit in der frühen Neuzeit*, Stuttgart.

HÖLSCHER, L. (1980) 'Meinung, öffentliche' in RITTER, J. and GRÜNDER, K. (eds) *Historisches Wörterbuch der Philosophie*, vol. 5, Basel/Stuttgart, pp. 1023–33.

Other studies

ALMOND, G. A. (1988) 'The intellectual history of the civic culture concept' in CANTORI, L. J. and ZIEGLER, A. H. (eds) *Comparative Politics in the Post-Behavioral Era*, Boulder, Colorado/ London, pp. 162–89.

ADORNO (1961/62) 'Meinung, Wahn, Gesellschaft' in: *Monat*, **14** (159).

BAERNS, B. (1985) *Öffentlichkeitsarbeit oder Journalismus? Zum Einfluss im Mediensystem*, Cologne.

BAIER, H., KEPLINGER, H. M. and REUMANN, K. (eds) (1981) *Öffentliche Meinung und sozialer Wandel. Public Opinion and Social Change. Für Elisabeth Noelle-Neumann*, Opladen.

BAUER, W. (1914) *Die öffentliche Meinung und ihre geschichtlichen Grundlagen*, Tübingen.

BAUER, W. (1930) *Die öffentliche Meinung in der Weltgeschichte*, Wildpark bei Potsdam.

BERELSON, B. and JANOWITZ, M. (eds) (1966; 2nd edn) *Public Opinion and Communication*, New York.

CAYROL, R. (1991) *Les médias (presse écrite, radio, télévision)*, Paris.

CROTTY, W. J. (ed.) (1970) *Public Opinion and Politics: a reader*, New York.

DAVISON, W. P. (1985) 'Public Opinion', in *The New Encyclopaedia Britannica*, vol. 26, 16th edn, pp. 352–58.

DOOB, L. W. (1948) *Public Opinion and Propaganda*, New York.

DOSSIER (1991) *Dossier: Médias, sociétés et démocratie*, Le Monde Diplomatique, May 1991, pp. 21–28.

DUBIEL, H. (1988) *Kritische Theorie der Gesellschaft*, Weinheim/Munich.

FLAD, R. (1929) *Der Begriff der öffentlichen Meinung bei Stein, Arndt, Humboldt: Studien zur politischen Begriffsbildung in Deutschland während der preussischen Reform*, Berlin, Leipzig.

FOWLER, J. and FLOYD JNR, J. (1984) *Survey Research Methods*, Beverly Hills, London, New Delhi.

FRIEDRICHS, J. (1985; 13th edn) *Methoden empirischer Sozialforschung*, Wiesbaden.

FUNKKOLLEG (1990/91) *Medien und Kommunikation. Konstruktionen von Wirklichkeit*, Deutsches Institut für Fernstudien/Universität Tübingen, Weinheim/Basel.

GAYER, K. (1969) *Kritik der bürgerlichen Sozialwissenschaften*, in *Das Argument*. No. 50, Berlin.

GERHARDS, J. and NEIDHARDT, F. (1990) *Strukturen und Funktionen moderner Öffentlichkeit, Fragestellungen und Ansätze*, Berlin. (MS)

GRISET, P. (1991) *Les révolutions de la communication: XIXe–XXe siècle*, Paris.

GUIZOT, F. P. G. (1852) *History of the Origin of Representative Government in Europe*, trans. A. R. Scobie, London.

HABERMAS, J. (1981/1984) *Theorie des Kommunikativen Handelns*, 2 vols. Frankfurt. Jürgen Habermas *The Theory of Communicative Action*, trans. by Thomas McCarthy, Heinemann, London.

HABERMAS, J. (1989b) 'Ist der Herzschlag der Revolution zum Stillstand gekommen? Volkssouveränität als Verfahren. Ein normativer Begriff der Öffentlichkeit?' in *Die Ideen von 1789 in der deutschen Rezeption*, Forum für Philosophie Bad Homburg, Frankfurt, pp. 7–36.

HEGEL, G. W. F. (1821) *Grundlinien der Philosophie des Rechts;* trans. KNOX, T. M. (1942) *Hegel's Philosophy of Right,* Oxford, Clarendon Press.

HEIDEGGER, M. (1927) *Sein und Zeit*, Halle; trans. MACQUARRIE, J. and ROBINSON, E. (1980) *Being and Time*, Oxford, Blackwell.

HEINRICH, P. (1969) 'Meinung, öffentliche', in EICHHORN, W. (ed.) (2nd edn) *Wörterbuch der marxistisch-leninistischen Soziologie*, Opladen, pp. 424ff.

HENNIS, W. (1957) *Meinungsforschung und repräsentative Demokratie. Zur Kritik politischer Umfragen*, Tübingen (issue 200/201 of *Recht und Staat in Geschichte und Gegenwart*).

HOINVILLE, G. *et al.* (1988) *Survey Research Practice,* London.

HÖLSCHER, L. (1978) 'Öffentlichkeit', in BRUNNER, von O. *et al.* (eds) *Geschichtliche Grundbegriffe. Historisches Lexikon zur politisch-sozialen Sprache in Deutschland*, vol. 4, Stuttgart, pp. 413–67.

HÖLSCHER, L. (1984) 'Öffentlichkeit', in RITTER, VON J. and GRÜNDER, K. (eds) *Historisches Wörterbuch der Philosophie*, Vol. 6, Basel, Stuttgart, pp. 1134–40.

KAASE, M. and SCHULZ, W. (eds) (1989) *Massenkommunikation. Theorien, Methoden, Befunde*, Opladen.

KARMASIN, F. and KARMASIN, H. (1977) *Einführung in Methoden und Probleme der Umfrageforschung*, Vienna/Cologne/Graz.

KISSLER, L. (1984) 'Produktionsöffentlichkeit als Lernstrategie. Die Bedeutung des Partizipationslernens für die Organizationsöffentlichkeit der Arbeit', in KOUBEK, N and SCHREDEL-SEKER, K. (eds) *Information, Mitbestimmung und Unternehmenspolitik*, Frankfurt.

KISSLER, L. (1989) 'Zwischen "Refeudalisierung" und neuer Produktions öffentlichkeit. Entwicklungstendenzen im System der industriellen Beziehungen', in KLEINFEL, R. and LUTHHARDT, W. (eds) *Westliche Demokratien und Interessenvermittlung*. Beiträge zur aktuellen Entwicklung nationaler Parteien – und Verbändesysteme. Course No. 3223 der FernUniversität Hagen, pp. 58–76.

KOSELLECK, R. (1973) *Kritik und Krise. Eine Studie zur Pathogenese der bürgerlichen Welt*, Frankfurt. Reinhard Koselleck (1988) *Critique and Crisis: enlightenment and the pathogenesis of modern society*, Oxford, Berg.

KROMREY, H. (1986; 3rd edn) *Empirische Sozialforschung. Modelle und Methoden der Datenerhebung und Datenauswertung*, Leverkusen.

LANG, E. and LANG, K. (1983) *The Battle for Public Opinion: the president, the press, and the polls during Watergate*, New York.

LANGENBUCHER, W. R. (ed.) (1986) *Politische Kommunikation. Grundlagen, Strukturen, Prozesse*, Wien.

LAZARSFELD, P. F., BEREISON, B. and GAUDET, H. (1944) *The People's Choice*, Chicago.

LIPPMANN, W. (1965) *Public Opinion*, New York.

LOWERY, S. and DE FLEUR, M. L. (1988; 2nd ed.) *Milestones in Mass Communication Research: media effects*, New York.

LUHMANN, N. (1975; 2nd ed.) *Politische Planung. Aufsätze zur Soziologie von Politik und Verwaltung*, Opladen.

MACBRIDE, S. (1981) *Viele Stimmen – eine Welt. Kommunikation und Gesellschaft – heute und morgen. Bericht der internationalen Kommission zum Studium der Kommunikationsprobleme unter dem Vorsitz von S. MacBride an die Unesco*, Konstanz. MACBRIDE, S., ABEL, E. *et al.* (1984; abridged ed.) International Commission for the Study of Communication Problems: *Many Voices, One World: communication and society, today and tomorrow*, Paris.

MARTENS (1969) *Öffentlichkeit als Rechtsbegriff*, Bad Homberg.

MERTEN, K. (1990; 2nd ed.) *Inhaltsanalyse. Einführung in Theorie, Methode und Praxis*, Opladen.

MERTEN, K. and TEIPEN, P. (1991a) *Empirische Kommunikationsforschung. Darstellung, Kritik und Evolution*, München.

MERTEN, K. (1991b) *Allmacht oder Ohnmacht der Medizin? Erklärungsmuster der Medienwirkungsforschung*, in *Funkkolleg* 1990/91, Studienbrief, 9, pp. 38–73.

MEYN, H. (1988) 'Massenmedien: politische Funktionen und Bedeutung für die Demokratie' in Bundeszentrale für politische Bildung (ed.) *Grundlagen unserer Demokratie*, Bonn, pp. 293–343.

MISCHKE, R. (1958) *Die Entstehung der öffentlichen Meinung im 18 Jahrhundert* (doctoral dissertation), Hamburg.

NEGT, O. and KLUGE, A. (1972) *Öffentlichkeit und Erfahrung. Zur Organizationsanalyse von bürgerlicher und proletarischer Öffentlichkeit*, Frankfurt.

NOELLE-NEUMANN, E. (1982) *Die Schweigespirale. Öffentliche Meinung – unsere soziale Haut*, Frankfurt/Berlin.

OTTO, U. (1966) 'Die Problematik des Begriffs der öffentlichen Meinung', in *Publizistik*, **11**, pp. 99–130.

PATEMAN, C. and GROSS, E. (eds) (1986) *Feminist Challenges: social and political theory*, Sydney/London/Boston.

PATEMAN, C. (1988) *The Sexual Contract*, Cambridge.

PATEMAN, C. (1989) *The Disorder of Women: democracy, feminism and political theory*, Cambridge.

PREUSS, U. K. (1969) *Zum staatsrechtlichen Begriff des Öffentlichen*, Stuttgart.

PROKOP, D. (ed.) (1985/1986) *Medienforschung*, 3 vols., Frankfurt.

REIMANN, H. (1971) 'Öffentliche Meinung', in *Sowjetsystem und demokratische Gesellschaft*, **IV**, pp. 808–28.

RÜCKMANN, K. (1969) 'Meinungsforschung' in EICHHORN, V. W. (ed.) *Wörterbuch der marxistisch-leninistischen Soziologie*, **2**, Opladen, pp. 425ff.

SCHENK, M. (1987a) *Medienwirkungsforschung*, Tübingen.

SCHENK, M. (1987b) *Medienwirkungen. Kommentierte Auswahlbibliographie der anglo-amerikanischen Forschung,* Tübingen.

SCHMIDTCHEN, G. (1959) *Die befragte Nation. Über den Einfluss der Meinungsforschung auf die Politik*, Freiburg im Breisgau.

SCHMITT, C. (1923) *Die geistesgeschichtliche Lage des heutigen Parliamentarismus*, Berlin.

SCHRAMM, W. and ROBERTS, D. F. (1972) *The Process and Effects of Mass Communication*, Urbana/Chicago/London.

SCHULZ, W. (1988) *Massenkommunikation in den internationalen Beziehungen. Einführung aus dem Licht verschiedener Wissenschaften*, Deutsches Institut für Fernstudien an der Universität Tübingen, Tübingen, pp. 139–55.

SCHULZ, W. and SCHÖNBACH, K. (eds) (1983) *Massenmedien und Wahlen*, Munich.

SEIDEL, H. (1961) *Vom Mythos der öffentlichen Meinung*, Aschaffenburg.

SENNETT, R. (1977) *The Fall of Public Man*, New York.

SMEND, R. (1954) *Zum Problem des Öffentlichen und der Öffentlichkeit. Festschrift für G. Jellinek*, Munich.

SPEIER, H. (1950) *Historical Development of Public Opinion*, London.

STAAB, J. F. (1990) *Nachrichtenwert-Theorie,* Freiburg/Munich.

STAMM, K-H. (1988) *Alternative Öffentlichkeit. Die Erfahrungsproduktion neuer sozialer Bewegungen*, Frankfurt/New York.

TARDE, G. (1901) *L'Opinion et la foule*, Paris.

TÖNNIES, F. (1922; 1981 edn) *Kritik der öffentlichen Meinung*, Aalen.

TÖNNIES, F. (1963 8th edn) *Gemeinschaft und Gesellschaft. Grundbegriffe der reinen Soziologie*, Darmstadt (1st ed. 1935); Ferdinand Tönnies (1957), *Community and Society*, trans. and ed. by Charles P. Loomis, Michigan State University Press, East Lansing 1957.

Essay 6
Democracy as a critique of politics

Prepared for the Course Team by Gérard Duprat
Professor of political science at the Université
Robert Schuman de Strasbourg
Translated from the French by John Williams and
Noël Parker

Introduction

In this essay we shall analyse the critical dimension which is a distinctive feature of democratic practice in political institutions. The argument of the essay takes the following form:

(i)   We shall begin with some general considerations of method, examining (a) the notion of critique as a practice applied to political institutions and (b) the notion of ideology.

(ii) The second section of the essay goes on to establish two rules governing democratic practice in political institutions: 'the rule of democratic diversity' and 'the rule of democratic uncertainty'.

(iii) The third section explains why *pursuing aspirations, making demands,* or *posing requirements*[1] (rather than merely applying functional criteria to a system) can be said to be the distinguishing feature of democracy.

---

[1]   A key distinction underlying this essay is the difference between two ways of evaluating an institution – notably, of course, democracy. It is the difference between applying to it a measure that is internal – and hence a given – or one that is external – and hence not confined to the given reality. This distinction is hard to reproduce in English. The author refers to the former as *critères* (criteria), and to the latter by the more ambiguous expression *exigences*. There is no exact English equivalent for the term *exigences*, which includes three separate elements: 'demands' calling for something to be available; 'requirements' specifying what that something should be; and 'aspirations', the demanders' hopeful image of what might be obtained. Unless the immediate context renders it impossible, we have used 'aspirations' to refer to the second way of evaluating an institution, in which it is measured not against its given character, but against what it might become. (NP)

Sections (ii) and (iii) together work towards two specific aspirations of democracy, which are discussed in

(iv) The final section of the essay, which will offer an analysis of two specific aspirations: the critique of reason of state[2] and the critique of government.

This essay is closely connected with Alain-Marc Rieu's essay in this book. The existence and practice in a democratic society of a critical dimension (or 'critique') of its institutions brings into play a whole set of issues concerning the relationship between politics, democracy and knowledge. Here we pick up the main theme of Rieu's essay, which deals mainly with epistemological questions: questions of knowledge, its character, its form, its evolution and its internal dynamics. There is an equally close connection with Pierre Cot and Richard Corbett's essay, which gives an account of the 'democratic deficit' in the institutions of the European Community, and shows that the deficit in the political construction of Europe can be traced back to analogous deficiencies in the individual democracies contributing to European politics.

Through its choice of subject and its method, this essay will also address problems about the relationship between Europe and democracy. There is a need to identify the absolute, unquestionable value, from democracy's point of view, at work within each of the institutional configurations through which the European states have characteristically pursued democratization.

In analysing the critical dimension, this essay will aim to identify it as *that practice in political institutions which expresses the unique nature of democracy*. Through focusing narrowly on particular examples of democratization it is easy to view the critical dimension in an over-restricted way. The practice of critique is even ignored entirely by those doctrines that glibly present democracy as an entirely orderly, reasonable form of politics. In contrast, those who are opposed to democratic politics see this critical practice as the major justification for their conclusion that democracy may be fine in theory, but impossible in practice. Hence the need to begin this essay with a few brief statements of principle about how to tackle the notion of critique in a political context. The unique nature of democracy will start to become apparent because the issue between these opposed views is not merely a methodological one, about how to analyse politics. It is an issue that concerns the processes for acquiring knowledge and applying reason, a matter of principle.

Ideology and the practices of institutions

Because of the subject of this book, I will consider only those institutions which can be described as 'political' in the strict sense of the word: those institutions that

---

[2]   That is, the critique of the logic of the state's thinking when it acts in its own interests and for its own survival. Since the modern state is, formally speaking, sovereign, it does not readily admit any considerations other than its own 'reason of state' into its decisions and actions. Hence, the sense of hard-headed, amoral, or even brutal thinking which the expression has acquired in ordinary usage. To pursue a critique of reason of state is therefore to challenge the primacy of the state's interests and morality. (NP)

are provided for by the fundamental laws that determine the constitution of the body politic, or the state. Considered together, they can be seen to be arranged in a certain 'configuration'. I shall devote particular attention to the most important of the fundamental institutions within this configuration, considering them not merely for their own sake, as in a jurisprudential approach to politics, but from the point of view of their relation to democracy. The state, the government, and their subsidiary 'authorities' are major institutions by virtue of the primary constitutive role they play in these configurations, and the complexity of the functions devolved to them in practice.

This approach to political institutions is restrictive and excludes a number of institutions and organizations (e.g. the press, the media, and those mechanisms that sustain social accord[3]) that contribute to the particular character of public life in modern European states but are peripheral to the institutions at the core of the configuration.[4] The core institutions are strictly limited by the overall configuration in which they exist. The 'judicial power' of the state illustrates the relationship between core institutions: although, in the majority of European states, this 'power' is generally the subject of numerous, highly specific and powerfully symbolic provisions, it is in reality overlaid by a whole host of administrative, social or private institutions and organizations which implement justice in wider society.

The benefit of this narrow approach is that it makes us undertake a rigorous examination of the issues raised by the distinction between the political and the non-political in modern democratic states.[5] Only by adopting this restricted approach can we undertake an analysis of the relationship between democracy and political institutions.

The purpose of models of democracy

It is not easy to conceive a practical way of constructing institutional models of democracy within a purely sociological framework. Nonetheless, this is the classic objective of any jurisprudential approach claiming to be both 'pure' and

---

[3]   This would include social welfare agencies, health and education services, and other informal bodies that exist to take on the views of interest groups and pressure groups. (NP)

[4]   Though the latter in fact fulfill only a small part of the function for society that is their primary role: namely, to confirm, through processes of political symbolism, their own special character as the locus of state sovereignty.

[5]   It is worth noting at this early stage that, by adopting the confused and facile view which sees these states as 'complex social systems', others avoid such an examination. Once that method is applied, 'democracy' embraces indifferently both the product and the hallmark of the system. The question is no longer posed as to whether there is a democratic deficit, in a separate specific sense of 'democracy', in the organization and activity of the political institutions. The critical dimension of the practices of institutions is even more surely lost from view.

'applied'.[6] Kelsenism, with its juridical theory of the democratic state, is a highly instructive example.[7] But Kelsen was to a large extent anticipated, in an epistemological context where the distinctions between the social and human sciences were less clearly defined than nowadays, by the many modern theorists of the state under the rule of Law (or justice) who followed Grotius and Hobbes.

All activists, politicians, thinkers and writers seeking to steer public life in a democratic direction or seeking to shape public opinion should make the intellectual effort to reflect on institutions, taking account of how they operate in practice. Analyses of the conduct of public life in democratic states and opposition to non-democratic processes needs to be underpinned by reflections on public life that take account of the configurations of institutions and the constraints that democracy imposes on institutional practices. To formulate the intrinsic conditions for a just political discourse between *reasonable* individuals, with no social or institutional setting, is not sufficient. For any such discourse unfolds within the framework of public (or 'civic') life, which has its own rules and institutions. In a democracy, the way that dialogues are conducted depends on how the relationship between rules, institutions and practices is understood.

Political theory

Political theory and political philosophy[8] exist to deal with such questions. Rather than constructing institutional *models* of democracy, political theory has always been concerned with *forms of institutional configuration*. In so doing it has posed the question of whether democracy is a unique form of configuration, and investigated the particular relationship between democracy and political institutions.

There are two common approaches to these questions within political theory:

(i)   The first considers them from the point of view of a general theory of the major forms of institutional configuration. Such a theory is grounded in a 'first philosophy', which is in turn founded on the combination of a critique of knowledge (or 'epistemology'), a version of physics and an anthropology. A political theory in this sense provides the principles to examine, and make judgements on, the practices of specific configurations and the kind of public life they produce.

---

[6]   By 'pure' we mean that its methods are irreducible to those of any other science than that designed for matters of political 'right'. In the more specific language of jurisprudence, 'applied' is termed 'positive'.

[7]   See Kelsen (1920) *Vom Wesen und Wert der Demokratie*. For the state under the rule of Law, see F. D'Agostino's discussion of Kelsen in Essay 4 and the bibliographies of his and A.M. Rieu's essays, plus that in Barret-Kriegel (1989).

[8]   The recent practice of distinguishing between the two disciplines, introduced notably by Hannah Arendt, hardly matters here. See Leca (1985), vol. 1, ch. 2, and also Adelbert (1976), pp. 9–34.

Hobbes' *Leviathan* and Rousseau's *The Social Contract* are famous examples of this approach.[9]

(ii)   The alternative approach is to examine various forms of configuration in the light of some requirement placed upon political practice. A particular configuration is then evaluated in terms of whether it enables public life to fulfil that requirement. This is how Kant and Rawls proceeded when they identified, respectively, the requirements for *perpetual peace* and for *justice*.[10]

These two approaches differ from the modern, experimental form of a pure scientific approach in that they do not counterpose knowledge of practice with the development of theories. In addressing reality, practice and theory each refer back to the other, and the benefit of inquiry lies in thinking through the differences between them. The function of political theory (or philosophy) is not to say baldly what the body politic should be. Its function is to take stock of what really exists in the political domain: configurations of institutions and their concrete effects; Law and its implementation; theory as well as practice; the distinctions as well as the connections between all of these elements. Whatever strategy political theory adopts in order to state 'what really exists in the political domain', it distances itself both from empirical science and from mere trial and error. This is the result of its determination to mirror, in terms of its own practice as a theory, the actual relationship between the theory and the practice of politics.

Historical beginnings

Democracy's historical starting-point is the ancient Greek experience of the *polis* (city). Whenever modern Europe has asked questions about its own political and cultural identity – that is, about its own relationship to democracy – it has found a rich source of new meanings in the Greek experience. Long before the Copernican revolution, Greek thought diversified the ways of acquiring knowledge. It also thought through that differentiation, in a version of the discipline we now call 'epistemology'. Essay 1 showed how the diversification of forms of knowledge

[9]   Thus, for example, Hobbes (also considered in D'Agostino's discussion of the political meaning of sovereignty) might be said to argue along the following lines. Having established the proper terms for his inquiry (a critique of knowledge) and demonstrated that human nature was material (an anthropology and a physics), he can argue for a configuration of institutions in which power is concentrated in the sovereign. That is the necessary and sufficient basis for legitimacy in a body politic. Given Hobbes' theory, where the power of the sovereign individual/assembly is persistently challenged, the body politic can be judged according to criteria ultimately traceable to the anthropology, the account of configurations, etc. Likewise, Rousseau (also discussed in Rieu's section on the problem of sovereignty) worked from the nature of humans to a view of sovereignty as necessarily the property of the people as a whole. (NP)

[10]   In his 'Zum ewigen Frieden. Ein philosophischer Entwurf' of 1796 ('Perpetual peace, a philosophical sketch'; Kant, 1971, pp. 93–130), Kant postulates an absolute value for cosmopolitan accord amongst the human race as a whole, and advances its necessary constitutional and international conditions. John Rawls has developed the conception of justice as a principle to be realized in the body politic. (NP)

and epistemological reflections upon it were linked to the diversification of forms of government and the transformation of the city into a democracy.[11]

The idea of differentiating between bodies of knowledge (or ways, or routes to knowledge) was thus introduced into culture. So fundamental was it, that in Europe and other cultures drawing on the Greek tradition it became *part of the very notion of culture*. From that time, successive definitions of the relationships between the forms of knowledge (or 'epistemological configurations') have governed the various ways of acquiring knowledge, their mutual independence, and the competition between them. This has brought the differentiation of forms of knowledge to the level it is at today.[12]

An understanding of how changes in epistemological configurations determine changes in the forms of politics (and vice versa) is only possible against the background of these sharpening divergences. Against this background, too, we can consider the complexity of the relationship between epistemological configurations and institutional configurations. The most remarkable illustration of this approach is Leo Strauss's and Alexandre Kojève's celebrated attempt to comprehend contemporary forms of tyranny and the role these forms of tyranny assign to ideology on the basis of a reading of Xenophon's *Hiero*, by way of Machiavelli and the contemporary 'crisis' of political science.[13] Epistemological reflection on these divergences, therefore, constitutes an instrument through which the complexity of the relationship between politics and knowledge is perceived, even as it breaks down. In the final analysis, the true method of political thought is the rational usage of this instrument.[14]

Ideology

From this point of view, *ideology* is not a false or deceitful discourse that presents a doctrine. Nor is it a form of knowledge or inquiry. Rather, it is a *practice of domination* founded on obscuring the conditions of any discourse on methods. It therefore admits of a 'response' only on the level of practice. Marx drew attention to the fact that, in modern states under the rule of Law, the main pillar of ideology

---

[11]   In his section on 'An anthropological approach to science and politics', Alain-Marc Rieu discusses how the Greeks developed new forms of cosmology and science, while, in parallel, defining the topics of common public concern and the disciplines of debating them (the *logos*). (NP)

[12]   In which the divergences characterizing and shaping contemporary thought are so marked as to constitute a crisis, begun in the critical thinking of the Enlightenment (see Koselleck, 1959).

[13]   Strauss and Kojève (1954). Strauss's contribution to the debate, in its English version, 'Restatement of Xenophon's *Hiero*' appears in Strauss (1959). Xenophon (435–354 BC) was an Athenian nobleman, military commander and writer, and at one time a follower of Socrates. (NP)

[14]   See Duprat (1990).

is the political apparatus, and its main expression the discourse of the law. Marx demonstrated even more convincingly that a successful critique of ideology requires an analysis of how the ideology is rooted in the historical conditions that produced it. Such an analysis must focus in particular on the conditions generating the resources employed to extend knowledge.[15]

Political science, I suggest, should adopt this axiom: generally speaking, ideology is the distinctive feature of any discourse which, by appeal to its own authority, *conceals the way it produces and imposes 'truth' on democracy from the implications of the diversity of ways to acquire knowledge.*

Two derived rules

In the light of this axiom, and the various forms of this differentiation which have been familiar to us since the democratic *polis* and science have been part of our culture, a convincing case can be made for the first of the following rules.

Rule 1: Diversity

No society can be said to allow any kind of public life unless this rule, even though it is conditional, is obeyed. It is not enough for a society (whatever its motivation) simply to permit consideration of the political sphere by the various forms of knowledge, which hence contribute to the formation of public opinion. Nor is it enough for a society to lay down clear-cut provisions to ensure mutual competition between these forms of knowledge. It is more important that *the configuration of institutions* in a society should itself bring home to public opinion the need to protect these diverse routes to knowledge as a whole, in the face of any activity which would deny in theory, or suppress in practice, the irreducible differentiation between them. Without this diversity, no cultural life, private or public, is possible. Let us call this the 'rule of democratic diversity'. Vaclav Havel's admirable 'Letter to Gustav Husak', written during Czechoslovakia's 'normalization' in 1968, pursues this argument through to its logical conclusion.[16] This rule identifies one of the essential characteristics of democracy, without which it ceases to exist.

---

[15]   As Althusser clearly showed in his essay 'Ideology and ideological state apparatuses' (Althusser, 1971). See also both text and bibliography in Châtelet and Pisier-Kouchner (1985). Neither Marx's own critique of epistemology (which shaped his denunciation of ideology), nor its historical conditions, are of interest to us here. I merely contend that the half-century of European political history since 1945, which has been characterized by the gradual triumph of the 'democratic' discourse in states which qualify as 'states under the rule of Law', does not mean that ideological domination should be considered a thing of the past, despite the frequent predictions of the 'end of ideology' since the publication of Bell (1965). Nor should we expect to find ideology solely in the discourse of that whole host of formerly irreconcilable opponents of democracy who are now doubtful converts to it (the extreme right in Europe, for example). It is the nature and form of domination which leaders are sometimes able to exert over large sections of public opinion that matters, rather than their use of democratic discourse, honest or otherwise.

[16]   Published in Havel (1987 and 1989).

Vaclav Havel in the early 1970s (credit: Popperfoto/CNA/Jiri Bednar).

Even today this rule of democracy represents a highly controversial challenge to political theory. From Plato to Kant, and from Hegel to Heidegger,[17] political philosophy has been broadly unfavourable to the configuration required by democracy, mainly on account of the critical attitude towards institutions that democratic politics generates in the public mind. The theoretical legacy shadowed an opposition to democracy which left its mark on many currents of European political thought from the Enlightenment to the end of the nineteenth century. Advocates of Liberalism (including Republican ones) and even revolutionaries, have shared this legacy.

Only a few thinkers have been democratic on philosophical or ethical grounds as well as for reasons of social utility. Protagoras (of the Greek Sophists), Spinoza, the early Marx and Eric Weil[18] amongst modern thinkers are examples. In contrast

[17] See note 54 below. (NP)

[18] German Jewish philosopher (1904–77), who settled in France before World War II and survived imprisonment under the Nazis. His *Philosophie politique* (1956) pursued a reconstruction of the Hegelian ideal of the state, interpreting it as historically specific, but evolving to become the setting where rational individuals may find self-fulfilment in their diversity under a universal justice. (NP)

to other philosophers, these modern democrats took a positive view of the citizens' critical disposition towards political institutions in a democracy. But they also analysed the practices of domination which, by contrast, sustain public opinion in a view of the rational pursuit of knowledge that denies the necessary diversity, and supports a hierarchical (rather than equal) organization of the routes to knowledge. By implying that one form of knowledge or form of enquiry can be pre-eminent over others, such practices abandon the idea of reason to the grip of ideology or to theological authority. These modern democrats also undertook the task of revealing how the institutions of government typical of these practices are modes of domination. Both lines of thought become indispensable as soon as political theory moves away from abstraction and looks for practical applications. It then needs to take account of what actually exists (in terms of ideological domination and political oppression) as well as the underlying nature of politics and democracy, and the relationship between these in real states.

It is sometimes believed that one can side-step the challenge of the rule of democratic diversity by claiming that the kind of democracy to which the theoretical tradition was unfavourable is not the same as that experienced in modern Europe.[19] This argument has to be rejected for two reasons. Firstly, it would not dispose of the verdict of theory or the challenge inherent in democracy. Secondly, this way of juxtaposing the two 'democracies' is spurious. Political theorists are neither historians nor prophets. A theoretical conflict of this kind cannot therefore be dismissed so lightly. Moreover, there is a contradiction in both asserting a radical break with the past and, at the same time, demonstrating (as political debates about 'building the new Europe' usually do) that modern Europe's own democratic experience has deep roots in the so-called 'European' history of philosophical thought originating with the Greeks.

Avoiding this spurious debate, then, and confining ourselves for the moment to recent European history, let us note that the actual development of democracy has reinforced the theoretical challenge to democracy. Admittedly, this theoretical challenge has not been advanced within the states of western Europe, where there has been a near-unanimous conversion to democracy over the last half-century. The democratic experience of these states has nonetheless been thrown into question by the challenges of both events and theory.

Democracy has recently achieved an unforeseen success in the states of Central and eastern Europe. It has triumphed over institutions of government dating either from 1917 or from the period after World War II. These institutions acted on the principle of complying as little as possible with the rule of democratic diversity. Following popular unrest or during brief crises,[20] changes had from time to time been reluctantly introduced, and public life allowed to exist for a short while. But the concessions amounted to a mere semblance, or possibility, of public life.

---

[19] On Greek democracy, see Meier (1988) and also J.B. Euben (1986). I will return to this point several times in the text.

[20] See Dobry (1986).

Democracy is also likely to affect the politics of regions near to Europe. On the southern shore of the Mediterranean the 'democratic virus'[21] is every bit as active as it has been in the eastern bloc. Embryonic or fully formed, such processes of democratization follow varied routes in practice. But when it comes to the ultimate nature of the democratic form of politics they pursue, there is an element of uncertainty which is common to them all, which the political practices of western European states have done little to eliminate.

It is worth examining the reasons for this. Most people nowadays accept the principles of the state under the rule of Law, and the mechanisms and effects of the so-called 'social-market' economy.[22] In both these spheres, then, the states of western Europe provide globally acceptable (and frequently accepted, if not easily transposable) institutional models. Furthermore, the gradual framing of a schedule of political rights by the Council of Europe and the European Court of Human Rights has greatly contributed to clarifying the principles of the state under the rule of Law, and to spreading them to the states of eastern Europe.[23] During the late 1980s, those states wishing to join the Council of Europe so as to loosen their ties with the USSR and become 'European' accepted the obligation of bringing their institutions into line with these juridical principles. That was one of the first stages leading to the collapse of those same institutions.

On the other hand, it is clear that the uncertainty about the nature of democracy is in no way resolved by the example of the western states. This statement may seem surprising. It goes against the grain of the self-glorification of 'European democratic experience' at the time of the collapse of the East. Although it was widely shared in all of the western states (with the possible exception of Italy) this triumphalism is misplaced, and is contradicted by the facts. With this point in mind, we need to rebut a defective argument which follows on directly from the spurious debate which we dismissed earlier.

According to this argument, these recent revolutionary developments in the East drew their constructive inspiration and central ideas from 'western-European democracy', defined in terms of the three major components: the social-market economy; the state under the rule of Law, which provides the framework for managing that economy; and a specifically political complement to the other two components, identified as the proper meaning of the term 'democracy'.

This group of components, which is frequently referred to in debates, has two disturbing theoretical weaknesses. First, it relies on an historical and sociological paradigm devised to account for the type of development experienced by western European societies. This paradigm, however, possesses methodological

---

[21] The term 'virus' was used by the King of Morocco in an interview with *Le Monde diplomatique*, February 1991, during the Gulf War.

[22] That is, the free market economy modified to offset its socially undesirable consequences such as inequality, unemployment, etc. (NP)

[23] On the work of the Strasbourg Human Rights Court, see Delmas-Marty (1990).

difficulties, and met with failure when it was transplanted to other regions during the 1960s.[24] Secondly, to term this group of components 'democracy' is to rely on the rhetorical device of synecdoche, where the name of a part denotes the whole. Consequently, the extra ingredient which makes the system democratic becomes merely a 'spirit' needed as a supplement to the market economy, which is developed only in accordance with the requirements of the latter.[25]

In the doctrinal debate over the democratic character of the construction of Europe, this rhetorical version of democracy ensures complicity between the two main rival political discourses. The first vaunts the complexity of the social system as the rational and unsurpassable product of European history, and concludes that the *market economy*, rather than politics, has been the main unifying influence in these societies up till now. The other discourse prefers to attribute a common *organizational logic* to both the separate societies and the European Community as a whole: this is the logic of 'efficiency' referred to in the Preamble to the Treaty issuing from the Maastricht Agreements.[26] This discourse is content to deplore the logic of efficiency which it imposes on politics. But, in consequence, the only form of politics that can be envisaged for the Community is decided by default, by the complexity of the existing societies. The politics of the Community thus becomes devoid of the autonomy that comes from pursuing one's own purposes.

At each stage of the collapse of states to the East, the statesmen of democratic Europe and the Community (as well as the media) drew heavily on the above grouping of components in their public utterances. The same terminology had already been used (though more sparingly) during the earlier transitions from dictatorship to democracy in Greece, Spain and Portugal, which were then rapidly integrated into the European Community.[27] On the other hand, there was a difference stemming from the actual form of the process of democratization that took place in eastern Europe. In these states, the question of whether democracy was merely a political complement to the social system presented itself more directly and acutely than for the Mediterranean countries emerging from dictatorship. In eastern Europe, the same grouping of terms that makes democracy both the part

---

[24]   Dobry (1990) in Duprat (1990) [The 1960s saw many, ill-starred attempts to define a road to modernization for Third World countries, and the failure of many constitutions bequeathed by colonial powers on granting independence. (NP)]

[25]   Ultra-liberals view it as merely a juridical supplement to the market economy.

[26]   See the introduction to Part III, above.

[27]   See note 24 above. Michel Dobry's study of the sociology of political crises (Dobry, 1986) has shown that the historical and sociological analysis of these processes of democratization requires its own methodology, distinguishing between crises and problems. This distinction applies to the symbolic and material factors which were responsible for the institutional collapses in eastern Europe. I shall not attempt to assess, for these two sets of factors, the relative importance of internal dissolution (the ideological and material implosion of the states themselves) and external influences (relations with the West, etc.).

Boris Yeltsin addressing a crowd from the top of a tank during the attempted coup, 19 August 1991 (credit: Associated Press).

and the whole has been publicly examined within a generalized critical discourse, which is now expanding to embrace the whole of Europe's conception of its own democratic experience.

To what extent is this purely an exercise in political rhetoric? When that same group of terms is used to mark out the frontiers of 'a truly democratic Europe', does it not simply disguise the exercise of power relationships between states, and the protection of existing wealth? Is it not, in short, the traditional reason of state at work? Does European democracy therefore only ever exist in particular situations? Does it only exist when the masses revolt against oppressive governments, when (as in Russia) they stand in the path of a *coup d'état*, or when they 'vote with their feet' and emigrate westward? Or, closer to home, does democracy exist only when mass demonstrations secure the withdrawal of legislation, or the replacement of a prime minister?

Perhaps it would be better to speak of 'democratic situations'? These would be by definition short-lived, and anarchic in the true sense of the term, because not confined within institutions. Although a body politic might be constituted from within a democratic situation, it would take on a political form that would not itself be democracy. Much modern political theory has supported this. Alternatively, should democracy be seen as a *form of politics*? But in that case, what is the relationship between this form and the state, or between this form and the politics of running the state and regulating the economy? In short, we keep coming back to the same question: what is the relationship between the democratic form of politics and political institutions?

Western European states cannot ignore this question, for it harks back to their origins. The process of democratization in many of these countries began so long ago that its early struggles and the subsequent antagonisms have almost disappeared from memory. The chequered history of democratization has been overlaid with myths and rituals, enabling everyone to rally around the idea (or 'system') which now supposedly forms the object of consensus. Public life, rebuilt from the ruins and the horror of Nazi-dominated Europe, has enjoyed half a century of civil peace under the shadow of nuclear deterrence. Now that this supposed consensus and this peace have finally been attained, they can stave off for a while the anxiety prompted by questions raised elsewhere regarding the origins of democracy. European opinion, then, does not willingly recognize its own questionings in those expressed by (to name one example) crowds demonstrating in the countries on the southern shore of the Mediterranean.[28]

On the other hand, the public life of western states is directly confronted with the same issues about its origins, and will continue to be so for a long time to come. The democratization of eastern Europe raises the question and is radically modifying the process of forming institutions in a 'democratic Europe'.[29]

The chief issue is to examine the conditions needed in a democracy for a critique of democracy itself to arise. The challenges of theory and of recent history have each created conditions where, at the level of the state, *the critique of the reason of state* remains the primary democratic practice required of political institutions. Experience confirms that this requirement deserves particular attention.

The rationale for a radical critique of reason of state is found in the very form of democracy itself. It follows from the guiding principles of this form of politics and

[28] Those crowds may occupy a neighbouring region, but their states are still underdeveloped and their economic, financial, cultural and material survival depends very much on Europe. Europeans may not even realize that proclaiming to these crowds 'an international order of states subject to Law and prosperity' undermines the 'democratic virus' they are imbued with. That grouping of terms to define democracy takes on an unbearable air of condescension when, as in 1991, Western weaponry is also having its say.

[29] Denunciations of the democratic deficit in Europe now concern not just the apparatus of the Community, but also that of each state. Pierre Cot and Richard Corbett make the same point in Essay 8. One way forward is to examine this deficit through an internal critique of the various existing institutional mechanisms.

distinguishes it so profoundly that it leads to the most important question of political theory: Rather than simply being one form of government among others,[30] is democracy itself the general form of political life? Public life in democratic states seems at odds with itself when measured against this aspiration. Only under exceptional circumstances, like those mentioned earlier, is public opinion even dimly aware of the need for a critique of reason of state. In accepting reason of state, public opinion acquiesces to a form of argument that ought to be banished from democratic debate. Instead, it appears to validate those practices on the state's part which are justified by this very form of argument.

Public opinion, however, is not so hesitant as regards the *critique of government*. This second aspiration of democracy is fully satisfied: public opinion sees criticizing the actions of the government – in its role as manager of the affairs of the public – as a practice inherent to the democratic state. The practice is so commonplace and widespread that public opinion sometimes turns against itself, judging that its liberty to criticize may degenerate into destructive opposition, or 'licence'. Public opinion has difficulty in setting limits to its criticism of the government as an *agent* for public affairs. Yet it may not realize that a link exists between this uncertainty over limits and the inevitably ambiguous status conferred on government *as a political institution* by democracy – and by democracy alone.

Rule 2: Uncertainty

We have thus reached a point where we are able to derive a second rule of modern democracy, 'The rule of democratic uncertainty'. Like Rule 1, it is not as readily perceivable from a purely juridical or sociological approach. Unlike Rule 1, which concerned the cultural principle of the diversity between routes to knowledge, this second rule is not conditional. It lays down what a properly democratic public life, conducted within institutions affected by that cultural principle, is actually like.

In a democratic state under the rule of Law (or 'republic',[31] to borrow the exact term used by modern political theory from Hobbes to Kant) the configuration of institutions is strictly regulated by the logic of jurisprudence and subtly adapted to the historical and social characteristics of the given body politic. However, neither legal rigour nor adaptability to circumstances allow democratic states to ensure that political institutions are 'transparent', that is to say, plain and comprehensible. Part of the essence of democracy is that it is not transparent; hence the rule of democratic uncertainty. Since the democratic form of politics is also a critique of the political as such, it forces public life to come to terms with this structural ambiguity, whose practical consequences are visible on two levels. Firstly, those acting within political institutions know that their actions will meet limits in the face of the public criticism they are destined to confront. Beyond that criticism a more radical critique is threatened: one which questions their very function. They cannot help but acknowledge the legitimacy of this. Secondly, the very configuration of institutions through which public debate takes place imposes uncertainty.

[30]   For further explanation, see note 1 to the introduction to Part III. (NP)

[31]   This is further discussed in note 1 of the introduction to Part III. (NP)

Political actors are forced to admit that, because of the form of the culture, 'truths' in politics are relative and limited. These limitations are all the more constraining for the uncertainty which necessarily figures in any public debate about the political sphere itself. The prime example of this is the 'constitutional discourse' which underpins the public status of political institutions.

In a 'republic' the constitution is derived from general principles of Law and lays down various specific arrangements. These two aspects of the constitution justify the existence of both the state and the government, and explain how they operate in practice. *Only democracy questions the democratic state about the very need for its existence.* Only in democracy does public life openly ask the question: 'What is public life?'. Its doing so does not at all demonstrate that the rule of democratic uncertainty in political institutions implies the need for ideology to fill the gap of uncertainty. On the contrary, it is an attempt as far as possible to restrict recourse to ideology.

Is it, therefore, in the nature of public life in a democracy to be more difficult than in any other kind of society, on account of the additional constraints and demands that democracy imposes? Political theory has always been clear on this point. Whenever it returns a favourable verdict, the utility of democracy in functional terms and criteria derived from this never figure very highly. To be sure, political theory has sometimes justified social ties in those terms and constructed 'society' from criteria of utility and self-interest. This has been so particularly when political theory has built on economic theory – as in the tradition defining a modern, liberal 'civil society'[32] which stretches from Ferguson and Smith to Hayek.[33] However, it is worth recalling that Hegelian philosophy, even as it assimilated the new science of economics, conducted the most radical critique of liberal civil society and the science analysing it. Hegelian theory showed how liberal civil society, from the point of view of practice, enshrined a specious kind of politics: it left no space for the state. Hegel also demonstrated, from the theoretical point of view, the limits of economics as a science of politics.[34] Moreover, political theory

---

[32] Or, in German, *bürgerliche Gesellschaft* (bourgeois society).

[33] Adam Ferguson (1723–1816) and Adam Smith (1723–90) were leading figures in the development, during the middle of the eighteenth century, of a speculative history describing how society might have grown up on the basis of evolving economic links between people. (Smith, of course, is also credited with the invention of economics itself.) In the mid-twentieth century, Friedrich von Hayek (1899–1992) revived the primacy of economic ties between individuals by making them the starting point for fundamental principles to ensure liberty and limit the scope of the state. His account of the nature of society now underpins the politics of the Right. (NP)

[34] See *Grundlinien der Philosophie des Rechts* (1821) (Hegel, 1952) and Bourgeois (1989). [Briefly stated, Hegel's position – also discussed in the section on the organicist model of society in D'Agostino's essay – is that a society made up of individual economic actors with no more than superficial links of mutual self-interest pursued in the economic market would be no society at all. There would be no basis on which permanent state institutions and principles could emerge. (NP)]

has never justified the democratic form of politics in this way, nor credited it with a greater capacity to satisfy the demands of efficiency, utility or convenience. Hence political theory never adopts an apologetic tone for democracy – and it has yet more reason to reject the short-sightedness of contemporary triumphalism about democracy and the free market.

The history of democracy has at times been graced with such figures as Pericles, who was able to extol democracy in Athens with a measured grandness. But for every Pericles there has always been a Socrates blocking his path, wielding his critical doubt.[35]

The era of Pericles and Socrates is the origin of democracy and remains emblematic of it. The fate of modern democracies is above all publicly to encounter uncertainty in the realm of politics. Public life regulated along democratic lines is an acute case of that 'demystification' of the world which Max Weber identified as the major cultural factor shaping modern Western societies. By contrast, for Weber, the democracy of antiquity, rooted in an ontology of natural law and sustained by mythology,[36] had supposedly been self-confident, clear in its criteria and steadfast in its aspirations. The last part of this essay will link those two lines of enquiry: on the one hand, the character of European modernity; on the other, the criteria and the aspirations which have been pursued in democracy. Here too, considerations of method and substantive points will be closely interconnected, and it will become clear that we are touching on the problems surrounding the distinctive character of politics in European culture.

Aspirations and criteria

Political theory (provided that it is not confused with the regulated and rationalized catechisms of doctrine) is in itself neither democratic nor anti-democratic. To be either would be a contradiction in terms. However, under the pressure of circumstances and in the pursuit of knowledge, the political theorist may come to pose the question public opinion poses: What is, or is not democracy? If we focus on the identity of democracy, and are concerned to give priority to the practical perspective, then we may be less inclined to propose internal *criteria*, in the traditional manner of political theory. Rather, we should seek to establish what meaningful *aspirations* are expressed in the idea of democracy.

[35] Pericles (490–429 BC), military leader and patrician head of the democratic party, was the dominant figure in the Athenian state from 444 BC until his death. The quizzical style of reasoning developed by Socrates – also Athenian, and a near contemporary of Pericles – runs quite counter to the kind of certainty proclaimed by such a leader. Socrates' style of reasoning is considered further in Rieu's section on the emergence of democracy. (NP)

[36] The contrast between ancient and modern in terms of natural law, etc., is discussed in Alain-Marc Rieu's essay above. (NP)

Systems Theory

Criteria of the kind produced by the 'Systems Theory' analysis of politics[37] are unacceptable. If that type of analysis resembles mine but without any reference to the sociology of knowledge, that is precisely because the criteria it establishes are intended, by their purely formal nature, to eliminate just the problems that I wish to pose. Being a version of positivism,[38] Systems Theory considers these problems to be 'undecidable' and happily classifies them as 'philosophical'. This confuses the question of meaningful aspirations with that of arbitrary norms, lumping them all together as 'value judgments'. The most sophisticated example of this approach is currently provided by Niklas Luhmann's general Systems Theory.[39] Striking as it may be in the complex (but shallow) web of references it makes to philosophy, and in the breadth of material that it synthesizes, Systems Theory is a sociological method applied to public affairs. It pushes aside differences between modes of government, seeing only differences between the various interlocking systems in a society, which it distinguishes according to whether they intervene in political activity, or constitute the environment in which it takes place. Using this method, the problem of which institutions sustain democracy becomes (along with others) difficult to conceptualize.

Comparative government

Nor is it sufficient, in order to make judgements about self-styled democratic states, to compare their public life with that of states under other types of government – theocracy, dictatorship, oligarchy or polyarchy, to mention the most common ones. The method and the criteria used in the study of 'comparative government' can never be totally adequate for the task.[40]

Ever since Plato pioneered the comparative method,[41] much of political theory has been devoted to the enumeration of criteria of this type. But, in Plato's use of the

---

[37]   See note 40 of Hans-Joachim Schmidt's Essay 5 for a definition. David Easton, arguably the first to apply Systems Theory to politics, has described it thus: 'The study of politics is concerned with understanding how authoritative decisions are made and executed for a society. We can try to understand political life by viewing each of its aspects piecemeal. We can examine the operation of such institutions as political parties, interest groups, government and voting; we can study the nature and consequences of such political practices as manipulation, propaganda and violence; we can seek to reveal the structure within which these practices occur. By combining the results we can obtain a rough picture of what happens in any self-contained political unit.' (Easton, 1957) (NP)

[38]   See note 23 of Hans-Joachim Schmidt's Essay 5 for a definition. (NP)

[39]   For recent Systems Theory, see Tinland (1988), Lagroye (1991), Niklas Luhmann (1990) and Amsellek (1968). [Luhmann is further discussed in Hans-Joachim Schmidt's essay. (NP)]

[40]   For comparative governmental studies since Gabriel Almond, see Lagroye (1991).

[41]   It was Plato, rather than Aristotle (as is too often believed), who first developed this method in a rigorous fashion, and posed the questions of method which it gives rise to.

approach, forms of government are not categorized solely on the basis of their institutions. Nor does the typology derive from the science of Law. Rather, as I have already observed, the object is to distinguish forms of institutional configuration as a prelude to bringing forward criteria of judgement and arranging them in a hierarchy. The capacity to last over time; effectiveness in territorial defence; effective fulfilment of political (or, more properly, governmental) functions; the obedience obtained towards laws; the safeguarding of individual security; and suitability as a setting for private life have thus become the usual criteria. There is no denying that a skilful use of these criteria can yield illuminating comparisons, particularly from the point of view of a sociology of the practices of political domination. Unlike the abstractions of Systems Theory, these criteria address matters of substance and to arrange them rigorously prompts enlightened judgment in place of an arbitrary choice.

Yet, for all that, the comparative method in political theory is less than entirely satisfactory. For the *aspirations* that are particular to each configuration of institutions do not lend themselves to this sort of comparative measure. This is particularly so in the case of the democracy, since, as we all instinctively feel, democracy is not just one mode of government amongst many. We do not judge the public life of democracy by how it compares on such and such a criterion with 'public life' under tyranny, oligarchy or theocracy. Although this may seem at odds with what I said earlier about him, Plato had in fact already perceived that the comparative method was fundamentally inadequate. Acquainted with (or perhaps chastened by) a century of Greek experience of the democratic city, he had already begun to question the efficacy of the comparative method once democratic states were included in the comparison.[42]

Foreshadowing the democratization of western states, modern political theory from the outset rejected the comparative method and its criteria. For this body of theory democracy is certainly more than simply one mode of government: it is *the form of politics from which all government is derived*. This was the view taken by Hobbes – contrary to widespread prejudices against him.[43] His positive 'geometric' method made him the first modern theorist of this form of politics, as well as of human rights in the form of positive political rights. The democrat Spinoza was fundamentally in agreement with the position of the monarchist Hobbes on political rights, though he expressed himself differently. He characterized democracy as the form of government that is the natural direction of public power when it remains faithful to its ultimate purpose: the organization of an authentically human public life. That is, one oriented towards the exercise of that

---

[42]   See, in particular, Plato's *The Statesman.*

[43]   Although Hobbes commends firmness and power in the sovereign above all, the purpose of that is to secure the compliance of individuals to the power that protects them, and Hobbes is very much concerned with the active persuasion of subjects to sustain their support. In an unexpected way, therefore, he can be said to explore the processes found in a democracy. (NP)

liberty which individuals possess by virtue of their nature as human beings.[44] Rousseau had read Spinoza attentively before writing *The Social Contract* and analysing the relationship between democracy and political institutions. The problem is summed up, but also surrendered to, in his famous formula: 'If there were a nation of Gods, it would govern itself democratically. A government so perfect is not suited to men'.[45] We shall return to this formula when we look at the conflictual relationship between democracy and government.

Political theory and the demystification of politics

For the moment, Rousseau's formulation will serve simply as an indicator of that 'demystification' of politics undertaken by modern political theory – even when, as with *The Social Contract*, it is moving in the direction of democracy. The methods of the history of political ideas do not directly shed light on this development in modern political theory. Hence, in the midst of its recent successes, the history of political ideas sometimes views modern political theory too cursorily, even summarily. For this approach, which involves situating 'ideas' in 'their' history, focuses principally on currents of opinion whose appearance is linked to wider patterns of thought, or to antagonisms in national politics and the conflicts of doctrine (or ideology) within them. In so far as political theory does not really think in those terms, its development largely eludes this approach to history.

There is a second reason why demystification is not easily grasped by the history of ideas. The epistemological foundations of political theory constitute a sort of early deconstruction of the enterprise of the history of ideas. For political theory undermines the political significance of the very things that the history of ideas deals in: ideas themselves. In the wake of Machiavelli and well in advance of Marx, modern political theory challenged the notion that groups of ideas, opinions, or (still less) ideals might determine the course of events, or explain their causation. Moreover, modern political theory offers a critique of historical understanding and is, in itself, the refutation of nineteenth- and twentieth- century philosophies of history with their notions of social and political destiny.

The theocratic strand of modern Christian Europe has never been mistaken about modern political theory. Like the Islamic theocracy of the Middle East, it recognizes in political theory[46] the foundation of a *specifically European political culture*. It is a culture which serves as a vehicle for human rights, democracy, and, more generally, for a secular foundation to political life, which theocracy condemns on all counts. Despite the shortcomings of the theocracies, they have

---

[44] See Tinland (1988). [Spinoza's central political work, the *Theological-Political Treatise* (1670), is primarily a defence of freedom of opinion, as the setting for greater self-knowledge on the part of the subject (the true content of freedom) and more rational understanding of the people on the part of government. This could be regarded as the first statement that free, autonomous debate (which is here said to be what makes democracy the fundamental form of all politics) is also the essence of the state. (NP)]

[45] *Du Contrat Social*, book 3, ch. 4. See Rousseau (1968), p. 114.

[46] Much more so than in the Enlightenment, whose critical endeavours are rightly judged less radical.

asked what unique character European political culture derives from its various components. It is clear that this coincides very precisely with the widespread concern about the European 'identity' and democracy's place in it.

To anchor the development of modern political theory in the European political experience, and in the various cultural strands which European democratic culture possesses as a result, requires a different point of view from that of a history of narrowly political ideas. Political theory must provide the overarching point of view, not so much for its own sake (for the various systems of political 'ideas' elaborated by successive theories) as for the connections these theories have had both with unfolding democratic experience, and with a succession of ways for organizing knowledge. Theorists from Leo Strauss onwards have usually looked back to the 'Machiavellian moment'[47] of European political culture and to the scientific revolution underway since the Renaissance, with the aim of identifying the starting point of modern political theory and the 'demystification' of politics. This approach is not wrong, but the time-scale on which it is predicated is still too short. It is shaped by an obsessive preoccupation with the problem of the origins of the modern state, from which it draws its historical and sociological concepts. If the aim is not simply to define the modern state by studying various cases, but really to consider *political and democratic culture*, then the time-scale changes. As the historians themselves point out, origins need to be traced back through a quite different, longer history, though they remain equally decisive for the contemporary perception of democracy in Europe. The *demystification of politics* found its earliest and most forceful expression in Greek philosophy, and the resultant conflict with the democratic politics of the city was sometimes fatal for both.

Two symbolic figures will be sufficient to give the flavour of this conflict, in which the crises of the city and of philosophy arose and interacted. Both belong to Athenian public life before Plato, and typify an extreme situation. On one side, Critias: oligarch and implacable enemy of Athenian democracy,[48] whose idea of power, marked by an exceptionally tragic sense of the human condition, foreshadows Nietzsche's philosophy of the 'will to power' and the problems of its exercise in politics.[49] On the other side, Protagoras: democratic sophist and the

---

[47]   That is, the historic turning-point in European development when secular authority, the sociability of urban life and the importance of the elites' response to government were recognized together in the Renaissance Italy of city states. Niccolò Machiavelli (1469–1527), whose writing defined reason of state and revived the ideas of classical republicanism, epitomizes this 'moment' of European development. (NP)

[48]   460–403 BC, one-time student of Socrates, Critias participated in a coup in 411 BC and in the subsequent oligarchic governments. (NP)

[49]   Friedrich Nietzsche (1844–1900), German philologist and philosopher, identified an exhaustion in European thought due to its inability to create new values as history overturned those of the past. He traced this to the theoretical turn taken at the time of Socrates, and consequently admired the alternative: the courage of those who, in the celebratory spirit of the god Dionysus, could express their life-affirming 'will to power', rise above the existential vapidness of human life, and *create* new values and meaning in energy and joy. Rightly or wrongly, this view of the human condition has been linked to various versions of twentieth-century totalitarianism. (NP)

first 'positivist' theorist of justice, who asserted that 'respecting the Gods, I am unable to know whether they exist or do not exist'.[50] Protagoras' prime objective was the development of a public consciousness, to be achieved through the education of 'citizens'. In other words, his aim was to form, by reasoned discussion alone, beings able to govern themselves and to be governed. However, he was forced to flee by the Athenians, Pericles notwithstanding. One is tempted to recall, as an additional and more anecdotal piece of evidence, the political iconoclasm and cynicism of Alcibiades.[51]

But it would be more useful to emphasize the fact that Platonic idealism does not, by itself, preclude the demystification of politics. On the contrary, it shows it to be viable, *if accomplished in, and through the democratic city.* Platonic philosophy attempted to define politics via an enquiry into the conditions for a just and authentic public life in a city where the common measures of justice and truth had disappeared, and where politics was inevitably *tied to* knowledge reached through public opinion. Plato thus drew up an assessment of a century-long relationship of mutual criticism between philosophy and politics.[52]

Like many modern states, the Greek city had its links with the gods, just as its public life was infused with myths.[53] Equally, the invention of politics and, specifically, the formation of Greek democracy was plainly linked to the Greeks' elaboration of the critical mode of thinking as a route to knowledge, and with the development of a demystified view of the world. The tragic, glorious and turbulent history of democracy in the city was grounded in the public pursuit of that type of knowledge.

Earlier I noted that modern opponents of democracy can be recognized by their frequent denunciations of this pursuit of knowledge. Likewise, the enemies of democracy reveal themselves through their continual efforts to hold back this

---

[50]   Protagoras (c.490–c.411 BC), Athenian teacher and associate of Pericles (see note 35). He was the first to develop the discursive mode of teaching of the so-called 'Sophists', which culminated in Socrates – though the latter condemned his predecessors' too open-ended use of it. Protagoras was banished from Athens in 411 BC, at the instigation of the oligarchic leadership to which Critias belonged, and his books burnt. The quotation, almost his only known surviving utterance, is the first sentence of his work *On the Gods*. (NP)

[51]   Athenian politician, born in 450 BC, and one-time disciple of Socrates, who, having allied himself with Athenian oligarchs and democrats, as well as with Spartans and Persians, was assassinated in 404 BC. (NP)

[52]   It is worth reminding ourselves that this 'demystified' assessment of politics, which opened the way to Aristotle's 'prudential' account of the management of public affairs, encompassed a political and cultural area stretching from Sicily to the Black Sea coast of so-called Asia Minor. For these symbolic figures, see Dumon (1988). For the Platonic philosophy mentioned at the end of the paragraph, see G. Duprat, 'La résistance de la cité' (The resistance of the city) in Duprat (1990).

[53]   See Veyne (1985).

Holland House damaged by air raids on London, 1940 (credit: Hulton Deutsch).

critical pursuit of knowledge, confining it within the differentiated forms of knowledge of today. I can now complete the picture. The most astute enemies of democracy are those whose knowledge of European political culture leads them to assert that the struggle against it must be extended back beyond the Enlightenment and even beyond modern political theory. According to them, if modern thought is to survive its current (supposedly fatal) crisis, it must dig deeper for the origins of the crisis and attempt to re-establish itself on foundations from *before* that 'Greek moment' when the critical pursuit of knowledge and democracy were first formulated. For them, such a renewal would once again allow philosophical thinking to play its leading role in European culture and politics. In the German cultural and political situation in 1933, that meant that the philosopher was to become a member of the National-Socialist Party - as Heidegger did, without ever subsequently repudiating this membership.[54]

[54] Martin Heidegger (1899–1976), German philosopher in the phenomenological and existentialist traditions, who declared his support for Hitler in 1933 – though he may subsequently have regretted it. His philosophy sought to identify the possible meaning of human life in the underlying being of the world as it exists. He argued, somewhat like Nietzsche, that being in this sense has been obscured by the western rationalist tradition stemming from Socrates. (NP)

196

Democracy is not, then, any kind of ideology (although the democratic state cannot prohibit public discourses from making appeals to ideology). Nor is it just one political theory amongst others, providing support for the doctrinal discourses which compete in public life. It is an irreducibly unique form of politics, because its particular configuration of institutions makes public its own self-questioning. It directs this self-questioning onto every other form of government, and so injects it into the life of any social formation constituted as a body politic. One cannot draw from this the currently fashionable conclusion that any institutionalized democracy must either be a state[55] or an 'empty space': the graveyard of now dead democratic situations, their hopes betrayed. The experience of democracy, and the culture which has made it possible and sustained it are defined not by criteria inherent to the system, but by the aspirations it manifests.

The critiques of reason of state and of government

It is not necessary to undertake a detailed commentary on Aristotle in order to identify, as early as Book Three of his *Politics*, the two aspects of the practice of democracy in which the major political institutions of the city of antiquity played just as strong a critical role as do those of the modern state.

First, democracy does not simply recognize all the members of the body politic as equals, in the sense of all being citizens of identical status, and, by the same token, both *rulers* and *subjects*. The democratic form of politics puts this citizenship into effect. It ensures that everyone can enjoy a human being's natural right to be a citizen. In short, whether one goes back to the Aristotelian theory of politics or to the history of the Greek city, the situation is no different from that of modern democracy: in practice, democracy signifies a *process of democratization*. The process is a complex one: it is 'social' (to use the modern term) in the sense that it calls on the entire resources of a society. However, its central principle is that it is regulated by institutions and controlled by the law.

Alongside the empowerment of all citizens to exercise the narrowly political right to govern, democracy is also distinguished by the widest possible exercise of another civic right: that of speaking freely in public on public affairs. The freedom of speech that is granted entails not only the absence of institutional constraints on public discussion, but also that discussion is focussed on the *common good* (as the city of antiquity would express it) or the *general interest* (as the modern state would express it). The public authorities ensure that these conditions are respected by positive laws, which define the boundary where liberty becomes licence.

A third aspect of democratic practice is simply the product of the two preceding ones. The Greek city took pride in it. According to those who live elsewhere, it is the particular virtue of the European democratic state. By contrast, those who advocate a different sort of state see it as the irremediable weakness, the constitutive

---

[55]   In which case the Europe now under construction, since it is certainly not a state, will assuredly never be 'truly' democratic.

vice of the European model. I refer to the practice of reasoned critique. The obligation to pursue it cannot be prescribed by law. In a democracy, you cannot legislate reason. However, it follows from the rule of democratic diversity that positive law must sanction the practice (through a series of mediations) whenever its provisions explicitly affect freedom of speech or citizenship. It is logical that this sanction should appear primarily in the form of legal provisions covering the public expression of reasoned criticism regarding the institutions which govern the process of democratization itself. Such expression of criticism is universally identifiable in its two principal manifestations: a critique focussing on the use of state power – the critique of 'reason of state', to use the modern term – and the critique of government as the administrator of the general interest.

Naturally, the way these two critiques are pursued is strongly influenced by the social and cultural context, and by the development of knowledge. Although they belong to the domain of political theory (which is not the same as that of the sociology of knowledge), the critiques are bound to reflect the historical growth of forms of knowledge.

The critique of reason of state

Like most political concepts, reason of state, and the critique of it, need to be delineated on an historical basis. But neither can be adequately explained or understood in terms of history alone. It is not sufficient to identify and interpret the successive layers of meaning over three centuries: from the earliest usages of 'reason of state', as political theory tried to understand the formation of the modern state, to its contemporary uses, commensurate with the evolution of the state over the last two centuries. A number of recent studies have been devoted to the history of this idea, first proposed by Botero in the sixteenth century, in opposition to Machiavellianism, and to its sometimes paradoxical shifts in meaning. These studies follow the path marked out by Meinecke's famous work.[56] While recognizing its very great merits, Carl Schmitt demonstrated that the concept nevertheless requires to be delineated as a concept. Otherwise genuine knowledge of politics is abandoned, and, in particular, the radical opposition between reason of state and democracy is obscured.

Without departing from Schmitt's approach, if we take the construction of a democratic Europe as our central point of reference, we ought first to make a proper assessment of the present situation of European democracies, which has profoundly modified the radical opposition of democracy and reason of state.

The European states have in fact just emerged from the severe crisis provoked (initially during the 1960s in the USA) by the radical critique of the beneficent welfare state. As it spread to European states, this neo-liberal critique[57] denounced the

---

[56]   See Senellart (1989), Meinecke (1924) and Schmitt (1926).

[57]   Associated in UK politics with the name of Margaret Thatcher, this was an attack on the capacity and the appropriateness of the state to offer security against individual responsibility and the vicissitudes of life in the free market. Its theoretical roots lie with Friedrich Hayek – see note above 33 above. (NP)

'leviathan' of the state for its excessive interventionism, and declared it to be anti-democratic on account of its excessive desire to bring society under collective democratic control. The state must now respond, as a matter of urgency, to precisely the opposite criticism: the deterioration of the state sector and inadequate support for democratic control. However, for the states involved in the construction of the European Community, the original conception of the state – as the repository of public authority and national or popular sovereignty – is now merely a myth. The discipline of Community law, European decision-making and the European institutions of justice (the European courts at Strasbourg and Luxembourg) are all helping to build a previously unknown type of political organization on the principle of subsidiarity. It is clearly understood that, in practice, this new organization will entail not just drastic modifications of sovereignty (and hence of state power), but also the construction of a form of politics quite unlike that of the existing democratic nation-state.[58]

In those European countries that are already democratic, or are becoming so, the sheer diversity of relationships between people, nation and state precludes any general claims (of fact or of principle) about the real link between democracy and the state. No particular case can or should be taken as exemplary. In the case of France, the democratic situation of today has come about through a history linking the gradual elaboration of a national identity by the monarchical state, the sovereignty of the people acquired through revolutions, and the construction of the republican state. Yet this example can no more be set up as a 'European' model of democratic citizenship than the entirely contrary case of Germany. A very telling instance is the willingness of the current leader of the Social Democratic Party to set aside German national identity when addressing questions of participation in the construction of a democratic Europe.[59] To express such a view would be unthinkable in French public life, as in other European nations.

The historian may set about defining two, three or four processes in the construction of modern European states and their democratization, estimating the part played in the latter by the different national and liberal-parliamentary traditions. The sociologist, in turn, may emphasize the 'social' nature of the process, and show it to be irreducibly specific to the history of each society and each state as it structures society politically. Neither approach provides a theoretical overview of the direction given by Europe's democratic past and present in the construction of Europe as a political and democratic entity.

It is worth noting that it was in fact by transcending this historical and sociological diversity that Max Weber was able to construct his now familiar concept of the modern European state: that it is the agent in the real, historical world of the reason of state which is immanent to political processes. The state is the supreme authority for the mobilization of power in the political order. Within this order, it is the agent of the movement to bring individual and collective (or 'social') action

---

[58] See issues of the journals *Droits* (no. 14, 1991) and *Philosophie politique* (no. 1, 1991), devoted to the question of Europe.

[59] Interview with Björn Enghowm in *Le Monde*, 13 November 1991.

under rational rules – which has been the driving force of western societies throughout their history. The state thus behaves in accordance with what Weber called 'the objective pragmatics of "reasons of state" '.[60] The law of the reason of state is its ultimate law. This 'objective pragmatics' is the political manifestation of the broader process of demystification of the world. In formulating this law, Weber makes the state the ultimate social reality in the political order and confers upon it the right, according to historical and sociological circumstances, to have the final word in opposition to other states as well as over its own citizens.

However, it is also worth noting that Weber was pursuing an explicit political objective: in the name of practical rationality, he was attacking the anarchism of his day, as well as earlier communal ethics (the Christian ethic in particular) which were, in his eyes, forerunners of this anarchism. When it comes to our present-day concerns, one might take the contrary view that the anarchism Weber opposed was directed not so much at the reason of state as at the state itself (or at the government). Weber's thinking was off-target. Overwhelmingly preoccupied with the defence of the state, Weber left outside the scope of his sociological theory of politics the question of contemporary democracy in the state.[61]

The same cannot be said of Carl Schmitt, who defended reason of state as much as Weber. Schmitt argued that right must be something which is publicly declared at the highest level to be just and which must be obeyed. As a jurist, Schmitt supports his case for the necessity of a sovereign and absolute decision at the highest level by two arguments. First, an explicit reference to theology: metaphorically speaking, the final decision-maker, therefore the sovereign, therefore the state, is *a deo excitatus* (inspired by God).[62] Secondly, a radical critique of liberal representative democracy: since, in this form of state, there is no authority which possesses any ultimate truth, it allows free rein to all sorts of manipulation, it reduces any public judgment on public affairs to a mere expression of opinion, legitimates endless debate, and prevents decisions being taken as to what is right (even when public safety demands it). By its very nature, therefore, this form of politics is a negation of reason of state. Its configuration of institutions suits only the economic and technical modes of thinking. Eric Weil (though he was in every respect an opponent of Schmitt, and constructed a general model of modern democracy)

---

[60] Max Weber (1922–3), vol. 1, pp. 436–73; (1948; 1991) pp. 323–359. (The quotation appears on p. 334 of Gerth and Mills' translation. For a French translation, together with the passages concerning 'the demystification of the world', see Colliot-Thélène (1990). The concept of the state as 'a human community which (successfully) claims the monopoly of the legitimate use of physical force' is also described in Weber (1921). See also Colliot-Thélène (1992).

[61] According to Duprat, the *democratic* state is so because it sanctions precisely that element of anarchism which Weber, thinking about the state as such, opposed: the continual critique of reason of state. Therefore Weber's concept of the state would be overturned by the democratic state as Duprat conceives it, which incorporates the critique of reason of state. (NP)

[62] The following lines deserve to be quoted: reason of state 'implies the recognition of actions and interventions which are out of the ordinary, like those which are *a deo excitatus*; [it] also implies dictatorship' (Schmitt, 1926, p. 176).

was saying much the same thing in support of democracy when he affirmed that a 'good government must have the firmest possible convictions and no convictions at all'.[63]

Nobody would argue with the following views: there is an apparent paradox in the uncertainty built into the functioning of democratic political institutions; the solution to this paradox lies in the use the citizens, as rulers and subjects, make of their liberty and their reason (as they must); and this paradox is burdensome for certain types of mind and certain social groups who subordinate the use of reason in politics to a dogmatic view of liberty and reason, rather than a pragmatic one. Now I can add the final stone to the democratic edifice. We have reached the point at which the uncertainty of democracy can attain justification as a principle of 'Law'. Amongst the fundamental political principles of democracy is the *right to resist oppression*. It is completely paradoxical to postulate this right: it admits the limitations of positive law (when power is abused), then immediately transcends these limitations by re-affirming the concept of Law and the duty of the citizen to uphold political life under and through Law. Democracy thus builds its ultimate defence against reason of state. It affirms that, in exceptional circumstances, reason is, and remains, on the side of the citizens, who have a duty to uphold the idea of citizenship, which has no other foundation but the citizens themselves.

It is therefore not difficult to understand why the jurists, when they consider the legal mechanisms for guiding Europe towards democracy, are unable to include in their list of positive rights a specific right (and duty) to conduct a critique of reason of state.[64] As with the critique of government, we are dealing here with a political right (or, in jurists' terms, political principle of Law) that can only be embodied *indirectly* in positive law. Yet it is clear that public life, for its part, takes direct advantage of this right to pursue a critique of reason of state. Currently, this finds expression in public opinion, in the legitimate possibility (exclusive to contemporary democratic states) of a public debate over 'civil disobedience'.[65]

To borrow from Weber an example of the political import of theology, the scriptural basis of the Christian ethic of community includes an obligation to 'render unto Caesar that which is Caesar's'. There are no grounds for public debate about it: it is a commandment. By contrast, from its very beginnings, the democratic city expressed its identity by encouraging a collective reflection on the *limits* of the authority of politics and its laws. By organizing a public debate about the tragedy

[63]   Weil (1956), pp. 220 ff. He added that this was 'clear' – but only 'in principle'.

[64]   See the 'portrait of democracy' according to the jurisprudence of the European Court, as painted by Delmas-Marty (1990), p. 441.

[65]   For 'civil disobedience' in the German context, see Habermas (1990), in particular the essay on 'Recht und Gewalt' (Right and might), pp. 88–104, dating from 1983. [From time to time in democracies, an open debate is held about the citizen's right to refuse to obey the state, in spite of the latter's claim to act through indisputable 'reason of state'. Refusing the draft, obstructing military installations and revealing secrets are all, then, discussed as possible matters of conscience, higher purpose or 'public' interest. Such principles challenge the priority of reason of state. (NP)]

of Antigone,[66] Greek democracy educated its public opinion with a discussion of the various forms of servitude. Only democracy holds such discussions necessary for the education of the citizen.

The critique of reason of state is not, therefore, an obsolete civic right that it is no longer worth drawing attention to. The state and its mystique of sovereignty have by no means disappeared from Europe. The view that 'democracy stops where reason of state begins'[67] is still held by many people, who believe themselves to be democrats. But it is the proper functioning of European states, with their ongoing democratization, that remains the surest guarantee of the possibility that Europe will be constructed along democratic lines.[68]

The critique of government

We can now deal fairly briefly with the critique of government. The ground has been sufficiently prepared for this point, which is difficult to explain, though clear in principle. If citizens are both rulers and subjects, why, or rather how do governments come about? The Greek city was aware of the problem, thought it through, and found answers to it. The problem became inescapable with the formation of the modern state and its subsequent democratization. At the turning-point in this history, Rousseau expressed the problem in concise terms. If the people are both rulers and subjects, he proposed to call them 'sovereign' in the first role and 'state' in the second. A 'government', as a special body of persons not to be equated with the body of citizens, is necessary not so much because of the sheer numbers in modern society, as for articulating and executing particular decisions. In other words, a government is 'an intermediary body between the subjects [or state] and the sovereign'.[69] The earliest exponents of European political theory (Hobbes and Spinoza, for example) concluded that democracy could exist only momentarily – in logic, rather than in history. The democratic 'moment' was the moment when the body politic decided to create its own constitution. Whether decided by contract or in some other way, it gave birth to government ('sovereign powers', or 'the state', as the theorists called it). Rousseau did not remove the

[66] Mythical heroine of the play of that name, written c.441 BC, by Sophocles. Antigone disobeyed the explicit orders of the king by burying the body of her brother, who had been killed in an act of rebellion. For this she too was executed. The tragedy therefore confronts the conflict between the duty to family or custom and the obligations imposed by the state. Hegel's use of Antigone as the epitome of a certain stage in the growth of the conflict between public and private morality (*Phenomenology of Spirit*, ch. 6, part A; see especially Hegel, 1931, p. 491) made Antigone the classic figure for this issue. (NP)

[67] A remark made by the Charles Pasqua, French Minister of the Interior, in 1986 and immediately retracted.

[68] We must not disregard, either, those European states aiming to draw on these developing structures to consolidate their own recent internal democratization. We also need to take full account of the needs of those states, in the vicinity of Europe or elsewhere, that wish to move towards democracy, even though their public opinion has not experienced the logic of citizenship, or acquired the culture to confront its paradoxes.

[69] *Du Contrat Social,* book 3, ch. 1; see Rousseau (1968), p. 102.

Lithuanians saying 'No' to the Red Army in Vilnius, January 1991, as Soviet troops attempt to stop the independence movement (credit: Associated Press).

obstacle represented by the determinate existence of a constitution and a government. He showed it to be just as necessary as it is insurmountable. No body politic, no democracy can dispense with government, even though it supplants the sovereign and so leaves democracy in ruins.

Therein lies not only the true meaning of political servitude, but also the unique quality of democracy amongst forms of politics. It alone creates a special sphere called the political, since it alone makes simultaneously necessary both a form of servitude and the recognition of it as servitude. Servitude becomes the necessary condition for the exercise of freedom. In the political sphere, the government is the institutionalized form of the relationship between necessity and freedom. Criticism of government, as commonly practised in the states of modern democratic Europe, is the citizens' way of living out that relationship.

Our final point will be this. The ultimate purpose of democracy is not merely the pursuit of democratic political activity. That is why politics is a form of democracy, not its essence. The purpose of democracy is to struggle against the various kinds of servitude; its role is to organize the perpetual public debate over the meanings of servitude. Until such time as an autonomous European form of politics takes responsibility for the organization of this debate (and this will be some time yet), European politics will not satisfy the conditions for democracy. It will not be practising being free. It will merely continue to react in emergencies and at times of necessity.

203

References

ADELBERT, R. (1976) *Geschpräche mit Hannah Arendt* (Conversations with Hannah Arendt), Munich, Piper.

ALTHUSSER, L. (1971) 'Ideology and ideological state apparatuses' in *Lenin and Philosophy and Other Essays*, London, New Left Books.

AMSELLEK, P. (ed.) (1968) *Controverses sur l'ontologie du droit* (Debates on the ontology of law), Paris, Presses Universitaires de France.

BALIBAR, E. (1985) *Spinoze et la politique* (Spinoza and politics), Paris, Presses Universitaires de France.

BARRET-KRIEGEL, B. (1989) *Les Droits de l'homme et le droit naturel* (Human rights and natural rights), Paris, Presses Universitaires de France.

BELL, D. (1965; 1988 edn) *The End of Ideology*, New York, Free Press.

BOURGEOIS, B. (1989) *La Pensée politique de Hegel* (Hegel's political thought), Paris, Presses Universitaires de France.

CHÂTELET, F. and PISIER-KOUCHNER, E. (1985) *Les Conceptions politiques du XXe siècle* (Political ideas of the twentieth century), Paris, Presses Universitaires de France.

COLLIOT-THÉLÈNE, C. (1990) *Max Weber et l'histoire* (Max Weber and history), Paris, Presses Universitaires de France.

COLLIOT-THÉLÈNE, C. (1992) *Le Désenchantement de l'état de Hegel à Max Weber* (The demystification of the state from Hegel to Weber), Paris, Presses Universitaires de France.

DELMAS-MARTY, M. (1990) *Raisonner la raison d'état* (Thinking about reason of state), Paris, Presses Universitaires de France.

DOBRY, M. (1986) *Sociologie des crises politiques* (The sociology of political crises), Paris, Presses FNSP.

DOBRY, M. (1990) 'Les Avatars de la démocratization' (The phases of modernization) in Duprat (1990).

DROITS, journal, Paris (No. 14, 1991).

DUMON, J.-P. (1988) *Les Présocratiques* (The pre-Socratics), Paris, Gallimard.

DUPRAT, G. (1990) (ed.) *Connaissance du politique* (Understanding politics), Paris, Gallimard.

EASTON, D. (1957) 'The analysis of political systems', in *World Politics*, vol. 9. no. 3, (reprinted in Pizzorno, A. (ed.) (1971).

EUBEN, J.B. (1986) *Greek Tragedy and Political Theory*, Berkeley, University of California Press.

HABERMAS, J. (1990) *Kleine politischen Schriften* (Shorter Political Writings); French translation, *Ecrits politiques*, Paris, Cerf.

HAVEL, V. (1987) *Living in Truth: Twenty-two Essays Published on the Occasion of the Award of the Erasmus Prize to Vaclav Havel.* ed. J. Vladislav, London, Faber.

HAVEL, V. (1989) *Essais Politiques* (Political essays), Paris, Gallimard.

HEGEL, G. (1931) *Phenomenology of Spirit*, J.B. Baillie (ed.), London, Allen and Unwin.

HEGEL, G. (1952) *Hegel's Philosophy of Right*, ed. T.M. Knox, Oxford University Press, Oxford.

KANT, I. (1971) *Kant's Political Writings*, ed. H. Reiss, Cambridge, Cambridge University Press.

KELSEN, H. (1920; 1929) *Vom Wesen und Wert der Demokratie* (On the nature and value of democracy), Tübingen, Mohr.

KOSELLECK, R. (1959) *Kritik und Krise*, Freiburg, Verlag Karl Albert, trans. (1988) *Critique and Crisis: the Enlightenment and the Pathogenesis of Modern Society*, Oxford, Berg.

LAGROYE, J. (1991) *Sociologie politique*, Paris, Dalloz.

LECA, J. (1985) 'La Théorie politique' (Political theory), in *Traité de science politique* (Treatise on political science), Vol. 1, ch. 2, Paris, Presses Universitaires de France.

LUHMANN, N. (1990) 'Développements récents en théorie de systèmes' (Recent developments in Systems Theory), in Duprat (1990).

MEIER, C. (1988) *Die politische Kunst der griechischen Tragödie* (Greek tragedy as a political art-form), Munich; French translation (1991) *De la Tragedie grècque comme art politique*, Paris, Les Belles Lettres.

MEINECKE, F. (1924) *Die Idee der Staaträson in der neueren Geschichte*, Munich, Oscar Beck; Translation (1957) *Machiavellism: The Doctrine of raison d'état and Its Place in Modern History*, London, Routledge and Kegan Paul.

Philosophie politique, journal, Paris (No. 1, 1991).

PIZZORNO, A. (ed.) (1971) *Political Sociology: Selected Readings*, Harmondsworth, Penguin.

ROUSSEAU, J.-J, (1968) *The Social Contract*, trans. Maurice Cranston, Harmondsworth, Penguin.

SCHMITT, C. (1926), 'L'Idée de raison d'état selon Friedrich Meinecke' (The idea of reason of state according to Friedrich Meinecke), reprinted in Schmitt, C. (1940) *Positionen und Begriffe*, Berlin, Duncker & Humblot. (French translation in Schmidt, G. (1988): *Parlementarisme et démocratie,* Paris, Seuil.) See also Kervegen, J.-F. (1992) *Hegel, Carl Schmitt: le politique entre spéculation et positivité* (Hegel, Carl Schmidt: politics in between speculation and reality), Paris, Presses Universitaires de France.

SÉNELLART, M. (1989) *Machiavélisme et raison d'état* (Machiavellianism and reason of state), Paris, Presses Universitaires de France.

STRAUSS, L. (1959) *What is Political Philosophy? And Other Studies*, Glencoe, Free Press: 2nd edn. (1988), Chicago, University of Chicago Press.

STRAUSS, L. and KOJÈVE, A. (1954; 2nd edn 1983) *De la Tyrannie*, Paris, Gallimard (*Les Essais* LXIX).

TINLAND, F. (1988) *Droit naturel, loi civile et souveraineté à l époque classique* (Natural right, civil law and sovereignty in the classical period), Paris, Presses Universitaires de France.

TINLAND, F. (ed.) (1991) *Systèmes naturels et systèmes artificiels*, Paris Champ Vallon.

VEYNE, P. (1985; 1988 edn) *Les Grecs ont-ils cru à leurs mythes?* (Did the Greeks believe in their myths?), Paris, Seuil and Meier.

WEBER, M. (1921) *Gesammelte Politische Schriften* (Collected political writings), Munich; translated as 'Politics as a Vocation', in Weber (1922–3; 1991 edn).

WEBER, M. (1922–3) *Gesammelte Aufsätze zur Religionsoziologie* (Collected essays on the sociology of religion), Vol. 1; Translation (1948; 1991 edn)) *From Max Weber: Essays in Sociology,* trans. H.H. Gerth and C.W. Mills, London, Routledge.

WEIL, E. (1956) *Philosophie politique* (Political philosophy), Paris, Vrin.

Part IV
The institutions of democracy

Introduction to Part IV

Prepared for the Course Team by Gérard Duprat
Translated by Noël Parker

The essays you have read so far have their own interest as a contribution to understanding democracy as a general form of politics. But they also sketch out a framework for the analysis and also the evaluation of the various forms of European political institutions described in Part IV.

In the first essay of this final part, Pierre Avril describes and explains the principle organizational features of the political institutions in the states of western Europe. These are states where democracy is indisputably a major organizing principle – though only alongside others: freedom of opinion, social co-operation founded on the right to some level of state welfare, and the so-called free-market economy. The inegalitarian effects of this 'freedom' are tempered by social policies; and where the consequences of the production and circulation of goods are at odds with the general interest, those too are limited by economic policies.

Essay 8 by Jean-Pierre Cot and Richard Corbett is devoted to a study of institutional arrangements for 'the construction of Europe' as a political entity. The political form of Europe has gradually taken shape on the basis of the institutions which contributed to the creation and development of a 'Europe of the Communities'.[1] The Maastricht accords established the term 'European Union' to refer to the newly created political Europe, which will now absorb the Europe of the Communities. In the preamble, the Treaty defines the nature of the institutions as 'democratic'. At the same time, it calls for them to enhance their 'efficient functioning' and to respect other principles, such as the free circulation of goods and of people, and subsidiarity.[2]

---

[1]   That is, the legally distinct communities for which the 'European Community' has now become the generic term: the European Coal and Steel Community (founded in 1951), the European Atomic Energy Community (1957), and the European Economic Community (1957). The major components of EC administration (the Council of Ministers, the Commission, the European Court of Justice, and the European Parliament) were all originally set up under these communities, though modified by later treaties and agreements. (NP)

[2]   Title II, Article 6 of the Maastricht Treaty adds to Article 3 of the Treaty of Rome (a list of the areas of activity of the Community and its Member States acting together, now supplemented to include a common economic policy and fiscal exchange rates) the following explicit limitation:

'The Community shall act within the limit of the powers conferred upon it by this Treaty and of the objectives assigned to it therein. In areas that do not fall within its exclusive competence, the Community shall take action, in accordance with the principles of subsidiarity, only and in so far as the objectives of the proposed action cannot be sufficiently achieved by the Member States and can therefore, by reason of the scale or

The institutional arrangements set out by the Treaty are important for the future of the states that comprise Europe, and for their evolution towards a more explicit political union. But it must be emphasized that when it comes to precise details about the 'democratic' character of these institutional arrangements, the Treaty remains deliberately discreet. It is content to refer to general 'principles of democracy', and to the ways in which the member states express their 'attachment' to these principles in their own political processes.

The construction of a political Europe is certainly an arduous task for which no model exists to guide the Union towards democracy. Everything will have to be invented gradually, both to constitute the Union and to adapt the member states. But according to the terms of the Treaty itself, the process of invention can in no way avoid reflecting on the 'principles' of democracy, and on the experience that Europe has had of democracy. Only a far-sighted and rigorous analysis of the relationship between democracy and the fundamental notions of politics allows us to determine these principles and evaluate this experience. No less indispensable is a profound knowledge of the diversity of political processes in the member states and of how they fulfil those principles while remaining 'efficient'.

It is noticeable that this notion of efficiency, combined with the reference to democratic and other principles, poses a question in its turn. What does 'efficiency' mean from the point of view of democracy? Does democracy need to be chosen, or wished for, because of its greater 'efficiency' compared to other political set-ups? And, if so, what are the criteria of 'efficiency'? Does the Maastricht Treaty not indicate the contrary view: that the requirements of efficiency come into competition with the requirements that flow from the principles of democracy? Are the reasons for constructing a democratic form of politics unrelated, then, to considerations of efficiency in political life? Thus the debate on 'European' institutions leads back to the essays in the earlier parts of the book, which raised this last question from a number of points of view, marrying rational inquiry (which provides generalizations) to historical knowledge (which takes care to notice the differences between cases).

Pursuing such a method, I believe I was able to show in Essay 6 that efficiency depended upon criteria, whereas democracy arose from 'aspirations'. I also explained the rationale in a democracy for the difference between these two perspectives on political institutions. The ongoing construction of Europe seems to confirm this theoretical difference. Yet it also shows that, once the process of building a body politic is really under way, 'criteria' are in practice subordinated to 'aspirations'. For if functional efficiency were the only issue, the construction of Europe ought reasonably to exclude any extension of the powers of the Union.

effects of the proposed action, be better achieved by the Community. Any action by the Community shall not go beyond what is necessary to achieve the objectives of this Treaty.'

Thus, where the Community and the Member States acting together may consider *going beyond* the explicit areas laid down in the Treaty, this provision places on them a burden of proof to show that the extension is necessary to achieve the goals of the existing areas of activity. There is no expectation that Community activity will decline; rather it will be a brake on any extensions.

It is already over-burdened with Community business, which currently includes monetary policies, social policies, cultural policies, and so on. Furthermore, it ought to be necessary to reject all idea of enlarging the number of countries in the Union. In the opinion of Europe's 'governors', it is clear that the critical threshold of governmentability[3] has now been reached for the Union. Yet these perspectives are laid down in the Treaty, which explicitly anticipates that the conditions for their practical realization will be examined during the period up to 1996.

It must be admitted that the attempt to construct a political Europe transcends the present bounds of the modern western state. This process of transcendence has been undertaken following the European peoples' painful experience of the limits of that form of state. These limits arise, in particular, from its claim to absolute sovereignty, and the link formed between this absolutism and the historic experience of the 'nation', the 'people', the 'race', etc., when these are erected as the basis of an unchanging identity. When it comes to the treatment of outsiders, who are the 'other' of the nation, that version of national identity is a deadly object of worship. However, we have to admit that several guiding ideas (such as nationalism) which are in competition with democracy are contributing to the direction of European construction, and to decisions on its institutional arrangements. Yet this European process of transcendence, taking place slowly, with difficulty and in different ways, in the heart of the different polities of Europe, is in itself an endeavour to re-invent democracy as a form of politics.

---

[3]   For this term, see note 3 in the introduction to Part III. (NP)

Essay 7
The democratic institutions of European countries

Prepared for the Course Team by Pierre Avril
Professor of Public Law, University of Paris II
Translated by John Williams

Introduction

The 12 countries of the European Community share, first and foremost, a common historical heritage. All have experienced monarchy in some form[1] and half of them – Belgium, Denmark, Spain, the UK, Luxemburg and the Netherlands – still retain it today. In contrast, France, Greece, Ireland, Italy, Portugal and Germany have adopted the republican system (the most recent of these being Greece, which rejected monarchy in the referendum of December 1974 following the restoration of democracy).

The British model of parliamentary monarchy enjoyed intellectual pre-eminence among the élite of nineteenth-century Europe. But it did not always find fertile soil on the continent, where it conflicted with the idea of national sovereignty inherited from the French Revolution. That idea demanded universal suffrage and national independence. Whereas the British parliamentary monarchy, through the electoral reforms of 1832 and 1867–85, gradually came to accommodate an ever-greater level of participation on the part of the mass of the people, on the continent the progress of democracy was frequently interrupted by periods of authoritarian reaction (even before the upheavals arising out of the First World War led to the dictatorships Europe experienced between 1919 and 1945). The Second World War brought an end to dictatorships in Germany and Italy, but others survived until 1974 (Portugal) and 1975 (Spain). 1974 also saw the fall of the Greek 'colonels', in power since 1967. Since then western Europe has managed to recover its unity and, as it were, pick up the threads of its own history. At the same time, the way has been cleared for these last three southern European countries to become members of the EC.

---

[1] Even if only before independence as in the case of Ireland, which belonged to the United Kingdom until 1922.

The European political model

The institutions of the EC's 12 member states present, in all their diversity, a sufficiently homogeneous character for us to be able to speak of a 'European political model' without this being a purely arbitrary term.[2] This political model falls under the general heading of constitutional democracy, which is common to most western systems of government. But we can characterize it more precisely by its specifically European variant – the parliamentary system.

Constitutional democracy

Constitutional democracy arose out of the conjunction of two distinct historical currents: popular sovereignty and political liberalism. Popular sovereignty represents a principle of legitimacy, nowadays beyond dispute, which finds its practical application in universal suffrage: all 12 countries of the Community grant the right to vote in general elections to all citizens, male or female, from the age of 18. This democratic legitimacy takes its place within a constitutional framework inspired by liberalism, which is founded on the principle of the separation of powers, formulated by Montesquieu in *Spirit of the Laws* (1748) and applied for the first time in written form in the American Constitution of 1787.

Montesquieu drew his inspiration from the British example – which he systematized and somewhat distorted – of a monarchy with limited powers as it prevailed in the first three decades or so of the eighteenth century. What he admired in the British system was its liberalism, as opposed to the absolutism which held sway on the continent. As Benjamin Constant[3] observed in 1800: 'A constitution is, in itself, an exercise in mistrust, since it prescribed limits to authority.'

The idea that power must be divided in order to be 'reined in' is nowadays combined with the democratic idea, which is antipathetic to it insofar as in theory democracy does not admit any limitation on the will of the sovereign people. Constitutional democracy reconciles these two traditions by organizing political power in a manner that imposes limits on it, making it subordinate to the law yet accountable to the electorate in the last resort.

All EC states have a written constitution except for the United Kingdom. The oldest are those of the Netherlands (which dates from 1815 but underwent major revision in 1983) and Belgium (dating from 1831, last revised in 1988). The most recent are those of Portugal (1976) and Spain (1978). The text adopted in 1949 by the West German state was not given the term 'constitution', but was known instead as the *Basic Law* until the reunification of Germany, which was not achieved until 1990.

---

[2]   See Quermonne (1990, p. 192).

[3]   French author and politician, 1767–1830. He was a supporter of limited government and one of the founding fathers of French liberal thought. (NP)

The European constitutions are said to be 'rigid' where they can be modified only by means of special procedures, which, in the case of the most recent constitutions, involve the direct intervention of the electorate through a referendum. Here, too, the UK is the exception, precisely because its 'constitution' is not set down in a written document but is the result of a complex set of rules. Some of these are written, ranging from ancient texts such as the Bill of Rights of 1689 (or the Habeas Corpus Act of 1679), to the Parliament Acts of 1911 and 1949, to the Representation of the People Acts of 1949 and 1983. All of these are laws that were passed in the normal manner. Other rules come under the heading of common law, notably the royal prerogative, which is what remains of the authority traditionally recognized as belonging to the Crown (for example, international relations or the right to dissolve Parliament). These legal rules, applied by the courts, are supplemented by political rules which Dicey[4] has described as constitutional conventions and which concern the exercise of the powers conferred by the legal rules. These conventions apply in particular to the appointment of the Prime Minister, to cabinet government, etc.

Being written and rigid, the European constitutions have an authority superior to that of ordinary laws passed by parliaments, and this superiority shows up in the creation of an apparatus to monitor the constitutionality of laws – a court, tribunal or constitutional council. Based on ideas of the Austrian jurist Hans Kelsen,[5] this type of monitoring is becoming a distinctive characteristic of the European political model: a special constitutional court exists in Germany, Spain, France, Italy and Portugal, and also in Belgium for questions concerning the communities and the regions. In Denmark and Greece, the ordinary courts monitor the constitutionality of laws, while in Ireland the role is fulfilled by the Supreme Court. No such monitoring function exists in the UK (since it does not have a written constitution), nor in the Netherlands or Luxemburg.

The parliamentary system of government: dualism and monism

The features common to the political institutions of the EC states have as their foundation the shared heritage referred to above. Whether monarchies or republics, all of them practise parliamentary government, whose modern-day form is the culmination of a long process which began with a pragmatic accommodation between the power of the Crown and the principle of representation. Initially the preserve of the moneyed classes, representation took on a more democratic character and, in so doing, gradually acquired a unified legitimacy and the authority derived from it.

At first, the exercise of power was shared between the Crown and Parliament; the monarch chose his or her ministers from among the major groupings in the parlia-

---

[4] A. V. Dicey (1835–1922), English jurist and professor of law at Oxford. His *Law of the Constitution* (1885) authoritatively laid down the English consitution of his day. Dicey is further discussed in Francesco D'Agostino's essay in this volume. (NP)

[5] Extensively discussed in Francesco D'Agostino's essay. (NP)

mentary chamber, thus ensuring their co-operation. The ministers, including the chief minister who was in charge of the cabinet, were accountable both to the monarch, who could dismiss them, and to Parliament, which could express its lack of confidence in them. This double accountability has given rise to the term 'parliamentary dualism', which is applied to the initial phase of this form of government. During this phase, the legitimacy of the monarchy was still strong enough for Parliament, elected under a franchise based on property and thus resting on only a narrow popular base, to allow the Crown direct political influence over the government.

This phase came to an end in Great Britain following the resignation of Lord Melbourne in 1834, after he had been repudiated by King William IV. This was exactly two years after the electoral reform of 1832, when a wider and clearly defined franchise gave greater elective legitimacy to the House of Commons. Subsequently, the confidence of the Commons was established as the sole basis of cabinet authority, with the Crown giving up the pursuit of policies in its own right and obliged to accept whatever was supported by Parliament. Because it unifies the exercise of power under the aegis of the parliamentary majority, this second phase is termed 'parliamentary monism'. Under this set-up, the formal separation of powers is qualified by the common political interest that links the executive and legislative branches.

Nowadays, in those countries which still retain a monarchy, the king or queen represents no more than a symbol of unity and historical continuity, while the powers that traditionally belonged to the Crown are exercised, *de facto* or *de jure*, by a government accountable only to Parliament. In the republics, an elected president fulfils this symbolic function, standing for the necessary continuity of the state over and above the government, whose period in office, since it depends on a parliamentary majority, may be interrupted at any moment. Parliamentary monism has become the customary legal basis for government in the countries of Europe.

However, dualism, which had all but died out as an expression of shared legitimacy, has re-emerged in a democratic form in France where the President of the Republic, directly elected by universal suffrage, derives his own authority from this popular mandate. This enables him to take charge of the general political orientation of the country by appointing a government which, although it remains accountable to the National Assembly, is in fact the President's own.

Nevertheless, direct election by the people is not a sufficient condition for dualism to arise, since this tendency can be cancelled out where the presidency is not seen as the prize in a decisive political contest. Thus, in Ireland, where the President of the Republic is also elected by universal suffrage, the constitution provides for a popular vote only when there are several candidates. On four occasions since 1938 the parties have agreed on a single candidate, and hence there have only been four elections, the most recent won by Mary Robinson in 1990.

In France, on the other hand, election by universal suffrage was introduced in 1962 in order to confirm the presidential authority exercised by Charles de Gaulle and disputed by most of the political parties. But to be effective, dualism requires the majority which elects the president to correspond to the majority in parliament.

It cannot be maintained for any length of time if the parliamentary majority openly opposes the policies of the president. This situation arose exceptionally in France between 1986 and 1988, but is the norm in Portugal, the third EC country where the president is elected by universal suffrage. As a consequence the presidency, forced to 'cohabit' with parliamentary majorities that are not allied to it, has to take up a relatively neutral position in politics. Elected president in 1985, the Socialist leader, Mario Soares, found himself faced in 1987 with an Assembly where the main rival to the Socialist party, the centrist Social Democratic party, held an absolute majority. So successfully did he act as an arbiter above party politics that he was re-elected almost unopposed in 1991, supported not only by the Socialists but also by the Social Democrats – who thus gave their seal of approval to the President's conduct. Under these conditions, the Portuguese system of government is getting closer to Irish monism than French dualism.

Representation

Representation, the cornerstone common to the institutions of all the European countries, is a political device designed to reconcile the unity of the state and the natural diversity of society. The government of the country must reflect this diversity in order for the population to identify with it, but the government must at the same time convey to the population an image of its own unity. That is the reason why representation presupposes that the legislators elected by the citizens are representatives not just of their constituents, but of the nation as a whole. They exercise the sovereignty of the nation. As Edmund Burke[6] stated in the speech he addressed to his Bristol constitutents in 1774: 'Parliament is not a congress of ambassadors with differing and hostile interests....Parliament is a deliberative assembly of one nation, with one interest, that of the whole' (Burke, 1878, p. 447).

But although unity and diversity have to be reconciled, the way representation operates inevitably gives greater emphasis to one or other tendency. In the one case, priority is given to the affirmation of a national will: to determining a majority charged with carrying out the tasks of government. The majority must explicitly assume this responsibility, so that voters have a clear idea of what is at stake when they make their decision. The responsibility cannot be shared because the role of the opposition is – precisely – to embody the possibility of choosing an alternative. The possibility that the electorate could make a different choice legitimizes the majority's present claim on power. Where affirming the national will is not the prime consideration, priority is given to accurately representing all strands of opinion, implying that they should all take part in political decision-making in proportion to their relative strength. This means coalition government is the rule. In the extreme case, it embraces all the major parties as in Switzerland, but in any event parliamentary debate enables the parties which are not part of the coalition to play a role, and thus be associated with the decision-making process.

Historical conditions show through, in part, in the priority given to one or other of the two tendencies inherent in the concept of representation. In Britain the rep-

[6]   Irish writer and politician at Westminster, 1729–97. An early opponent of the French Revolution, he nonetheless favoured enlightened conservative government and was a founding father of the British constitutional conservative tradition. (NP)

resentative system of government came together in a form of participation in the exercise of the powers of the Crown by the 'Lords Temporal and Spiritual' (the House of Lords) and the elected representatives of the boroughs and counties (the Commons). The purpose of this association lay more in upholding the monarch's government than in challenging it. An oppositional role was also recognized: reserved precisely for 'Her Majesty's Opposition'. From revolutionary France onwards, by contrast, parliaments in the absolutist monarchies of continental Europe quite naturally took up the role of adversary to the Crown, which up to that point had rejected any form of power-sharing. Parliament had set up a rival claim to power and it seemed logical that the executive power, identified with the monarch's government, should be made subject to parliament's will, since that represented the will of the sovereign people. In the first case, representation developed as a kind of top-down movement of power into society, whereas in the second it meant the struggle between the newly emerging power of the people's representatives and the traditional power of the monarchy.

Though the principle of representation is the cornerstone of constitutional democracy, the modern era has produced forms of immediate and direct expression of the popular will in order to legitimize exceptional decisions or make choices which cut across party lines. The approval of a new constitution or the decision to join the European Community have thus been subject to referenda in France, Spain, Denmark, the UK and Greece, whereas in Italy recourse to mechanisms of direct democracy has become more or less commonplace.

Majority democracy and consociational democracy

Up until the 1960s Anglo-Saxon political science, which identified democracy with the two-party systems characteristic of the UK and the USA, tended to consider multi-party states which diverged from this model as 'imperfect' – and therefore fragile – democracies. This ethnocentric attitude prompted European political scientists to draw their colleagues' attention to the qualities – in particular the stability – of certain continental European states, such as those of the Benelux countries and of northern Europe. They gave these the name 'consociational democracy' (Lijphardt, 1984) or 'concordant democracy' *(Konkordanzdemokratie)* (Lehmbruch, 1967).

Lijphardt has produced a systematic analysis where he distinguishes two ideal types: majoritarian democracy, which he calls the 'Westminster model', and the 'consensus model'. He organizes the definition of these two 'pure' types of democracy around eight pairs of opposing terms:

- government by a single party/broad coalition

- domination by the executive branch/balance between the executive and legislative branches

- two-party system/multi-party system

- one issue-dimension party system/multi-issue-dimension party system[7]
- voting system favouring majority rule/proportional representation
- centralization/decentralization[8]
- single-chamber system/two-chamber system
- unwritten constitution/rigid constitution.

Put schematically, these eight pairs of terms indicate that, in the case of the Westminster model, there exists no obstacle to domination by the majority, while the characteristics of the consensus model place limits on such domination.

Lijphardt's theory provides an interpretive grid which allows us to classify systems of government according to whether they show a tendency towards one or other of the ideal types. As we have already seen, we can locate the earliest origins of this tendency, which determine the overall character of the representative systems of government, in the conditions under which they were established. But historical traditions alone cannot explain what these forms of government mean in practice today. We need to take into account the nature of the conflicts which democracy is supposed to provide the means to resolve.

When hostile communities come into conflict or when unbridgeable differences have to be reconciled, the majoritarian formula can be incapable of providing the peaceful methods of arbitration needed, because centrifugal forces may prevail over forces of unity. The solutions offered by consociational democracy are then sought, as they allow for a constant process of negotiation and compromise between partners, none of whom is in a position to impose their will.

But we also have to reckon with the trend in modern societies to expect policy initiatives and efficient management from government; this requires that the government enjoy a degree of support and autonomy which will enable it to carry out its functions. This has resulted in an evolution in political behaviour towards the formation of stable coalitions – organized around powerful, disciplined parties – which is modifying the practice of consensus democracy and bringing it closer to majoritarian democracy.

Applied to the EC states, Lijphardt's typology shows that the UK, as the term 'Westminster model' indicates, represents the archetype of the majoritarian model,

---

[7]   Where one 'issue dimension' predominates, parties are subsumed under a single main issue; they can be distinguished by policies and beliefs grouped into a single range of positions. For example, there may be parties advocating more or less welfare, or there may be parties more or less attached to traditional religion. In a multi-issue-dimension system, parties exist to reflect a number of cross-cutting ranges of position: Catholic advocates of welfare distinct from Catholic opponents, anti-Catholic advocates and anti-Catholic opponents of welfare, and so on. (NP)

[8]   The term used in the French original is 'fédéralisme'. However, the byways of British politics in 1991 altered the sense of the direct transposition of that term (i.e. 'federalism') to mean the very opposite of 'fédéralisme'. In the British context, 'federalism' has come to mean centralization. (NP)

elaborated precisely on the basis of this example. The French Fifth Republic,[9] founded deliberately on majoritarian principles, has this much in common with Britain (though its original constitutional blueprint, unlike Britain's, was dualist). In contrast, Belgium (with its different linguistic communities which have led to something approaching a federal structure), the Netherlands and Denmark fall within the consensus model. Germany occupies an intermediate position: Bundestag elections combine proportional representation with a 'personalized', majoritarian element,[10] and its party system approximates to the two-party model, though it is necessary to resort to coalitions.[11] The term 'Chancellor-democracy' (*Kanzlerdemokratie*), which emphasizes the dominance of the Chancellor, likens German government practice to British cabinet government, but the Bundestag acts more as a balance to the executive than does the House of Commons, and federalism puts additional limitations on the power of the centre. Spain, which combines majoritarian government with a strong element of decentralization, provides a further intermediate example.

The organs of state

The head of state

The existence of a politically unaccountable head of state, distinct from the head of government who is accountable to parliament, derives from the very nature of parliamentary government. This contrasts with the American system of government, which is not parliamentary, where the head of state (the President) is also the head of government. In the six EC monarchies, the hereditary sovereign fulfils this function, whereas in the six republics, a president is elected for a certain term of office (seven years in France, Ireland and Italy; five years in Greece, Portugal and Germany). The manner in which he or she is chosen varies. In Greece the president is elected by the Chamber of Deputies (by a two-thirds majority in the first two rounds, or by a three-fifths majority if a third round is necessary, failing which parliament is automatically dissolved). Direct universal suffrage comes into play in France, Ireland (if there is more than one candidate) and Portugal, while Italy and Germany rely on a special electoral college. In Italy this consists of all members of parliament and senators, plus three delegates for each of the 20 regions (except for the Valley of Aosta, which has only one). The federal character of the German state is evident in the fact that members of the Bundestag meet in

[9]   That is, the set-up created by the 1958 constitution which introduced, among other things, direct elections for the president. (NP)

[10]   German voters have two votes. They cast one vote for an individual standing for their constituency, and the other for a list of candidates put forward nationally by each party. The proportions of total 'list' votes cast determine the relative numbers of each party in the legislature. The votes for individuals give priority to successful candidates when it comes to the question of who, from the parties, actually takes up the seats. (NP)

[11]   Jean Blondel (1969) has dubbed this a 'two-and-a-half-party system'.

joint session to elect a president with an equal number of delegates elected by the parliaments of the 11 *Länder*[12] (16 since unification), each *Land* being represented in proportion to its population.

Embodying the permanence of the state, the queen or the president normally stands aside from party politics, and her lack of accountability obliges her to observe a certain discretion with regard to matters of political debate. This deference to an accountable government is expressed, in Britain, through the custom of the Queen's (or King's) Speech, drawn up by the Prime Minister and delivered by the Queen, who is thus called upon to present impartially to Parliament the programmes of Labour and Conservative governments, as the case may be.

The symbolic character of the office of head of state is no doubt more obvious in the case of monarchies where, alongside legitimacy conferred by law, the head of state retains the vestiges of what Max Weber calls traditional legitimacy. Precisely for that reason, this symbolic character can be particularly effective when the sovereign intervenes during a crisis in the name of the national unity which he or she embodies. Just such a case occurred in Spain when King Juan Carlos opposed the attempted military coup in 1981.

The rebellion leader, Colonel Antonio Tejero, in the Spanish Parliament during the attempted coup in February 1981 (credit: Hulton Deutsch).

[12]   The name given to the federated states of Germany. (NP)

Under a parliamentary system of government, the head of state possesses a certain number of established prerogatives in international relations (such as the ratification of treaties and the accreditation of ambassadors) and in internal affairs (such as the ratification of laws and the nomination of senior public officers). But these notional powers are all exercised *de facto* by the government, usually in the form of a countersignature whereby documents officially signed by the head of state are also signed by the head of government. It follows from the logic of parliamentary monism that the head of state never refuses his or her signature, although the extent of this obligation may vary according to the political situation. When no clear majority exists to impose the decisions of the politicians, the head of state regains some room to take initiatives and arbitrate (as does the Italian President, for example). We shall see below what margin of discretion this leaves when it comes to forming governments.

Furthermore, the logic of monism accommodates a number of exceptions connected with the head of state's role as arbiter. On the question of dissolution, for instance, a constitutional convention obliges the British Queen to comply with the Prime Minister's recommendation, but this system of 'ministerial' dissolution (as it is known) has not entirely removed from the head of state a certain power of discretion, at least as regards the right of refusal. The Italian President is even entitled to take the initiative, as is the Portuguese President in certain conditions. In addition, the Portuguese President has the power to dismiss the government, a power also possessed at one time by the Greek President. But it is significant that the 1975 Greek constitution and the 1976 Portuguese constitution, prompted by the 1958 French constitution, have both been revised (in 1982 and 1986 respectively) along lines which limit the president's political prerogatives, now partially taken back by the government.

Hence, the French Fifth Republic offers the only real example of genuine dualism. As well as carrying out all the classic functions of a parliamentary head of state, which in other countries would be purely nominal, the French President possesses powers of his own which he effectively exercises alone: dissolution of the National Assembly, referenda, and his special powers under Article 16 (authorizing all necessary decisions in the event of a serious crisis). In this connection, it is revealing that the President represents France at meetings of the European Council of Ministers, where all the other nations are represented by their heads of government. Similarly, he chairs cabinet meetings, whereas his counterparts in other countries do not even attend, or do so only at the invitation of the prime minister (as in Portugal).

The head of government

The executive in a parliamentary system is a collegiate body whose members are, at one and the same time, the administrative heads of the various ministries and collectively the officials in charge of the country's political affairs. This collegiate character varies, however, according to the structure of the parliamentary majority and the development of personal power which characterizes modern democracies. The British and Spanish Prime Ministers and the German Chancellor possess

State opening of Parliament in the United Kingdom (credit: House of Commons Public Information Service).

genuine power to direct, whereas the Italian President of the Council of Ministers[13] is, in spite of the recent strengthening of his role, merely *primus inter pares*[14] and obliged to negotiate with the coalition parties in the government.

The head of government is formally appointed by the head of state in accordance with procedures which fall into two main categories. Either the nomination takes effect without parliament being called upon to ratify it (as in the UK, Denmark and France) or alternatively a parliamentary decision is necessary. In Germany the Chancellor is elected by the Bundestag and then officially appointed by the state President. The principle of inauguration by parliament is enforced in the form of a

---

[13]   This title for the prime minister was deliberately adopted by Italy after World War II, when the powers of the head of government were reduced. (NP)

[14]   First among equals. (NP)

vote of confidence for the head of government in Italy, Spain and Greece. In other countries, parliamentary confirmation is not explicitly required by the constitution but has arisen through political custom and practice.

Only in France does theory coincide with practice, insofar as the President's power of nomination is discretionary, though limited by accountability to the National Assembly – which forced François Mitterrand to appoint Jacques Chirac, the main leader of the opposition, as head of government after the opposition had won the elections of March 1986. In the UK, constitutional convention obliges the Queen to send for the leader of the party that wins the election, who forms a government without a vote in the House of Commons, since he or she usually holds a majority by virtue of the electoral system. Where the Prime Minister re-signs during the lifetime of a parliament, the MPs belonging to his or her party choose the new leader, who is then immediately sent for by the Queen (as we saw following the resignation of Margaret Thatcher and her replacement by John Major in November 1990). The Queen's liberty of action is thus as circumscribed as that of the German President after the Chancellor has been elected by the Bundestag. In Denmark the absence of any parliamentary inauguration allows minority governments to be formed, but only on the initiative of the parties them-

Queen Beatrix presents the new Dutch government to the press in 1989 (credit: Bert Verhoeff, Hollandse Hoogte).

selves. The Greek constitution specifies in minute detail the steps that the President must follow: he sends first for the leader of the party with an absolute majority or, failing that, the leader of the largest party – then, if unsuccessful, for the leader of the second largest party. He regains freedom of choice (subject to a vote of confidence) only if none of these attempts bears fruit.

In all cases, the head of state's range of options is conditioned by the political make-up of the assembly. He or she does not possess any discretionary power when there exists a predetermined majority able to secure the appointment of its own leader as head of the government. This is the situation in Britain, Germany and Spain. By contrast, the Italian President is able, through his own initiatives, to orchestrate the formation of a coalition. Prior to the election of Sandro Pertini as President of the Republic in 1978, the Prime Minister was, by convention, chosen from the ranks of the Christian Democrats. But in 1981 Pertini called on Giovanni Spadolini, from the small Republican Party, and then in 1983 on the Socialist leader Bettino Craxi.[15] In 1987 his successor, Francesco Cossiga, fell back once more on leading Christian Democrat figures. In Belgium and the Netherlands, a government is formed only after what often turn out to be very lengthy consultations, and before appointing the Prime Minister, the monarch assigns a leading political figure to explore the possible combinations.

In every country apart from France, the head of government alone chooses the ministers – but, here again, his or her freedom of action is conditioned by the political make-up of the majority. Though unrestricted in Britain, this freedom is necessarily reduced, in the case of coalitions, by the demands of the parties involved. They divide up the ministries between themselves and their leaderships sometimes remain (as in Italy or Belgium) the real centres of decision-making, producing compromises that the government simply endorses. Members of the government are generally chosen from among the members of parliament. This is obligatory in the UK, but in France, Luxemburg, the Netherlands and Portugal, these roles are considered incompatible, so members of parliament (or senators) are obliged to resign their seats on their appointment as ministers.

Parliament

In four of the 12 EC countries, parliament consists of only one chamber: the Folketing in Denmark (since 1954), the Chamber of Deputies in Greece and Luxemburg, and the Assembly of the Republic of Portugal. The other eight operate a two-chamber system. But while the first chamber is, in every case, elected by direct universal suffrage – like the single assemblies of the four countries named above – the second chamber represents a response to different concerns. With the exception of the British House of Lords (which is made up of hereditary and life peers, and thus appears in this context to be something of a historical remnant), all consist of elected members (plus in the case of the Irish Seanad a number of figures nominated by the Prime Minister and members representing economic, social or cultural groups).

[15]   See Giustino d'Oragio (1985).

Federal government involves a special kind of two-chamber system in which the first chamber represents the people, while the second chamber provides for the direct participation of the federated communities. This is the situation in Germany, where the Bundestag is elected by direct universal suffrage and the Bundesrat is made up of members of the governments of the individual *Länder*. This concern to represent the different parts of the territory occurs in other countries which do not have a federal structure, but which practise forms of decentralization having much in common with federalism: the French, Belgian and Dutch senators are elected indirectly by electoral colleges made up of local councillors (though the Belgian senate also includes directly elected members), while the Spanish senate includes members elected directly from each of the 47 provinces (plus others who are appointed by the parliaments of the autonomous communities). Italian senators are elected by universal suffrage, but within a framework of the 20 regions. Unlike the other second chambers, whose powers are always of a lesser nature than those of the chambers representing the population, the Italian second chamber enjoys equal status with the first.

The Belgian and Italian senates are the only ones that can call the government to account, a prerogative which normally belongs to lower chambers. Conversely, if challenged, the executive can have the assembly dissolved. This gives the executive a lever over the assembly; if it votes the government down, its members may be subject to the risk of re-election, unlike the Bundesrat or the French and Italian senates.

Relationships between government and parliament

Confining our attention to lower chambers, we can identify two main functions which they perform: political supervision and legislation. Political supervision, which concerns the government's accountability, is exercised from the moment of its formation according to the principle of parliamentary inauguration. It continues throughout the government's lifetime, which the lower chamber can cut short by passing a motion of censure. On a formal level, those more recent constitutions which are informed by the concept of 'rationalized' parliamentary government lay down in precise detail the conditions and procedures necessary to challenge the government's right to govern. In the UK constitutional convention leaves it to the Prime Minister who finds himself in a minority to judge whether he still enjoys sufficient parliamentary support to allow him to remain in office: only when he is explicitly censured, or when his budget is rejected, is he obliged to stand down. By contrast, the German Chancellor can be removed from office only if the Bundestag passes a motion of 'constructive censure'; it must also nominate his successor.

The exercise of these procedures depends on the political character of the parliamentary majority involved. The British two-party system makes the onset of a crisis exceptional. When James Callaghan was censured on 28 March 1979, one had to go back as far as 1924 to find the previous precedent for a crisis precipitated by a vote in the House of Commons. The 'constructive censure' allowed for under

Article 67 of the German Basic Law has been exercised twice, in 1972 and 1982. But only on the latter occasion did it result in the resignation of the Social Democrat Chancellor, Helmut Schmidt, and his replacement by the Christian Democrat Helmut Kohl, due to a switch in allegiance by the Liberal party – which up to that point had been allied to the Social Democrats. Conversely, coalitions formed at a purely parliamentary level – rather than prior to the election – turn out to be a lot more fragile, and the survival of the government essentially depends on the decisions of the parties involved. When one of them decides to withdraw, the government falls apart from within, without a vote by members of parliament. This is what happens in Italy and Belgium.

The other main function of parliamentary assemblies is to pass laws. Bills put forward by the government and proposals emanating from parliament itself are normally examined by committees, either standing committees specializing in a particular policy area or ones set up specifically to study a particular text. In two-chamber systems, both chambers take part in the process of debate. But the powers of the second chamber are generally more limited because, in the event of a disagreement, the decision rests with the people's elected representatives (either after a certain lapse of time as in Britain or after conciliation as in France). In single-chamber systems, several successive readings by the one assembly generally replace readings by both chambers, which ensures a more rigorous examination. In Italy the committees can pass laws, as can one of the sections of the Spanish Congress.

Generally speaking, it is mainly the government that initiates legislation, and it often has priority in the examination of bills. This dominance, a consequence of the often highly technical nature of legislation, also reflects the fact that the government's general policy line is put into practice through the medium of legislation. So the interdependence which characterizes parliamentary systems leads logically to a situation in which the government is recognized as having a leading role in drawing up legislation. This lay behind Article 49, paragraph 3 of the French constitution – a bill on which the Prime Minister has staked the government's authority is considered to have been adopted unless a motion of censure is put down for debate.[16]

In addition to parliament's powers, most European countries have procedures for delegating legislative powers, whereby parliament authorizes the government to modify or abolish certain laws, subject to subsequent ratification.

---

[16]   The motion requires a simple majority of deputies, counting only those taking part in the vote in order to nullify the effect of abstentions.

Elections and parties

Impact of electoral systems

All citizens have the right to vote from the age of 18 (for elections to the Italian senate, this age limit rises to 25). The minimum age to stand for election is generally higher: from 23 to 25 (and from 35 to 40 in the case of certain second chambers).[17]

Elections are conducted according to two main voting systems: those favouring majority rule or proportional representation. In its simplest form, practised in Britain, majority voting means a single round, in which the candidate who obtains the most votes is declared elected. In France, on the other hand, in order to be elected on the first round, an absolute majority of the votes cast is required; otherwise a second round is needed, this time requiring a simple majority.[18]

Unlike the British and French systems, where there are as many constituencies as there are members of parliament, proportional representation requires constituencies to fill several seats. In brief, it involves two phases. The first allocates the seats to parties on a 'quota' basis – that is, by dividing the total number of votes cast for each party by the number of seats to be filled (plus 1 in the case of Droop's quota method, or plus 2 according to Imperiali's formula). The second phase distributes those seats not allocated in the quota process. This operation is generally carried out using Hondt's system (or the system of the 'highest average'), which favours the major parties. It can be done either at the level of the individual constituency or on a national basis (in the Netherlands the entire country forms a single constituency). In order to prevent the representative assembly being too fragmented, a minimum number of the total votes is generally required to obtain any seats (3 per cent in Spain, 5 per cent in Germany, while in Italy the threshold in practice is less than 1 per cent), and a bonus is sometimes awarded to the winning party (as in Greece).

Unique voting systems are used in Ireland, where proportional representation is combined with the transferable vote, and in Germany, which operates a personalized form of proportional representation. In the latter, citizens have two votes: the first votes elect half the members of the Bundestag by a simple majority in each constituency; the second votes, to fill the other half of the seats, are cast for party

[17]   The word 'senate' comes from the Latin *senex*, meaning old man, with its connotations of wisdom!

[18]   An 'absolute' majority is greater than half the votes cast; a 'simple' majority is merely a larger number than those votes cast for the next most popular candidate (e.g. in a three-horse race). (NP)

Voting under proportional representation in the Netherlands – note the extensive list of candidates (credit: Werry Crone, Hollandse Hoogte).

lists within each *Land*.[19] Each party's total number of seats is determined by its proportion of the second votes, but the seats filled directly by the first votes count towards this number, the rest being made up of candidates drawn from party lists.

The voting system obviously affects the level of representation the parties enjoy in parliament, and thus the way the system of government operates. A comparison between the UK and Germany illustrates its effect on the fate of the smaller parties. Single-round majority voting has consistently denied the Liberals a place in the political process, because candidates from the two major parties come first in most constituencies; the proportional element in the German system has made smaller parties indispensable partners to form a majority in the Bundestag. In fact, German voters have used their second votes to benefit the Liberal party, so as to moderate the victories of the Social Democratic party up until 1982, and subsequently those of the CDU-CSU[20] (to whom the Liberals have been allied since that date). The consequence is that since 1969 the Liberals, with between 7 and 11 per cent of the votes, have occupied an important place in every government, and even brought Chancellor Kohl to power in 1982 by breaking with the Social Democrats. In contrast, the British Liberals, who receive on average more than double that number of votes, win only about 20 of the 632 seats in the House of Commons, and exercise little influence on national politics.

Here we come back to the dilemma of representation mentioned earlier: it privileges either the need to bring together a strong enough political will to provide the foundation for strong government, or the expression of diversity of opinions and interests. Though appropriate electoral techniques can balance these conflicting preoccupations, in the long term they can only be truly reconciled through a process of change in the political culture that should be the responsibility of political parties.

Party systems

Giovanni Sartori (1976) has shown that, to define a party system concretely, we must take account of only the 'relevant' parties – that is, those which play a role in institutions thanks to the size of their parliamentary representation or to the strategic position they occupy when it comes to forming majorities. (By way of example of the latter, the Italian Republican party, which obtains on average no more than 2 per cent of the votes, is included in nearly every government and has even headed one.) As for parties lacking 'governing potential', they are considered as part of the party system only if their importance in terms of popular support gives them a 'blackmail potential' to deter the government from some courses of action. This capacity is shown by the French and Italian Communist parties, for example, and indeed in certain circumstances by extreme right-wing movements. The 'Greens' seem to have acquired neither of these capacities.

---

[19]   See note 10 above. (NP)

[20]   A longstanding alliance of two parties, the Christlich Demokratische Union and the Christlich Soziale Union. (NP)

The party systems of the 12 EC states appear to offer a great diversity of configur-ations, all the more difficult to grasp insofar as they are not stable. However, they can be ranged within a functional classification based on the criterion of political change. Democracy is defined in practice by the possibility of peacefully replacing leaders with whom the people are dissatisfied. This cannot be evaluated in terms of a supposed 'will of the people', which cannot be known in its own right but only divined negatively after the event.[21] At one extreme of this classification stands the British two-party system; at the other the immobilized multi-party sys-tem in Italy. The UK operates on the basis of two parties alternating in power, which is always possible once the voters are given a choice. Italy depends upon the existence of what Jean-Claude Colliard (1978) calls a 'pivotal party' on which the whole political system turns. The Christian Democrats have been included in every government since 1949 and have led them almost continuously.

Between these two poles, a spread can be observed. In some cases, one dominant party controls the government as long as its opponents do not manage to put it into a minority position. In other cases, there are alternating coalitions of either the centre-right or the centre-left. Thus, Belgian politics has long rested on a suc-cession of majorities formed between either Christian Democrats and Liberals, or Liberals and Socialists, or indeed Christian Democrats and Socialists – until these groupings were complicated by the fragmentation due to the language issue. Similar groupings can also be found in German and Dutch politics.

The structure and cohesion of the system formed by the 'relevant' parties consti-tutes an essential element of the way institutions operate. When there are only two main parties (as in Britain), or when coalitions are formed in advance of elections (as in Germany), or when one party outstrips its rivals (as in Spain or Portugal), the leader of the winning party or coalition is in effect chosen by the voters to head the government. By contrast, in the looser multi-party systems, coalitions to achieve a majority are formed after elections on the basis of the relative strength of the parties and through negotiations between leaders. This is the model which fits Italy, Belgium and Denmark (where minority government is sustained thanks to the neutrality of the minor parties). Greece offers a different kind of example: since 1988 the Socialist party has lost its pre-eminence, and unstable coalitions have replaced majority government.

Finally, France differs from the others in that presidential elections by universal suffrage play a decisive role in structuring the political system. The parliamentary majority is organized, indeed, around the political forces which supported the President, and provides the support necessary for the government he appoints and leads (apart from the period of 'cohabitation' between 1986 and 1988). The party enjoying presidential support (the Gaullists up to 1974, the Socialists since 1981) occupies a dominant position in relation to its rivals. This means that the French party system is essentially dependent on the presidential election, and differs in this regard from other European systems, where the decisive role is played by elections to the legislature in accordance with the logic of parliamentary monism.

---

[21] The author derives this critique of the idea of the will of the people from the work of Joseph A. Schumpeter, especially *Capitalism, Socialism and Democracy* (1942). (NP)

Conclusion

The 'European political model' exhibited in the institutions of the EC countries is all the more worthy of this term since it applies equally to the Nordic countries and Austria, which, though not members of the EC, practise parliamentary government with the same characteristics (monist in the majority of cases, dualist in the case of Finland). The 'directorial' system of the Swiss Confederation[22] is the one exception to this rule but only in a formal sense: as far as its functioning is concerned, it can be classified as a 'consociational democracy' on the model of Belgium, Holland or Denmark.

From this point of view, the historical watershed of the last decade of the century, in which we have seen the countries of eastern and central Europe reunited with their western neighbours, represents the final stage in the unification begun in the 1970s following the collapse of the dictatorships of southern Europe. On the whole, the states liberated from communism are turning to parliamentary institutions, picking up the threads of the democracy they once practised. We note the attraction of solutions tried successfully in France and Germany, but also the search for original formulas, of which the mixed voting methods applied in Hungary and Bulgaria already provide an illustration. Through these variations on common themes, the European political model continues to bear fruit across the geographical and cultural space of Europe, which was divided at the end of the Second World War.

[22]   Where, formally speaking, the confederated cantons remain sovereign. (NP)

References

BLONDEL, J. (1969) *An Introduction to Comparative Government*, London, Weidenfeld & Nicolson.

BURKE, E. (1878) *The Works of the Right Honourable Edmund Burke*, vol. 1, London, Bohm's Standard Library.

COLLIARD, J.-C. (1978) *Les Régimes parlementaires contemporains*, Paris, Presses de la Fondation Nationale des Sciences Politiques.

LEHMBRUCH, G. (1967) *Proporzdemokratie: Politisches System und Politische Kultur in der Schweiz und in Österreich* (Proportional democracy: political system and political culture in Switzerland and Austria), Tubingen, Mohr.

LIJPHARDT, A. (1984) *Democracies: Patterns of Majoritarian and Consensus Governments in Twenty-one Countries*, New Haven, Yale University Press.

D'ORAGIO, G. (1985) *Presidenza Pertini (1978–85): Neutralità o Diarchia* (The Pertini presidency (1978–85): neutrality or divided government), Rimini, Maggiori Editore.

QUERMONNE, J.-L. (1990) 'Existe-t-il un modèle politique européen?', *Revue française de science politique*, Paris.

SARTORI, G. (1976) *Parties and Party Systems: A Framework for Analysis*, Cambridge, Cambridge University Press.

SCHUMPETER, J. A. (1942) *Capitalism, Socialism and Democracy*, New York, Harper.

Bibliography

General works

VON BEYME, K. (1970) *Die parlamentärischen Regierungssysteme in Europa*, Munich, Piper.

BLONDEL, J. (1969) *An Introduction to Comparative Government*, London, Weidenfeld and Nicolson.

CHALVIDAN, P.-H. and TRNKA, H. (1990) *Les Régimes politiques de l'Europe des Douze*, Paris, Eyrolles.

COLLIARD, J.-C. (1978) *Les Régimes parlementaires contemporains*, Paris, Presses de la Fondation Nationale des Sciences Politiques.

LAUVAUX, P. (1990) *Les Grandes Democraties contemporaines*, Paris, Presses Universitaires de France.

LIJPHART, A. (1984) *Democracies: Patterns of Majoritarian and Consensus Governments in Twenty-one Countries*, New Haven, Yale University Press.

MÉNY, Y. (1978, 1991) *Politique comparée – les démocraties: Allemagne, États-Unis, France, Grande-Bretagne, Italie*, Paris, Montchretien; trans. J. Floyd (1990) *Government and Politics in Western Europe: Britain, France, Italy and West Germany*, Oxford, Oxford University Press.

QUERMONNE, J.-L. (1986) *Les Régimes politiques occidentaux*, Paris, Editions du Seuil.

SMITH, G. (1989) *Politics in Western Europe*, London, Heinemann.

DE VERGOTTINI, G. (1991) *Diritto costituzionale comparativo*, Padova, CEDAM.

Specialist works

LAUVAUX, P. (1983) *La Dissolution des assemblées parlementaires*, Paris, Economica.

LAUVAUX, P. (1988) *Parlementarisme rationalisé et stabilité du pouvoir exécutif*, Brussels, Bruylant.

LAUNDY, P. (1989) *Les Parlements dans le monde*, Lausanne, Payot.

MASTIAS, J. and GRANGÉ, J. (eds) (1987) *Les Secondes Chambres du parlement en Europe occidentale*, Paris, Economica.

ROSE, R. and SULEIMAN, E. (eds) (1980) *Presidents and Prime Ministers*, Washington, D.C., American Enterprise Institute for Public Policy Research.

SARTORI, G. (1976) *Parties and Party Systems: A Framework for Analysis*, Cambridge, Cambridge University Press.

By country

Belgium

DELPÉRÉ, F. (1986–9) *Droit constitutionnel*, Brussels, Larcier.

MABILLE, X. (1986) *Histoire politique de la Belgique*, Brussels, CRISP.

Pouvoirs (1990) No. 54, *La Belgique*.

Spain

MOLAS, I. and PITARCH, I. E. (1987) *Las Cortès Generales en el sistema parlementario de gubierno*, Madrid, Tunos.

Pouvoirs (1984) No. 8, *L'Espagne démocratique*.

France

AVRIL, P. (1987) *La Ve République. Histoire politique et constitutionnelle*, Paris, PUF.

GICQUEL, J. (1991) *Droit constitutionnel et institutions politiques*, Paris, Montchrestien.

QUERMONNE, J.-L. (1987) *Le Gouvernement de la France sous la Ve République*, Paris, Dalloz.

Pouvoirs (1989) No. 49, *La Ve République-30 ans*.

Britain

CHARLOT, M. (1990) *Le Pouvoir politique en Grande Bretagne*, Paris, PUF.

KING, A. (ed.) (1985) *The British Prime Minister*, London, Macmillan.

MACKINTOSH, J. (1977) *The British Cabinet*, London, Methuen.

MATHIOT, A. (1955) *Le Régime politique britannique*, Paris, Armand Colin.

NORTON, P. (ed.) (1985) *Parliament in the 1980s*, Oxford, Basil Blackwell.

Pouvoirs (1986) No. 37, *La Grande Bretagne*.

Italy

PASQUINO, G. (ed.) (1985) *Il sistema politico italiano*, Bari, Laterza.

MANZELLA, A. (1991) *Il Parlamento*, Bologna, Il Mulino.

Pouvoirs (1981) No. 18, *Italie*.

Germany

VON BEYME, K. (1985) *The Political System of the Federal Republic of Germany*, London, Gower.

MÉNUDIER, H. (1986) *Système politique et élections en République Fédérale d'Allemagne*, Berne, Lang.

Pouvoirs (1982) No. 22, *La RFA*.

SCHAFER, F. (1982) *Der Bundestag*, Opladen, Westdeutscher Verlag.

Essay 8
Democracy and the construction of Europe

Prepared for the Course Team by Jean-Pierre Cot
Professor of Law, University of Paris and President
of the Socialist Group of the European Parliament
and Richard Corbett
Adviser on constitutional affairs to the Socialist
Group of the European Parliament

Introduction

Reduced to its essentials, the concept of representative democracy boils down to three key points:

- the adoption of legislation by a representative assembly elected by and accountable to the people

- dependence of the executive on the support of the elected assembly

- rule of the majority within the framework of the rule of law respecting the fundamental rights of individuals.

Of course, there may be and there are nuances. The elected representative assembly is not necessarily alone: it may share its powers with another chamber. In federal-type systems, there is traditionally a body of equal status representing the component states. The executive may, as in the United States, be elected separately from the legislature and not emerge from its majority. Majority rule may be qualified, in some circumstances, to require particular majorities for certain types of action. Nevertheless, in essence these three features are present in systems commonly described as representative democracies.

Yet in the European Community all three exist only to a highly limited degree. The powers that national parliaments, in ratifying the EC treaties, conferred upon its institutions are not exercised in conformity with the same principles of democracy and representation that apply at the national level. Hence the term 'democratic deficit' that has arisen to describe where this lacuna occurs in the Community's system. Nevertheless, the embryo of these three principles exists and has grown over the years. There is every chance it will grow still further.

The adoption of legislation by an elected parliamentary assembly

The European Community has a number of important powers:

- It can adopt legislation which overrides national law (the role of the European Court of Justice[1] is particularly important).

- It has a substantial budget financed out of its own resources.

- It can adopt treaties with other countries and international organizations.

These powers apply to large areas of policy:

- the organization of a common market, including competition policy, environmental standards, consumer protection regulations, etc.

- a common external trade policy (with a common external tariff)

- a common agricultural policy

- transport

- some fiscal harmonization

- regional and social policies (with substantial funds available), and so forth.

The introduction of a common currency in the framework of a monetary union is being considered. In addition, the foreign ministries of the member states and the European institutions work together to coordinate their positions on foreign policy matters, including political and economic aspects of security. In all, the Commission President, Jacques Delors, has estimated that up to 80 per cent of economic and social legislation will be of EC, rather than national, origin by the mid-1990s. Even if the percentage is not as high as that, it will nevertheless represent a substantial proportion of public policy-making.

To ensure democratic scrutiny of those policy sectors in which national parliaments in effect transferred responsibility to the European Community, the treaties progressively creating the Community have included a parliamentary body among its institutions. It was not merely symbolic but related to the exercise of important powers, helping to avoid a 'democratic deficit' which would have undermined the legitimacy, and therefore the effectiveness, of the Community. In the process of integration, it is important to have a balance between the effective integration of policy-making and democratic accountability.

Nevertheless, the member states were originally cautious about giving the European Parliament itself much power. Under the original treaties, they vested legislative power primarily with the Council (composed of government ministers from the different nations), and the member states and the Council kept the power to nominate and mandate the executive Commission in their hands. Parliament was given the right to scrutinize the executive (via debates and questions), to be

---

[1]   Court made up of 13 judges sitting at Luxemburg, which decides on the legality, in terms of Community law, of legislation enacted by national governments or the Community's own bodies. (NP)

consulted on proposals for legislation and on the budget, to act as a forum, and to dismiss the Commission. (A new Commission is, however, appointed by the member states.)

These limited powers have been increased over the years in five main stages:

(1)   The Community budget

Two treaties amending the budgetary provisions of the original treaties were signed in 1970 and 1975. They gave the European Parliament the right to make changes to the budget, and to determine the allocation of expenditure for certain categories (within the limit of EC resources and providing the overall increase from one year to the next does not exceed a certain rate). Parliament can also reject the budget outright. Once the procedure of consideration is complete, the President of the Parliament ratifies the budget.

Over the years the European Parliament, unlike some national parliaments in Europe, has frequently amended and gradually reshaped the EC budget. It can also use its budgetary powers in other ways: for instance, by freezing certain items of expenditure where it is dissatisfied with the way the Commission is carrying out policy, or by creating new budget lines when it wishes to initiate new action.

(2)   Conciliation procedure

In 1975 the EC's institutions jointly agreed to establish a conciliation procedure for legislation with budgetary consequences. They recognized that if the European Parliament was dissatisfied with such legislation, it could (at least theoretically) withhold the necessary funding. The procedure therefore provided that for budgetary proposals, if Council wished to depart from the opinion expressed by Parliament, they would refer it to a conciliation committee composed of each of the national ministers in the Council and an equal number of MEPs (Members of the European Parliament) delegated by Parliament. The committee has three months to find a compromise on the text in question.

In practice, the procedure is a negotiation between unequal bodies, as it remains Council's prerogative to adopt the legislation after the three-month deadline, and Parliament is unlikely to use its budgetary powers to block the implementation of EC programmes, which it is normally keen to develop. Nevertheless, the procedure was a first step beyond a purely consultative role for the Parliament in the adoption of legislation.

(3)   Direct election

The third step forward was not, strictly speaking, an increase in the powers of Parliament, but was nevertheless a major reinforcement in its democratic legitimacy and influence. In 1979 the European Parliament became a full-time directly elected body. Not only was this significant in terms of the democratic legitimacy it conferred, but it also had a number of other major effects:

- Being a member of the European Parliament became a full-time job. The number of members holding a dual mandate (membership of both the European Parliament and a national parliament) declined. It was not forbidden, but it became increasingly difficult and impractical to carry out both functions. As a result, there came into being a group of politicians whose main interests and careers depended upon the success of the European dimension in politics.

- The advent of regular European elections forced national political parties to consider their positions on European affairs in considerably more detail than they had before. In adopting their positions, they were inevitably influenced by the MEPs from within their party, who acted as an ongoing 'lobby' on European issues within each national party.

- The growing politicization of the European Parliament strengthened the importance of its political groups. The fact that members sit according to political and ideological affiliations rather than in national delegations means that the Parliament examines each controversial issue not so much from a national viewpoint as from an ideological one. When seen in the context of the Community's decision-making process as a whole, this has the benefit of diminishing public perception that conflicts are between member states. Most political issues have MEPs from each country on various sides-of the argument: rarely do they vote as national blocks. As a result, most issues have lost the appearance of being one national interest against another.

(4)   Delaying power

In 1980 a ruling of the European Court of Justice struck down a piece of Community legislation adopted by Council on the grounds that the European Parliament had not yet delivered its opinion upon the proposal.[2] This ruling made it clear that, in the absence of Parliament's opinion, Council could not take a final decision. It thus gave the Parliament a *de facto* delaying power.

[2]   Joined cases 138 and 139/79.

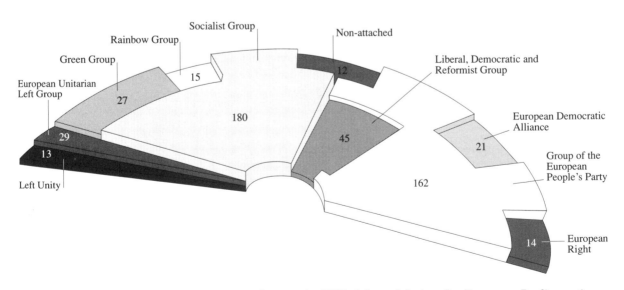

The political groupings of the European Parliament in 1992, left to right (credit: European Parliament).

The European Court of Justice in session (credit: Council of Europe).

Parliament immediately modified its internal rules of procedure to take advantage of this ruling. Now it votes first on any amendments it wishes to make to draft legislation; then, before taking a final vote on its resolution as a whole (which legally constitutes Parliament's opinion), it seeks an undertaking from the Commission to incorporate the amendments in a revised proposal. If the Commission's answer is unsatisfactory, Parliament has the option of not taking its final vote, referring the matter back to its internal parliamentary committee, and thus preventing Council from taking a decision. The committee will seek compromise solutions with the other institutions.

(5)   The Single European Act

When it came into force in 1987, this set of additions and amendments to the original treaties brought in two new procedures for involving the Parliament in the adoption of legislation:

- The *cooperation procedure* applies to certain categories of legislation, including that related to the establishment of the internal market.

- The *assent procedure* applies to the accession of new member states and the conclusion of association agreements with other countries.

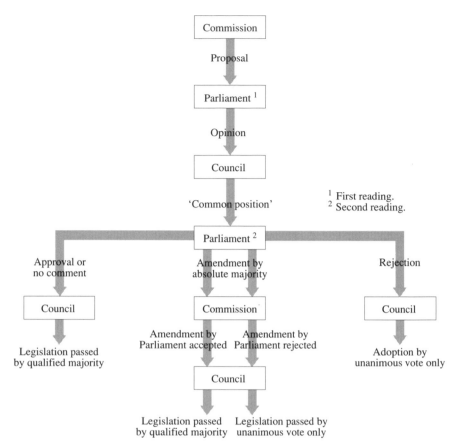

The cooperation procedure for Community legislation (credit: European Unification: The Origins and Growth of the European Community, *Office for Official Publications of the European Commission, Luxemburg, 1990).*

Essentially, the cooperation procedure adds a second reading on to the procedure for consulting Parliament. The first reading follows the traditional consultation procedure: Commission proposal, Parliament's opinion (possibly delayed in order to obtain concessions), Council decision. However, the Council's decision is now no longer final, but returns to Parliament for a second reading. Parliament then has three months to do one of three things:

- Approve the Council's text (in which case the Council is obliged to adopt it).

- Reject it by a majority vote (in which case the draft legislation will fall unless every member state within the Council agrees within three months, with the consent of the Commission, to overrule Parliament).

- Amend it again (in which case the Commission must table a modified proposal, taking Parliament's amendments into account).

    The Council can adopt this modified proposal by a qualified majority vote or amend it (e.g. back to the original Council position) by unanimity. The Council has three months to choose one of these options; otherwise the text will fall.

The *assent procedure* (or *avis conforme*) requires the approval of Parliament (by a majority of its members in a single reading), as well as the Council, for the adoption of certain types of agreement with other countries and for the accession of new member states.

Thus, the European Parliament's powers have developed well beyond their original, purely consultative role. Nevertheless they still fall somewhat short of Parliament's aspiration towards a system of *co-decision* in the Community, such that legislation would require the explicit approval both of Council (representing the governments of the member states) and of Parliament (representing the electorate as a whole). This would not allow either body to impose legislation upon the other, but would at least ensure that Community legislation be subject to the same democratic guarantees as at national level: approval in a public vote by a democratically elected assembly.

The 1990–91 intergovernmental conference on political union examined the issue of giving Parliament a power of co-decision. A majority of the member states have accepted the principle, but treaty amendments require unanimity. It is too early to say what compromise will emerge from these negotiations, but it seems likely, judging from the papers submitted by the presidency of the intergovernmental conference, that at least in certain areas Parliament will achieve co-decision powers with Council.

Parliamentary control over the executive

A second aspect of representative democracy is control over the executive. This usually involves the dependence of the executive on the support of a majority in Parliament, which plays a role in its appointment and is in a position to dismiss it. Such features are typical of representative democratic systems in western Europe, but not, for instance, in the United States or many Latin American countries, where an executive president is directly elected and does not necessarily need the support of the legislature. France has a mixed system with a directly elected president who appoints the government, but the Assemblée Nationale can dismiss it. Another variation can be found in Switzerland where, once appointed, the members of the government cannot be dismissed by Parliament before the end of their mandate. Thus the pattern varies, but at least in western Europe it is normally a prominent feature of democratic accountability for Parliament to have an important role in choosing or maintaining the executive.[3]

In the European Community the Commission is the executive branch. As in many federal-type systems, much implementation of policy occurs at the level of the member states rather than the common executive. But the Commission monitors implementation by member states, as well as carrying out those executive tasks assigned directly to it. Thus, the Commission executes EC programmes once they have been agreed, administers the budget, has the bulk of the Community's civil

---

[3]   Pierre Avril's essay in this volume contains a fuller discussion of these variations. (NP)

servants working for it, takes the member states to court if necessary, and initiates new proposals for legislation (a process on which it has a virtual monopoly).

Granted it is an executive kept under a tight leash. Few executive powers are attributed to it directly by the treaties: most derive from directives and regulations adopted by the Council, which specify the limits of its executive powers. The Council has often been very cautious in conferring executive powers upon the Commission, preferring to deal with controversial items through the legislative procedure (hence the spectacle of technical matters, such as the noise emission of lawnmowers, having to go through the full legislative procedure with two readings in Parliament and the Council!).

When the Council has delegated implementing powers to the Commission, it has done so under strict conditions. These conditions typically involve consultation by the Commission with a committee of national civil servants, and in some cases these committees have the right to block the Commission's decision and refer the matter back to the Council. Indeed, so many committees have been set up over the years that the term 'comitology' has been coined to describe the situation. The types of committee procedure were standardized in 1987.[4]

[4]   Procedures of Council committees:

Procedure I (Advisory Committees)

Commission listens to view of committee and then takes a decision taking account of the committee's opinion.

Procedure II (Management Committees)

If the Commission is *opposed* by qualified majority in the committee, then *either*:

Variant a):   The Commission *may* delay the application of its decision for up to one month.

Variant b):   The Commission *shall* delay the application of its decision for a period up to three months.

And, within these deadlines, Council may, by a qualified majority, take a different decision. (This and other forms of voting in the Council and its dependent committees are explained on pp. 244–250 below.)

Procedure III (Regulatory Committees)

If the Commission is *not supported* by a qualified majority in the Committee, the matter is referred to the Council, which may take a decision on a Commission proposal within a deadline not exceeding three months. If it fails to make a decision, then:

Variant a):   The Commission adopts its own proposal without further discussion.

Variant b):   the Commission adopts its proposal unless a *simple* majority in Council votes against, in which case no decision is taken.

Safeguard measures (mainly trade)

No committee, but any member state may ask for a Commission decision to be referred to Council. In that case:

Variant a):   Council has a deadline to take an alternative decision by a qualified majority.

Variant b):   Council must confirm, modify or annul the Commission's decision by a qualified majority. If it fails to act within a deadline, the decision is annulled.

Eurocats

Kipper Williams

Credit: Chris Williams.

The implications of this complex system are that it is not always clear who can be held to account for particular decisions, which tend to emerge as a compromise between the Commission and national civil servants. Although not unknown in federal-type systems (the German federal government can frequently only act with the approval of a majority in Bundesrat committees), it does mean that the executive is not fully and specifically accountable for its acts.

The Commission, then, is a weak executive, but it is nevertheless accountable to the European Parliament in the sense that the latter can adopt a motion of no confidence causing it to resign. Although Parliament has never adopted such a motion, it has threatened to do so on a number of occasions, and the *existence* of this power is more significant than the frequency of its exercise. Indeed, the fact that a two-thirds majority is necessary for it to be exercised probably inhibits its use.

Parliament also has lesser means at its disposal to put pressure on the Commission. Its members can ask parliamentary questions (written or oral). Parliamentary committees frequently call commissioners, or their civil servants, to account and subject them to cross-examination by MEPs. And Parliament can use its budgetary powers to freeze certain items in the Commission's budget, or deny it extra appropriations, unless and until Parliament is satisfied with the way the Commission is using them.

It is in the appointment of the Commission that the treaties gave no role whatsoever to Parliament. Nevertheless, there has been an evolution in the *de facto* situation, which began when Parliament started to organize debates and votes of confidence on the incoming Thorn Commission in 1981, and continued with the Delors 1 and Delors 2 Commissions in the 1980s. It was partially recognized by the Stuttgart Solemn Declaration of 1983, which provided for a new Commission to present its programme to Parliament for debate and a vote.

Significantly, the last two Commissions waited until they had obtained a vote of confidence from Parliament before presenting themselves to the Court of Justice in order to give the solemn undertaking required under Article 10 of the so-called

Merger Treaty.[5] This is the oath of office, swearing independence from national governments, taken by incoming commissioners. Implicitly the Commission recognized that, had it failed to obtain the confidence of Parliament, the commissioners would not have felt fit to take office.

The Parliament has also become involved in the initial choice of the Commission President, which the member states agreed in the mid-1970s to make before the other members of the Commission – theoretically in order to allow national governments to consult him or her before appointing the other members. The Stuttgart Solemn Declaration of 1983 provided for the Parliament to be consulted on the choice of the Commission President. This provision has since been aided by the practice of allowing the President of Parliament to attend the opening part of Council meetings.

The 1990–91 intergovernmental conference on political union considered whether to entrench these practices in the treaties and, perhaps, to go a stage further. Parliament suggested that the Commission President should be *elected* by Parliament on the proposal of the Council, and that he or she should have an equal say with the national governments in the choice of individual commissioners. The Commission as a whole would then present itself to Parliament for a vote of confidence. This whole procedure would take place at the beginning of each parliamentary term of office – in other words, the mandate of the Commission would run for five years (instead of four), and run concurrently with that of Parliament. Without changing any formal powers, this would strengthen the link between Parliament and Commission, and allow the public to observe the appointment of a new executive following each European election.

The Luxemburg Presidency[6] proposed that Parliament should be consulted on the appointment of the Commission President, and then take a vote of confidence in the Commission as a whole. Consultation on the President, in such circumstances, would be tantamount to a vote of confirmation, as it is difficult to conceive of a Commission President taking office should Parliament give a negative opinion. On the other hand, the proposals did not satisfy Parliament's aspirations concerning the change in the period of the Commission's office.

Decision-taking by majority

The European Parliament, of course, votes by majority – although, as in many national parliaments, certain types of decisions require a particular level of majority

[5]   The Treaty establishing a Single Council and a Single Commission of the European Communities, signed in Brussels in 1965. (NP)

[6]   The presidency of the Council rotates among the member states' governments. Hence, the Luxemburg Presidency is the Luxemburg government acting, within the institutions of the EC, as President of the Council and the Community as a whole for the six months of its turn. (NP)

The European Commission at its regular weekly meeting in Brussels. This Commission took office in January 1989 for a four-year term, and is the second to be presided over by Jacques Delors (credit: European Parliament).

(rules of procedure, some budgetary votes, etc.). In some cases, a specific majority is necessary to go against the views of Council. But, again, this is not unknown in bi-cameral systems, where one branch of a legislature can only overrule the other by a specific majority. The problem, when it comes to majority voting in the Community, does not lie within the Parliament: it lies within the Council.

The Treaty of Rome[7] laid down that decision-taking in the Council (notably for the adoption of legislation) required unanimity in certain areas, qualified majority voting in others, and for a small area (notably procedural points) simple majority voting:

- Unanimity was required for areas where national interests are particularly sensitive (e.g. taxation) or for the development of new policies not explicitly laid down in the treaties. It was initially also required for the harmonization of national legislation for the internal market.

---

[7]   The treaty establishing the European Economic Community, signed in Rome in 1957. (NP)

- Qualified majority voting was laid down as the normal procedure in those areas where the Community is supposed to be carrying out a common policy (e.g. agriculture, transport, external trade, some aspects of social policy, fishing, etc.). It was also laid down for the adoption of some measures necessary for the Community's functioning and implementing its policies (e.g. the budget) but not for others (e.g. the location of the institutions).

The procedure for qualified majority voting always contained two safeguards:

1   A qualified majority consists of over 70 per cent of the weighted votes in Council (currently 54 out of the 76 votes).[8]

2   A qualified majority can *approve* a Commission proposal; to modify it, however, requires unanimity. This is based on the notion that the Commission is constitutionally bound to examine the overall Community interest and the impact of its proposals on all member states from an impartial and independent point of view. The treaties therefore made it easier to adopt a proposal than to modify it. A majority of states cannot form a coalition to amend proposals in their interests.

Despite these safeguards and the limitation of majority voting to certain areas of policy, in 1965 Charles de Gaulle provoked a major crisis in the Community by insisting that no state should be outvoted if it considered that important national interests were at stake. After several months of crisis with France boycotting Council meetings, a special meeting of the Council took place in Luxemburg in January 1966. The minutes of this meeting are referred to as the 'Luxemburg compromise'.

The Luxemburg compromise is, in fact, not a compromise: it is an agreement to disagree.[9] Whereas the member states accepted that an attempt should be made to find a solution acceptable to all in a situation where important national interests were at stake, they disagreed as to what should happen if no solution was found within a reasonable period of time. France considered that the discussions should

---

[8]   Current (1992) weighting of votes in the Council: UK, Italy, Germany and France – 10 each; Spain – 8; Belgium, the Netherlands, Greece and Portugal – 5 each; Denmark and Ireland – 3 each; Luxemburg – 2.

[9]   Luxemburg Compromise majority voting procedure:

'I. Where, in the case of decisions which may be taken by majority vote on a proposal of the Commission, very important interests of one or more partners are at stake, the Members of the Council will endeavour, within a reasonable time, to reach solutions which can be adopted by all the Members of the Council while respecting their mutual interests and those of the Community, according with Article 2 of the Treaty.

'II. With regard to the preceding paragraph, the French delegation considers that where very important interests are at stake the discussion must be continued until unanimous agreement is reached.

'III. The six delegations note that there is a divergence of views on what should be done in the event of a failure to reach complete agreement.

'IV. The six delegations nevertheless consider that this divergence does not prevent the Community's work being resumed in accordance with the normal procedure.'

continue indefinitely. All other member states took the view that there should be a vote in accordance with the treaties.

In practice in the years following the Luxemburg compromise, very little qualified majority voting took place in Council. This was partly due to a reluctance to create a new crisis with France, but was reinforced in 1973 by the accession to the Community of new member states who essentially shared the French view on these matters. Together, France, the UK and Denmark constituted a large enough minority to prevent decisions even by a qualified majority. In other words, if a matter were put to the vote against the express national interest of *any* member state, it would not get through as these countries would not vote for a proposal in such circumstances. It therefore became habitual to negotiate on all texts, virtually line by line, until all member states agreed before putting the matter to a vote in Council.

By the 1980s this working method was coming under increasing strain. A number of negative consequences were becoming increasingly apparent:

- Such a decision-making procedure was inefficient (it took 17 years, for instance, to agree on a directive on the mutual recognition of the qualifications for architects).

- Virtually any EC policy or action could only be the lowest common denominator acceptable to all member states.

- The Commission's right of initiative and the role of the European Parliament were reduced.

- Such detailed and time-consuming negotiations could only be carried out by national civil servants, which led to a bureaucratization of the whole EC system.

- Above all, it became apparent that while unanimity when agreeing on *new* policies was one thing, unanimity for the management or revision of *existing* Community policies was another. In these cases, the Community as a whole had a vital interest in ensuring that it could take rapid decisions, and the blocking power given to individual member states was a threat to the continued existence of Community policies.

It was clear that national ministers were quite capable of deeming almost anything to be an 'important national interest' when their state had an advantage in the status quo. Reforms in the Common Agricultural Policy, for instance, were all too easy to block by any member state gaining from the system, even when this was at huge expense to the Community as a whole. This applied to varying degrees to all EC policies and member states. The right of veto proved to be the dictatorship of the minority, used for selfish national interests.

The first major crack in the practice of unanimity came in 1982 when the UK attempted to block the annual package of farm prices (details of which it had already agreed) in order to extract concessions in separate negotiations on the Community's budget. Other member states perceived this to be almost a form of blackmail. The Community had to decide urgently on the agricultural prices for that year, and Britain was not objecting to the contents of that decision but merely

The French farm lobby must be defeated if the Community is to survive, says **Nicholas Ridley**

Scandal of fortress France

*Collective decision on an 'important national interest'? In December 1992 French anger at the Community's agreement in the GATT negotiations to reduce subsidies to agriculture raised fears that France (here in the form of its President, François Mitterrand) would throttle Community decision-making (here represented by British Prime Minister, John Major, EC President at the time) (credit: Peter Brookes/*The Times, *11 December 1992*).

using its supposed right of veto to extract concessions on another matter. This attitude provoked a sufficient majority of member states – including France – to take part in a vote openly putting Britain in a minority.

A shift in the attitude of some member states became apparent in Stuttgart in 1983 when the Council adopted the Solemn Declaration on European Union. The declaration itself referred to a need to improve the Community's capacity to act by applying the decision-making procedures laid down in the treaties. In declarations appended to the minutes, however, each member state laid down its interpretation of when a vote should take place. Only Britain and Denmark supported the original French position of 1965. France and Ireland now spelt out that such an interest must relate directly to the subject under discussion and they, like Greece, took the view that the vote should only be postponed if a member state invokes an '*essential* national interest' *in writing*. Belgium, Germany, Luxemburg, Italy and the Netherlands took the view that a vote should be held *whenever* the treaties provide for it.

In 1984 the European Parliament put forward its proposal for a new treaty (on European union), which envisaged the introduction over ten years of majority voting without the right of veto for *all* existing Community policies (except foreign policy cooperation), but retained unanimity for the introduction of new policies. The response of the member states, in the form of the Single European Act, was to extend by ten the number of articles in the existing treaties which require majority voting. The articles in question were linked to certain already agreed policy objectives (such as the legislative harmonizations necessary for completing the internal market by 1992), and to Council decisions that follow up decisions already agreed unanimously (e.g. individual research programmes, following the adoption of the multi-annual framework for research; and Regional Fund decisions, following the adoption of the overall regulation for the structural funds[10]).

This change in the treaties did not in itself affect the Luxemburg compromise, as the compromise is a political agreement with no legal basis, let alone a treaty one. Indeed, Mrs Thatcher declared to the House of Commons that it remained in force. However, such a change to the treaties, duly ratified by all national parliaments, changed the constitutional framework for making decisions and signified at least a willingness to take majority votes more frequently. There would, after all, be little point in modifying the treaties if this were not the case.

The Council followed up this treaty change with an amendment to its internal rules of procedure. After a year of negotiations, it agreed to change its rules to oblige the President-in-Office[11] to move to a vote upon the request of the Commission or the representative of any member state, provided a simple majority of member states support the request. The context was also changed by the accession of Spain and Portugal to the European Community. It is no longer clear that states seeking to invoke the Luxemburg compromise would have sufficient support in Council to constitute a blocking minority.

The upshot of all these developments is that, for the areas now subject to qualified majority voting, member states have been reluctant to try to block majority votes. Interestingly, member states in the minority, rather than invoke the Luxemburg compromise during a vote, have in some cases challenged it in the Court of Justice on grounds of an incorrect legal basis – arguing that an article requiring unanimity should have been used.[12]

How have these changes worked in practice? There has been a striking increase in the number of votes taken in the Council. Over 70 took place in the first ten months after the Single Act. There were also, according to Council's answer to a

[10]   The EC's funds for various types of economic and social restructuring – namely, the European Regional Development Fund, the European Social Fund, the European Agricultural Guidance and Guarantee Fund. (NP)

[11]   The term 'President-in-Office' does not just refer to the head of the national government, but to any minister chairing the Council. (NP)

[12]   Forexample, cases 184/87 (Portugal v. Council), 68/86 (UK v. Council) and 51/89 (UK v. Council).

parliamentary question, many 'decisions without a formal vote where it is clear that the required majority exists'.[13] Indeed, this statement reveals what is probably the main impact of majority voting: most matters are still agreed by consensus, but the negotiations are very different in a situation where representatives know that they can ultimately be outvoted, as against a situation where they know they can sit back and block anything they do not like. The effect is that each delegation seeks to avoid isolation and accepts compromises more willingly.

As to the areas in which votes have been taken, they have included controversial issues. There have been important votes on subjects as varied as emission standards for car pollution, a ban on hormones in meat (leading to a 'trade war' with the United States), permitted radioactivity levels in foodstuffs, rules for transfrontier television broadcasts, several fishing controversies, some aspects of foreign aid, and some of the crucial reforms of the CAP.

By contrast, the areas which still require unanimity have continued to be subject to extremely lengthy negotiations, and even blocking by individual member states. This has not only included the headline-catching antics of Mrs Thatcher in a variety of policy areas. It also means that some essential Community policies are still subject to the rule of the lowest common denominator. This is particularly unfortunate in the fields of environmental protection, many aspects of social policy, harmonization of indirect taxation (allowing 'tax haven' countries to dictate policy to the rest), the framework programme for research, monetary integration, and most aspects of foreign aid.

Fundamental rights

In a democracy, rule by the majority cannot mean the dictatorship of the majority. In modern representative democracies, it is generally agreed that certain minority rights must be respected and, in particular, that the individual has certain fundamental rights which cannot be transgressed by the will of the majority.[14]

Although all member states are parties to the European Convention on Fundamental Rights and Freedoms of the Council of Europe, the Community itself is not. Does this mean there is no guarantee that the EC's institutions respect fundamental rights in their actions? This question has given rise to substantial academic and political debate as well as declarations by the institutions of their intentions to respect human rights.

The issue is not merely theoretical. As the Community begins to lay down provisions about matters such as what is allowed on television broadcasts across frontiers, under what conditions citizens can exercise their right of residence in one

---

[13]   Council answer to parliamentary question 2470/87 by Mr Megahy.

[14]   Francesco D'Agostino's essay in this volume discusses at length the issue of legal limitations on democratic politics. (NP)

member state or another, and equality of opportunity between men and women, it inevitably treads on areas where it could violate the European Convention. This would leave a curious situation in which member states were obliged to follow Community directives, but could then be in breach of their obligations under the Convention.

Several solutions have been offered to this quandary. One is that the European Community itself should become a party to the Convention. Another is that it should adopt its own declaration of rights. A third is that it should incorporate a reference in a treaty of its own to the need to respect the Convention. All of these solutions – which are not necessarily contradictory – have advantages and drawbacks.

Community accession to the European Convention would require a change in the provisions of the Convention to be made at the Council of Europe level. The Community is not yet recognized as a state. It cannot sign the Convention without a change allowing entities other than states to do so and to take part in the machinery established for its enforcement: the European Commission of Human Rights and the European Court of Human Rights.

Adoption by the Community of its own declaration of rights would involve negotiating a new charter by states who are signatories to one already. It is not easy to convince them of the need to do this. The European Parliament has adopted such a declaration, along with the De Gucht report in April 1989, but the intergovernmental conference on political union of 1990–91 did not take up the proposal. We should emphasize that the European Parliament did not see this as an alternative to Community accession to the Convention, but as complementary: the Community Declaration would have the same relationship to the Convention as do the declaration of rights included in national constitutions.

The third possibility – making a reference to the European Convention in the Community treaties – would reinforce the basis on which the European Court of Justice has, in its case law, sought to draw on the Convention as a source of Community law. Starting in 1969,[15] the Court stated that the general principles of Community law enshrined fundamental human rights and were protected by the Court. In 1974[16] the Court specified that it could not uphold measures incompatible with fundamental rights recognized and protected by the constitutions of the member states. This has led many to conclude that, since the Convention on human rights applies to all member states, the Community is itself bound by the Convention in so far as it exercises authority in the place of the member states. The Court has not explicitly stated this, but in 1974 it said that 'international treaties for the protection of human rights on which the member states have collaborated or of which they are signatories can supply guidelines which should be followed within the framework of Community law'.[17] It therefore seems that, in

[15] Case 29/69.

[16] Case 4/73.

[17] *European Court Review* (1974), no. 491, p. 507.

practice, when the Court is called upon to give judgement, the European Convention can be regarded as providing a source of Community law.

Indeed, support for this is indicated by an interesting reversal of position by the German constitutional court (among all the member states, legal protection of fundamental rights is most developed in Germany). In 1974 the Bundesverfassungsgericht claimed jurisdiction to review Community regulations against the fundamental rights laid down in the German constitution, until such time as the process of integration had developed far enough for Community law to contain a codified catalogue of fundamental rights, decided upon by a democratically legitimate and elected parliament, which offered the same guarantees as the German constitution. In 1986, however, the Bundesverfassungsgericht reversed its position, stating that it was now convinced the aims expressed in 1974 had been achieved. The case law of the Court of Justice (referred to above), which the German court analysed exhaustively, together with the joint declaration by the European Parliament (by then directly elected), the Council and the Commission on fundamental rights (of 5 April 1977) and the 1978 Council declaration on democracy, were all cited by the Bundesvergassungsgericht. They persuaded the court that satisfactory and durable guarantees existed, and that the European Community now ensured an effective protection of fundamental rights against action by Community authorities.

We can therefore conclude that the Community's legal system probably does offer guarantees of fundamental rights of the same magnitude as those offered in the member states. However, the EC – unlike its member states who are signatories of the separate European Convention on Fundamental Rights – lacks a procedure whereby an external body tests its rulings using a framework common to over 20 countries. That will only be achieved once the Community as such accedes to the Convention on Fundamental Rights of the Council of Europe.

Afterword: The situation following the Maastricht Treaty (1992)

The intergovernmental conference of 1990–91 on political union, leading up to the Maastricht meeting of the European Council, was an opportunity for the European Parliament to press for an increase in its powers along the lines described above. Parliament was quick to put forward its own proposals for treaty revision in all the areas likely to be subject to negotiation, including the issue of its own powers.[18]

The new treaty agreed in Maastricht did not give full satisfaction to the aspirations of the European Parliament but nevertheless represented a significant step forward. Furthermore, the treaty itself provided for a new intergovernmental conference in 1996 which will again look at Parliament's powers.

[18]   Martin Reports, notably 11 July and 22 November 1990, minutes of the European Parliament of those dates. (Reports submitted to the Parliament by David Martin, MEP. See also David Martin, *Europe: An Ever Closer Union*, Nottingham, Spokesman, 1991.)

Legislative procedures

As regards the Community's legislative procedures, the new treaty laid down a co-decision procedure in Article 189b (though not actually called that in view of the opposition of one member state), which will apply to certain categories of legislation: most internal market legislation, consumer protection, education, research and technological development, some environmental measures, trans-European networks, public health, culture and equivalence between qualifications. This is similar to the procedure that Parliament had advocated, but contains an important difference. Parliament had asked for a procedure of two readings in each of the two bodies (Parliament and the Council), to be followed by a conciliation procedure should their positions diverge. The result of the conciliation procedure would have needed the approval of both bodies.

The intergovernmental conference accepted this procedure, but the Maastricht conference added a further provision: should conciliation fail, the Council could then act unilaterally and its text would become law unless Parliament were to reject it within six weeks by an absolute majority of its members. This extra provision loads the procedure in favour of the Council. Often, the Council will know beforehand that Parliament will not wish to reject a measure outright. It will frequently prefer a half measure to no legislation at all, or will not wish to take the blame for a procedure failing. The Council is therefore unlikely to give much ground in the conciliation negotiations. Nevertheless, the new procedure represents an important step forward for Parliament: no text can become law under this procedure if Parliament opposes it, and there are opportunities (two readings and a conciliation) to use this power to bargain with the Council.

In addition to this, the new treaty extends the assent procedure to a wider category of international agreements, to the uniform electoral system, to the definition of the aims and objectives of the structural funds and the creation of new funds, to the amendment of the Central Bank protocol, and to some other matters. The co-operation procedure is extended to most other significant categories of legislation not covered by the co-decision procedure.

Appointment of the Commission

As regards Parliament's involvement in the appointment of the Commission, the new treaty gives it almost complete satisfaction. Parliament had asked for the right to elect the Commission President, to take a vote of confidence on the College of Commissioners as a whole, and for the term of office of the Commission to be changed from four to five years and linked to Parliament. The new treaty takes up all these points except that, as regards the President, Parliament will only be consulted. However, a public vote on a nominated individual is tantamount to a vote of confirmation, as in practice it is unlikely that any politician would wish to take up office if rejected by Parliament. Under Maastricht the concurrent terms of office will begin after the next European elections, the months following the election being used to go through the new procedure and the new Commission taking office the following January.

Powers of control

The new treaty also adjusts Parliament's powers of control. The treaty acknowledges its rights to set up committees of inquiry, gives it the right to elect a Community ombudsman, enhances its powers of budgetary control, and makes it easier for Parliament to take the other EC institutions to the European Court if its own prerogatives are violated.

Conclusion to Book 3

Prepared for the Course Team by Gérard Duprat
Translated by Noël Parker

Liberty has to be learnt.

In the course of modern European history, both democratic and non-democratic states have ensured that the people in their charge were educated and informed, and that they have had legally guaranteed rights as citizens. As Europe emerged from the storm of revolution at the end of the Enlightenment, both Kant and Hegel explored the theory of this twin necessity for education and for legally guaranteed rights. With some reverses, European states under the rule of Law fell progressively into line over the course of the nineteenth and twentieth centuries. Kant and Hegel were important contributors to the philosophy of human rights and political liberty, but were far from advocating democracy. European states have become democratic only by the long-delayed and uncertain victory of the democrats.

The essays in this book clearly underline the lesson that democracy amounts to more than imposing human rights and the rule of Law upon the general legal framework to which all states conform. Yet democracy is a form of politics whose notion of citizenship generates and also resolves the paradox that, for humans, liberty has to be learnt.

It was Aristotle who, following the first experience of it, established the basic conception of democracy, the structure of which has not changed since. Democracy is built on the right to have rights (first and foremost the right to be governed and to be a governor), and on the aspiration that 'government' should have the sole aim of permitting the citizens to realize their ever-to-be-completed nature as human beings (that is to say, their nature as free people practising liberty among similarly free fellow humans). In its early days in the seventeenth century, with Hobbes and Spinoza, European political thought embraced this conception – though it substituted personal rights[1] for natural law, and the state (with its sovereignty) for the city (with its autonomy).

Modern political thought conceptualized a division unknown to the city of the ancient world: the distinction between the *sovereign state* – responsible for the general interest – and *society* – the creation of individuals, groups and classes.

---

[1] However, the personalization of law and rights did not necessarily imply an attachment to so-called 'liberalism'. This was a later idea and only took on real meaning in the context of the liberal conception of the economy and the transformation of the western economies by capitalism. Authentic liberalism has been a rare historical experience. It is confined to those few cases of a European body politic in which the state was never conceived primarily as a sovereign power (that is, as the ultimate rationality underlying the order between peoples) and never took precedence over law, justice, or indeed over society (which is the locus not only of conflict, but also of social solidarity and rights).

This division did not remove the idea of 'the people', however. The 'people' was distinguished from 'the mass of the population' (an aggregation with no political identity) and from the 'republic', and hence public opinion. But 'the people' was also distinguished from the state. The state's laws and government had no other authority than that derived from the consent which the citizens, as members of a 'free people', gave them. There followed from this the problems and issues surrounding the human *right* to resist oppression and, latterly, the citizen's *duty* of civil disobedience.[2]

Following the division of state and society in modern European culture, the conception of democracy was gradually articulated, and became the form of a certain kind of political life. It has been impeded by clashes between states, rivalries between ideologies, the self-glorification of nations, and conflicts of interest between groups or classes. The culture of political liberty and citizenship that the peoples of Europe enjoy today is the fruit of a history which makes no sense without those impediments.

Democracy, then, is far from being 'the worst form of government, except all those other forms'. This witticism does, however, recognize that democracy has drawbacks. The opponents of democracy have itemized them over two centuries: the 'reign of opinion' incapable of defining the 'common good'; the grumbling crisis of government created by the procedural problems of representation; the way that the separation of powers is perpetually undermined by the competition between them, by the confusion between their separate functions and by their mutability under the influence of social change; the effective exclusion of a portion of the citizens for the benefit of the majority (quite apart from the cynical exploitation of those who are not nationals of the given state); liberties and rights that remain purely formal for many, by virtue of their lack of resources to enjoy them in reality (in particular, because of inequalities in education, culture and employment); a complex and uncertain decision-making process, which carries the risk of an inadequate response to the dangers confronting the people and their liberty. The list of the democratic state's structural weaknesses and grounds for crisis is a long one.

The witticism has a second virtue: it turns these drawbacks and difficulties back against democracy's accusers. For the 'other forms of government' exhibit a still more limited capacity for social intervention. The thesis that democratic government suffers from structural weaknesses, making it unable to resist 'stronger' regimes, joins those propositions that the facts themselves disarm.

For all that, the matter is not yet settled. The second lesson of this book is that democracy is not just one way of governing among others – a more or less economical way for states to obtain obedience. Nor is it simply a 'form of government': an ensemble of institutions and procedures offering the best way for a 'general interest' to surface with least harm. Democracy is not content with such

---

[2]   This latter is evoked not only by those claiming a duty in conscience to resist certain state activities (such as the maintenance of nuclear weapons), but also by the general obligation of subjects to refuse obedience when ordered to commit war crimes. (NP)

functional criteria. For, in two ways, it renders the very idea of government problematic.

In the first place, democracy establishes the perpetual critique of government, because it postulates something which Aristotle brought to our attention: that the totality of citizens, the people as a body, are wiser and shrewder than their governors can be, either individually or collectively. Through elections as well as through all the other means developed by modern techniques for communication and the articulation of public opinion, the people exercise a control over government that is far from a purely negative critique. It is not just a reflex revolt or an act of defiance. This critique expresses the principle that, in a democracy, the real institutional arrangements of government are not beyond criticism: the people remain their final master. Thus the only aim of government is to maintain those arrangements by giving the governed the greatest degree of satisfaction – or, rather, by doing the least harm to their private interests, in the name of the body politic.

Second, the government in a democracy is not the 'governor' of the body politic, and the state is in no sense sovereign. Yet that does not justify scepticism or relativism, or bring any master–slave dialectic[3] into play. These two kinds of danger have often been evoked, one threatening the value of citizenship and the other relations between individuals. It has been said that their destructive effects can only be avoided by flights into utopian fantasy – be they political (society reconciled to itself through consensus over its institutions) or social (society producing prosperity for all through the free market or through a free association among autonomous collectives of producers). The democratic form of government means that the state, rather than the mode of exercising supreme power, is merely a way of governing. And the object of democracy is thus clear and unambiguous: the culture of the citizens, individuals who are by nature all free in the same way, and hence all equally responsible for their state.

If the 'people' constituted by the body of the citizens can be credited with an identity, then this must be understood in rigorous and strictly limited terms. In particular, identity must be purged of all elements drawn from the ethnic particularity which every social group carries with it. Democracy reduces the process of forming an identity to the essentials: the exercise by a people made up of citizens of its 'political will' that all should be free. Hence, 'identity' is demonstrated solely by the fact that society is regulated as required by the culture of liberty and citizenship, as regards relations both between individual members of the body politic and with other polities and peoples.

---

[3] In his seminal analysis of the basis of self-consciousness (*The Phenomenology of Spirit* (or *Mind*) of 1807, Part B, Chapter 4), Hegel explores how humans must, in his view, have originally defined their own self-consciousness via relations of domination and subservience with others. Turned by Sartre (in his *Being and Nothingness* of 1943) into a category of existentialist psychology, this so-called 'master–slave' dialectic is sometimes thought to identify a perpetual tendency in human personality. Thus, if the supreme position of the state were to be undermined, it is possible to argue that relations of domination between individuals would take its place. Duprat holds that this is not a realistic prognosis. (NP)

The Maastricht Treaty's proposals concerning the integration of the European peoples are clear – though they are somewhat impaired by the failures of expression due to the text being hastily drawn up. Besides, the proposals have to be understood across the formidable complexity of the Community apparatus envisaged by the Treaty, and according to the areas of competence allocated to the Union and the degree of intervention permitted within different sectors. The search for the 'European identity', which gives the Treaty its ultimate purpose, should be understood in terms of the rigorous logic of the concept of democracy, as set out above, and by the political culture that flows from it. European citizens must consciously define their own identity. This means that European identity will find its source only in the 'political will' of the citizens. As members of other polities already defined as 'peoples' (rather than nations), it is they who will decide how the integration of the states of the Union is to proceed.

It is clear that democracy's implicit critique of political institutions prevents us from attributing to them a sovereign or absolute mission to define liberty, and hence servitude. Democracy teaches the citizens its ultimate lesson in political culture: that the debate on liberty and servitude goes beyond the boundaries of politics. At the same time, it confers a framework of law – the exercise of freedom of opinion in the true sense – on the public organization of this debate. Democracy requires of government both that it should act in the best way to preserve that freedom, and that it should expect the citizens as a whole to govern themselves in the way that is best for their own liberation. Over and above political life, which is where the government judges its success by the reception of its policies, democracy makes its own contribution: by organizing and employing public institutions (the 'republic') so as to form and sustain social bonds.

The ways that European democracy has been put into practice in institutions vary according to historical conditions and the country in question. It has depended on past social conflicts, the idiosyncrasies of the different peoples and the processes of democratization that they have been through. But we have noted a growing uniformity in political institutions, and in the breadth of sectors covered by public policy in western European countries since the Second World War. During the phase when it was pursued through the various European 'communities',[4] the construction of Europe has contributed to those changes.

The uniformity will become more marked with the present attempt to move from that phase to one of enlarged areas of competence for the Community, now to be absorbed into a European Union whose guiding ideas include democracy and the development of European citizenship. But as in the individual states, so in this unprecedented political setting, which may bring about a European identity, a 'democratic deficit' is a corollary of putting democracy into practice in institutions. The deficit is irremovable in principle. Yet in either setting, public debate, conducted under the rule of Law and nourished by democratic culture, will determine the diminution of that deficit in the cause of social peace.

---

[4]   See note 1 and the text of the introduction to Part IV. (NP)

Acknowledgements

The work of the Humanities Programme Committee of the EADTU has been carried out with the support of the Commission of the European Community within the frameworks of the ERASMUS Programme and the Jean Monnet Project.

Notes on contributors

Pierre Avril

Pierre Avril (b. 1930) was from 1955 to 1962 an aide to the French Prime Minister Pierre Mendès-France. From 1962 to 1970 he was a journalist for the Société Générale de Presse. He has been a Professor of Public Law at the Universty of Poitiers and the University of Paris X–Nanterre, and is now Professor of Public Law at the University of Paris II. His publications include *Le Régime politique de la Ve République* (1969, 4th edn 1979); *Politics in France* (1969); *Essais sur les partis politiques* (1990); and *Droit parlementaire* (with Jean Gicquel, 1988).

Rodney Barker

Rodney Barker teaches political science at the London School of Economics. He is the author of *Education and Politics* (1972); *Political Ideas in Modern Britain* (1978); and *Political Legitimacy and the State* (1990). He is also opera critic of *Tribune*.

Jean Baudoin

Jean Baudoin is currently Professor of Political Science at the University of Rennes. In 1978 he presented his doctoral thesis (*thèse de doctorat d'Etat*), which examined the political and ideological evolution of the French Communist Party. In 1981 he passed the national competitive examination to be an *agrégé* in political science. He is the author of *Introduction à la Science Politique*; *Mort ou déclin du marxisme* (1991); *Karl Popper* (1990); and *La Philosophie politique de Karl Popper* (1993).

Richard Corbett

Richard Corbett is policy adviser on constitutional matters to the Socialist Group secretariat of the European Parliament. He previously worked in the European Parliament itself on the secretariat of various parliamentary committees and in the service of relations with national parliaments. He is the author or co-author of a number of works on European affairs, including *A Socialist Policy for Europe* (1985); 'The 1985 Intergovernmental Conference and the Single European Act' in *The Dynamics of European Union* (1986); *The Intergovernmental Conference on Political Union* (1992); and *The European Parliament* (2nd edn 1992).

Jean-Pierre Cot

Jean-Pierre Cot (b. 1937) was Professor of Law, then Dean of the Law Faculty, at Amiens from 1966 to 1969. He has been Professor of International Law at the Sorbonne since 1969. During his political career he has been Mayor of Coise-St-Jean-Pied-Gauthier (Savoy) since 1971; a member of the National Assembly for Savoy 1973–81; a member of the European Parliament 1978–9 and from 1984, chairing its budgets committee; Minister for Overseas Development 1981–2; a member of the French Socialist Party since 1969, a member of its steering committee 1970–1 and since 1973, and a member of its executive 1973–81. He is the author of various works on international law, political sociology and foreign policy.

Francesco D'Agostino

Francesco D'Agostino (b. 1946) graduated in jurisprudence from the University of Rome and has taught at the Universities of Lecce, Urbino and Catania. He is currently lecturer in the Philosophy of Law at the Faculty of Jurisprudence at the 'Tor Vergata' University of Rome and assistant director of the 'Rivista Internazionale di Filosofia del Diritte' (International Review of Philosophy of Law). His works include: *Diritto e secolarizzazione* (Law and secularization), 1991 and *La sanzione nell'esperanza giuridica* (The place of sanctions in the juridical idea) 3rd edn, 1993.

Gérard Duprat

Gérard Duprat (b. 1933), *agrégé* and *docteur d'Etat* in humanities (*ès lettres*), is Professor of Political Science at the Universities of Strasbourg and Paris. At Strasbourg he is director of postgraduate studies at the Institute of Political Studies (which is devoted to research on 'The political and cultural construction of Europe') and at the Centre for Political Thought. He is a member of the editorial board of the journal *Philosophie politique*.

Noël Parker

Noël Parker (b. 1945) is a Lecturer in European Politics in the Department of Linguistic and International Studies at the University of Surrey. From 1977 to 1993 he worked for the Open University as a Senior Counsellor, a Staff Tutor and a Lecturer in Arts. A graduate of UK and French universities, he has published a book and numerous articles, in English and French, on political and philosophical thought, notably in connection with the impact of the French Revolution. His *Portrayals of Revolution: Images, Debates and Structures of Thought on the French Revolution* was published in 1990, and he is currently preparing a second book, *The End of Revolution: Revolutions and History at the End of the Twentieth Century*, due out in 1994.

Alain-Marc Rieu

Alain-Marc Rieu (b. 1947) is a former student at the Ecole Normale Supérieure, *agrégé* and *docteur d'Etat* in Philosophy, University of Paris I-Panthéon-Sorbonne. When he edited this volume, he was Professor of Philosophy at the University of Strasbourg II, director of the *Centre d'Analyse des Savoirs Contemporains*. He is presently Research Fellow at the Maison Franco-Japonaise in Tokyo and Professor of Philosophy at the University of Lyon III-Jean-Moulin. His research is in contemporary philsophy and the interactions between science, technology and contemporary societies.

Hans-Joachim Schmidt

Hans-Joachim Schmidt (b. 1947) is currently Lecturer in Philosophy at the FernUniversität Hagen. He studied philosophy, history, political science and pedagogics at the Universities of Bochum, Köln, Bonn and Essen. He is also head of an institute of philosophy and peace research, as well as a member of a group of practitioners and theoreticians working on further developments in psychoanalysis. He is a member of the German and international peace movement and of other grass roots movements; in 1991 he was elected as a faculty member of the European University Centre for Peace Studies of UNESCO in Schlaining, Austria.

Index to Book 3